THE MODERN PROFESSIONAL
PLANTING DESIGNER

THE MODERN PROFESSIONAL PLANTING DESIGNER

ANDREW FISHER TOMLIN

New York · Paris · London · Milan

CONTENTS

FOREWORD

I first met Andrew when he was judging a garden I'd designed at my very first RHS Chelsea Flower Show. After awarding the medal, he'd come to give feedback to this very happy garden designer.

His words were typical Andrew: he gave me honest, critical advice. And he started off by saying this: "I don't understand how you do what you do with planting, but I like it."

This got me to thinking. I'd always designed planting in a way that suited my needs in terms of the atmosphere I wanted to create, the viability of a planting and how I knew plants to behave. Seeing planting design as an extension of what Nature does, rather than a complete imposition of my own ego onto those plants, I'd always planted in a loose, natural way which would encourage wildlife with offerings of habitat and food. But I'd never realised this; I knew only that for my own visions of a planting, other accepted ways didn't feel quite right. I needed planting which was sensitive to a site. And Andrew got this straight away.

It's heartening to note that in the decades since then, this approach has since become understood and accepted. At that time people were planting in blocks, monocultures and, dare I say it, swathes, but none of it resembled how I gardened. What I saw was often lacking in personality and atmosphere. I couldn't find within it any reflections of the garden, location and the custodian of the garden. Yes, the planting designs bore traces of the designer, but this was the problem: planting ended up as a heavy stamp of design, a self-serving imposition which repeated and repeated and repeated in garden after garden. I have tried to avoid this throughout my time working with gardens. It was clear that Andrew and I had a meeting of minds.

This meeting of minds was in numerous areas. Andrew's love of shrubs was one particular moment. These garden stalwarts, which provide the vital underpinnings for a garden, had been sharp-elbowed out of planting designs in the 2000s by that upstart newcomer: the ornamental grass. Now, I think an ornamental grass can look fabulous in the right place, with the right companions. But vast sweeps of them? Strange rectangular blocks of them wrestled into a form so at odds with their habit? We agreed that so much of this is about context: whilst a planting like this might look magnificent in an open space with the right light and perfect conditions, it just looks sad and dull in another. That flower bed seen in a German park might be magnificent in context, but when it's copied and transported into another country, with different light, different soil, different background—that's when and that's why it doesn't feel quite right. And yet if some thought is put into it, and a study is made of what will be happy in that context, you can end up with something original that feels to be at home in its place.

Over the years, Andrew and I have had countless and endless conversations about what planting design actually is. We have learned to separate fashionable planting designs from what is actually achievable, maintainable and, critically, sustainable. Those enormous swathes of naturalistic planting may look wonderful in the photo of a glossy magazine, but are they sustainable? Ask the people who garden them. They may surprise you.

What is it then that captivates me in a planting?

It isn't a collection of plants that follows a fashion. When a planting design sits in its place seamlessly, seemingly effortlessly, and intelligently but without forcing a message, that's enough to spark an interest. When the garden looks different to other gardens by the same designer and yet feels right—that's what keeps me looking. And when it feels right, and it works—that's the magic moment.

Originality and soul will have that magic.

A word to the garden designer: you're not a planting designer until you garden. Until you plant things. Until you understand how plants work. If you don't do these already, now is the time to start. A solid basis in plants is essential and should go hand-in-hand with reading this book.

If you are a prospective client, do check your designer does actually garden—you'd be surprised.

Planting design is an art and a science. You need to understand a plant and how it grows, how it behaves in certain conditions and how it will appear through the different stages of its life. You need to know the names and understand the history of a plant—for example, once you understand *Mathiasella bupleuroides* 'Green Dream' is from Mexico, you'll understand that it probably won't be happy on a soggy clay soil. Be interested in a plant's backstory.

You also need an appreciation of the form of the plant itself. The structure, the texture, the colour. And not just the obvious colour of the petals, but how the tones of those petals fade as they near the centre of the plant. And the foliage: Is it green? Is it silver? Is it blue?

And then, how does this plant work with another? How does it work in a mass? How it does it change in different lights?

In short, know your plants.

As you get to know them and understand them, you'll learn their preferences and their foibles. You'll also, most importantly, get to know their personalities, and how you can bring together a group of them to have the very best of parties, whilst hosting a party for Nature at the same time. For this is what the intention of planting design is. Of course it will be sustainable—this has always been part and parcel of what I do, so I don't need to separate it out. What I am trying to create is an atmosphere, an atmosphere appropriate to the planting in terms of the location, the house, the client, and, critically, the garden itself. Without atmosphere, a planting is already dead.

Get out there, learn your plants. And then apply everything you've learned to the way you read this book. If you forget to use plants, so will others, and then we'll lose them. Exploring the ways we can bring plants together to create a thousand different effects is a magical thing indeed. It's a gift—use it, enjoy it, grow it.

—JO THOMPSON

INTRODUCTION

◂ Naturalistic planting for a country home in England.

The fortunes for planting design are changing. Early on in my horticultural career, I recognised a need to put plants front and centre. I could see that there was always a planting solution to a landscape challenge. As my career developed, landscape architects and garden designers increasingly approached me to help design the planting for their projects. They told me that they had never had a proper or extensive training in planting design and asked me if I could do something about it in my role at the London College of Garden Design. Like me, some of these designers had started their careers with a horticultural training that had stood them in good stead to a point, but others had finished courses with only a limited knowledge of plants and certainly no training in the possibilities offered by planting design.

As our understanding of the impacts of a changing climate became more understood, landscape architecture and garden design offices began crying out for more knowledge that would take current realities into account and generally give them more support, and so in 2010 I began to write a course in professional planting design. The objective was to provide an extensive exploration of planting design with a view to making planting design a recognised career path. I didn't know if anyone would come, but with the support of some incredibly talented colleagues within our industry—and from many different countries—they came to learn, and since then professional planting designers have become recognised as playing an integral role within the land-based professions. This book emerged as the natural progression of years of course development and conversations with leading plant experts on what was needed to be taught.

Of course, for centuries our designed gardens and landscapes have been created by 'planting designers.' They were professional gardeners and the enthusiasts who delighted in plants and their composition. With the increasingly urbanised landscapes of the mid-twentieth century, we saw the development of the role of the landscape architect and then later the garden designer increase, professions that celebrate the materiality of landscape. But many landscape architecture courses gradually reduced horticulture and planting design to a single module, and in some cases removed both from their courses altogether. The advent of the celebrity garden designer created a new fashion for the 'outdoor room,' where the outside resembled the interior decoration of a home; plants were used to 'soften' the hard materials in these trophy gardens, reducing plants to mere decoration.

However, in the twenty-first century we are experiencing radical changes in climate and ecology. There is a prolonged and devastating impact from population growth, increased urbanisation and a substantial reduction in tree canopy coverage. People who have never really noticed or engaged with nature are suddenly looking to nature as a cure and so we are witnessing a renewed interest in nature and especially in tree protection and planting as a way of mediating a changing climate. Opinions differ about how engaged we are with nature, but we increasingly measure cultures that are more progressive as those that are working to protect and enhance their ecology and so we now quite rightly look at the quality of our landscapes as an indicator of natural wealth. It's tempting to believe that contemporary planting design is changing the quality of our landscapes to meet these challenges, but there is still plenty of evidence of a reliance on the old ideas of the past—limited experimentation and very little innovation—where new generations are enthralled by old ideas repackaged as something new.

We desperately need more radical thought. Fortunately for us, landscape designers are now climbing on board and giving at least equal importance to plants as to modern hard landscape features, fuelling a passionate return to plants as a key feature of our landscapes. It is therefore timely for this book that some forward-thinking universities and technology colleges have even placed horticulture and planting design back on the syllabus.

I have come to understand that you don't necessarily need to have extensive landscape design or architecture training to become a planting designer. The spatial and design awareness that comes with that training will certainly support an understanding of how plants interact with the built environment, but of foremost importance is a sound understanding of good horticultural practice and a curiosity about plants. Indeed, you will find that the careers of many planting designers were started first by training in natural sciences and horticulture in particular. Whilst the elimination of many horticulture courses is still a great cause for concern, I am optimistic that the fortunes for planting design are changing.

A FRAMEWORK FOR YOUR WORK

There's is no single way of designing with plants. Different projects call for different solutions, everyone is individual, every project unique. In the twenty-first century, the challenge for planting designers is that we must deliver engaging, resilient, and functional solutions that meet the need for human interaction but ideally also fulfil other ecological roles, such as reducing urban temperatures and pollution, improving and protecting wildlife habitat, creating biodiversity and even sanctuaries for plants themselves. But how do we bring our knowledge and understanding together into intelligent planting solutions? Where do we start?

I realised that there are many books on planting that are focused on individual or groups of designers who are creating planting within a particular style. These books are absorbing but seldom show the opportunities and the

▲ A native planting design for a country garden in New South Wales, Australia.

much wider range of design approaches that are possible. So, in this book I have taken a much wider view and aimed to explore the context for all these different processes and approaches. Today's professional planting designer must have a familiarity with all of them, and needs a framework for following a career in plants as well as a good range of proven tools in their toolkit for whatever project comes their way. It's a framework that will also work for skilled garden enthusiasts wanting to develop their own planting through the language of design.

This book's framework for planting design is based upon interviews and conversations with a very large number of designers over the past fifteen years. It is a process, if you like, that will give you the confidence to consider any project large or small, private residence or public space. Within this you will recognise the work of planting designers you know already, even if they give different emphasis in their own approaches. Crucially, it will show how through exploration, understanding, and a strong narrative or story, you can engage planting in ways that will enable you to develop your own planting designs that will respond to the requirements of each individual project and help you avoid using the same list of plants and the same planting design approach every time. That might mean slowing down and taking more time to discover, explore, and design with plants, but the reward will be unique, innovative designs for each project you work on.

With the support of many individual designers and constant updating to address the environmental changes we are experiencing today, the curriculum that I first developed many years ago that emphasised planting as key to landscape design has helped establish planting design itself as an actual career. At LCGD, we've developed opportunities to study with practicing professionals with a wide range of expertise and backgrounds who make a good living from planting design every day. And that's crucial. A professional in any area still needs to make a decent salary from a chosen career, and I'm supported by people who do just that. Their enthusiasm for a career that they love is infectious, and it is immensely rewarding to see graduates creating remarkable careers and finding their own voices with their own specialist enthusiasms and innovations through the opportunity to become a professional planting designer.

ALWAYS BE INNOVATING

Early on in my career I was fortunate enough to spend time with the painter David Hockney within a garden setting. Seeing a landscape and plants through the eyes of an artist revealed hidden qualities and opportunities for me, not just in what I saw, but how design was processed. My training allows me to understand the scientific horticultural process, and to pair it with an artist's eye. It opened new avenues of research to me. I began to understand planting as a creative, changing experiment where every design is unique and where, if I took the time to explore my ideas and create a strong narrative, I could innovate via planting design. My only constant has been to eschew big trophy plants and let nature set the speed limit.

I've always been interested in artists and designers from different design realms—especially fashion and textile designers, who create things in a kind of organic blur of motion and transport me from my familiar London landscape to another world. Someone else's perspective can be of huge benefit to your creativity and will help you see new opportunities for your work. However your own unique experiences have impacted your perspective or identity, I implore you to understand them and use them as a strength. For example, I am yellow-green colour-blind, which for many years I was told would be a drawback in my work. But in researching colour and vision impairment in relation to the planting I've created over a number of landscapes for Blind Veterans UK, a charity that helps vision-impaired ex-servicemen and women to rebuild their lives after sight loss, I discovered a lot about my own relationship with colour. I also discovered that some garden designers immediately don't like what they see of my schemes. Pressed on their reasons why, I realise it's usually because they haven't taken the time to consider my planting narrative. And so whilst I have some landscape architects and garden visitors congratulating me on my planting designs, other professionals will tell me they just don't like it. But at least I get a reaction.

Working with Blind Veterans UK, I experienced designing something innovative for what is a very distinct group of people. This was invigorating, and my firm continues to work with this charity today, developing a deeper understanding of what resonates, building on our shared experience.

▲ Innovation in our future planting designs will be crucial to meet the needs of a changing climate. In this small garden, nonnatives take centre stage.

Being asked to design planting for a project outside your comfort zone will always be a challenge, but try to accept that challenge. It will allow you to stretch your skill set to create something different and innovative, independent and fearless, not predictable but impactful. Make it immersive, make it different, even make a protest, but whatever you do, just make that planting happen.

KEEP LEARNING, KEEP COLLABORATING

The opportunity to write this book has allowed me to take a pause from many years creating my own planting designs and look at other successful contemporary planting designers' work, and to contextualize how we assess what success means. I've reconnected with designers who have moved their own work forward and made new connections with people that I have long admired to discover what they believe to be important in creating rich, engaging planting schemes. The designs in the case studies that you will discover throughout the book are theirs alone and recognise a wide range of experience, talent, and innovation worldwide. Many are not purely planting designers, but there is no doubt that the featured designers have become well known due to their planting. Some may not be so well-known to you; this was a deliberate choice, so that you might see that you don't have to work for a big office or be a celebrity to enjoy planting design as a career. I am grateful for all their collaboration in this book as much as their collaboration with the landscapers, nurseries, and technicians that make their work happen. They make a valuable contribution here by providing inspiration for how you might use and interpret each stage in the planting design framework. Their generosity in sharing their thoughts and projects as well as helping me formulate what counts as good design and great process has been awesome.

Times have changed, and those who work with plants within the land-based industries are in more demand than ever. In our modern world we cannot ignore the need for more sustainable actions, processes, and ideas within our designs. Plants give voice, belonging, and knowledge; they create individual and community identity, and our landscapes and lives are strengthened through plants. The horticulturist and planting designer are once more back at the forefront of a revolution in landscape design, and they need collaboration with the wider land-based professions to make things happen. So, when you've finished reading this book, please put it into practice, develop your own design voice, find your inspiration, write your narrative, and imagine the extraordinary impact you can have on other people and our natural world.

—ANDREW FISHER TOMLIN

A planting design for vision impairment that utilises contrasting colours to aid understanding.

CHAPTER **1**

WHAT MAKES A GREAT PLANTING DESIGN?

What is it that we intuit from planting that lifts our spirits, increases our sense of well-being, allows us to escape from daily pressures of life, and also tells us where to walk, where not to trespass, where to literally stop and smell the roses? How can we measure the success of our planting designs? Considering outcomes at the inception of the design process feels counterintuitive but is in fact critical to ensuring planting design success.

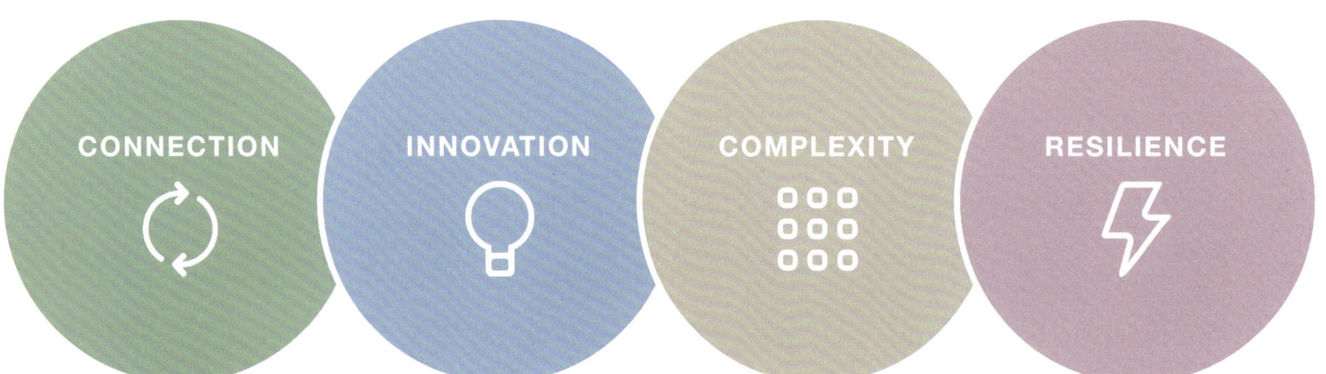

◂ The four attributes of planting design success.

New landscapes are commissioned by humans, but not all planting design is focused directly on how our planting engages with people. In a contemporary landscape it is quite possible that the brief for a landscape, and therefore the planting design, might have much wider objectives and priorities, including improving biodiversity of flora and fauna or creating new wildlife habitat. Yet even in these circumstances, the planting design will still have a secondary impact on the people who encounter it.

So, what are the attributes of planting design success? What measures of success can the contemporary planting designer use when assessing their work, whether it's focussed on engaging people or prioritises other objectives? If you study a range of successful contemporary planting designs and the landscapes that they sit within, you'll find that certain indicators of success repeat themselves. For each individual project some indicators might be more important than others, but successful planted landscapes will tend towards encompassing a mix of four key attributes.

CONNECTION

The attribute of connection indicates how we successfully engage people with plants and nature together in their place. It's about engaging people with nature but it's also about getting a response. If pleasure in planting design is subjective, then the response might be seen on a scale that allows for one person to be more enthusiastic than another, but it has nevertheless elicited a response. For example, you might love a certain planted landscape that someone else doesn't care for; both responses are valid, one just has a greater connection to the landscape and with the plants within it.

If people like our planting design, is that enough? For many clients it will be difficult to verbalise what it is they like about a planting beyond aesthetic descriptors such as colour and form, or maybe sensory descriptors such as fragrance. It may be that it contributes to their overall sense of well-being and for them that is enough. Understanding the planting further may require them to understand the story you are trying to tell through a planting narrative.

As designers we might aspire to intelligent planting where we use plants in a way that achieves functionality and practicality whilst inspiring the people who will benefit from this planting. Intelligent planting might, for example, mean planting that works for the user whilst also encouraging soil health. It might be a planting that fulfils a wider aim, such as improving biodiversity on a commercial office development.

The average person working at that office doesn't have to understand that somewhat invisible aim; they can just be happy that they can look out from their office window at an interesting, planted landscape rather than a car park. If their sense of well-being is improved by the planting, a successful connection has been made between plants and people.

▾ Communal gardens are a great way for people to connect with nature. Here, an innovative rooftop garden in Rotterdam proves a challenging growing environment but one that enables people to garden together.

INNOVATION

What are your expectations for a planting design? What are your client's? You should never be surprised if someone doesn't immediately seem to appreciate your work, as those outside the profession seldom have the tools to fully understand the subtleties inherent in a design. But that they know they cannot design is often why they called you in the first place. Learning to explain what your design will achieve is important, especially when it pushes your boundaries as a designer. The case studies in this book are by designers who each do a great job at explaining their objectives and narratives for the featured projects.

Ask yourself: Does your design push you to propose challenging planting that is stimulating and innovative? Has the project challenged you to innovate with new plants? If you just use the same plants from the same list of favourites you've used before, you'll become easily bored by your own work. So, does your design push boundaries for you and your client, *and* might it also contribute to how your planting meets other objectives, such as resiliency? It might be a planting design that is unique for that location, that uses a distinct planting palette, or that even exceeds the expectations of your client—but does it excite *you*?

Imagination and creativity are your tools for innovation. You need to be patient and flexible with your own design process to achieve this. We often have favourite places and planting designs, our own or others', that take our work in new directions and enable experimentation. Innovative planting designs can be simple and peaceful as much as they might be high-impact, immersive spaces, but if they are creative and imaginative, they will naturally engage people.

Communal gardens are a great example of how the simplest planting design, such as reintroducing a native mixed hedge to a space, might reinvent how local residents engage with nature. You don't have to change the world of planting design in every project, but you should understand how your work can push your own boundaries. Measuring innovation is not easy, but you can ask yourself how far you've stretched your imagination and creativity in achieving any planting design. Then ask your client if they like it, how it works for them, and whether they feel *engaged* by their newly planted landscape.

◂ A complex ecosystem including native flowering *Richea scoparia* at the Walls of Jerusalem National Park, Tasmania, Australia.

COMPLEXITY

Modern designed landscapes increasingly aim for ecological and biodiverse solutions. The development of a planting scheme that is both ecologically sound and complex will take time to discover and define. With the emerging changes in our climate and global loss of biodiversity, we should be able to talk about our planting designs in ecological terms and appreciate the level of control that we have within a landscape project, whatever its size or scale and in terms of how a project sits within its wider complex landscape.

Increasingly, planting design aims to mimic nature through 'naturalistic' planting aesthetics. That we are also part of that nature perhaps gives more credibility to what we are trying to achieve. Humans have been designing nature artificially for centuries, often as an attempt to connect with it. The use of natural materials in art, for example, is held in high esteem because it brings together the natural and artistic through human ingenuity. So this is not a new concept, but in times of climate crisis we should be careful not to just mimic nature for aesthetic reasons and consider how we can practically support and improve upon nature within our designs through goals such as improving soil health and avoiding chemical maintenance for aftercare.

We can demonstrate the complexity and ecological success of our designs in many ways. For example, as new measurement tools are developed, we might simply count the embodied carbon (carbon footprint) of creating a new planting and consider the impact that aftercare will have. You could focus beyond your own role within nature and design planting that is mutually supportive.

Use relevant data to assess success. If your aim is to encourage biodiversity, how would you measure it? Generate an initial definition of biodiversity that you can measure against to demonstrate the success of your planting design. Generalised objectives will not be enough to satisfy many clients, so aim to be specific. For example, is there a specific regional native plant under threat that you want to support by encouraging its use in your design? Are there particular insects and animals you want to attract? In both cases, it will be possible to provide a base measurement of what exists onsite before you plant, and then to return to measure them again after the planting has established.

RESILIENCE

Resilience is a relatively new term in planting design. It is often linked to a changing climate, and is generally associated with adaptive planting solutions. What we are aiming for is planting design that displays long-lasting success in the face of critical changes in climate. Long-term aims for successful, resilient planting can also be experienced in terms of meeting client needs for a planting that will stand the test of time, growing in a way that's desirable whilst also being adaptive to an increasingly unpredictable range of weather patterns. Of course, as planting designers we understand that what we plant will change in structure and form almost as soon as we have planted it, and that plants will interact with each other to form communities over time. To achieve resilient planting, ask yourself if your design takes these considerations into effect.

Native plants are often seen as a tool for resilience, as it's believed utilising plants that have developed alongside each other will help a garden connect with the wider native landscape. But native plants will not necessarily be resilient to climate change, and contemporary planting design has moved towards considering how native and nonnative plants can be used together in planted habitats to create resilient landscapes. There is still a place for solely native plantings, especially in areas of distinct climate or where that climate may be changing slowly, but the impact of people and other factors such as installed drainage, buildings, and hardscape will likely stress native plant communities since we're asking them to thrive in decidedly nonnative conditions.

This blended approach to creating resilient planting is actually not new. International trade has seen the migration of plant species around the world for centuries, and indeed nonnatives incorporated from places with even more extreme conditions may hold the key to climate resilience at home. Horticulture will often also embrace traditional methods of maintenance, such as better hygiene standards in aftercare, to support successful planting; our planting designs may indeed rely on traditional knowledge to support contemporary ideas of resilience in our future designs.

▾ The Taft Botanical Gardens in California utilise plants from similarly dry Mediterranean climates to create a spring bloom.

◂ This small residential garden in England has a distinct microclimate that allows for a high proportion of nonnative plants. It will likely require regular review to measure its success, but will also inspire a more diverse plant palette for future designs.

SUMMARY: MEASURING SUCCESS

These four attributes are useful metrics for assessing our own work. Our clients can provide some feedback, but we can and should also measure success ourselves. Is your planting design inspiring? Does it fulfil your objectives? Has it pushed your boundaries? Some of the results you achieve are measurable. You might measure the ecological benefit of your design through aspects such as the attraction of wildlife, sustainable approaches like no-waste construction, low-impact aftercare, or working with the site's existing plant layers. Some results are necessarily subjective, but are equally important. Do you *like* what you have created? Does your client like it?

It is equally important to revisit projects over time, in fact as essential a part of a planting designer's work as designing a new project. Clients will appreciate the continued interest in the health of an established planting, and we can achieve insights into where our successes lie both through our own observations and client feedback. Their insight is every bit as useful to you as that of another professional. Sometimes we might be surprised by the positive response that we receive from the simplest of designs. Other times we might see a way to enhance a client's experience even more.

There are also times when we might use these four attributes of success when assessing someone else's planting design. Sometimes we are called in to improve an existing planted landscape, for example, and our first inclination is often to retain the larger structural, established planting as something to build upon. Our first step should instead be to assess the original aims of that planting, and to decide whether the design is successful in achieving them. If we know that, *then* we can assess whether our new client's objectives will work and how we can sustainably adapt the existing planting to those new objectives. It will help us understand why we appreciate someone else's planting and how we can successfully develop and innovate in our own designs in the future.

CHAPTER **2**

FINDING YOUR PLANTING DESIGN VOICE

◂ An extensive Mediterranean-climate planting above Palazzo Parisi's swimming pool in Rieti, Italy, reveals the unique planting 'voice' of its designer, Arabella Lennox-Boyd.

Different projects call for different solutions. Every client is individual, every project unique. Planting design is not a static subject, and the professional planting designer will develop expertise over many years by honing skills and adapting to the demands of various settings and personalities. Although we start each project afresh, if we are to achieve imaginative, creative designs it is useful for a designer to develop a process or framework to use as a guide through the complex process of designing with plants. A larger framework for planting design allows you to find your own design voice and to develop your approach to planting over a body of work.

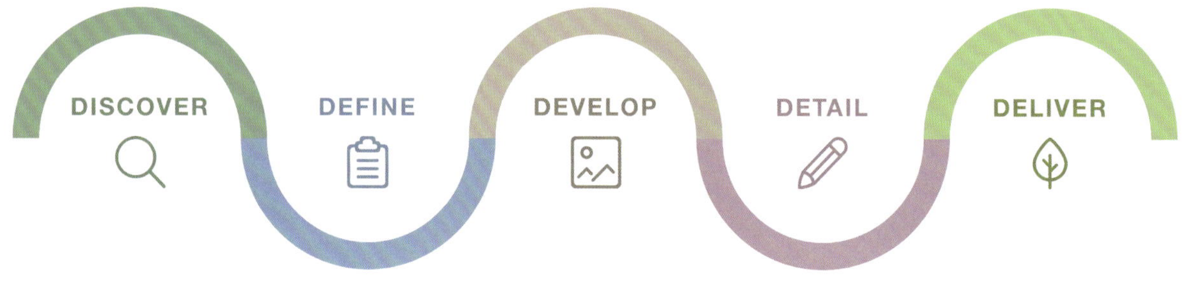

◂ This framework for planting design is based on a large number of successful designers' approaches to their work and aims to support creativity and innovation in your own designs. Some designers may place more emphasis on one area than another but if you observe others' work and your own design process, you will likely recognise these distinct design stages.

The framework for planting design presented here has been developed and tested over the years through my own projects, by working with and listening to some of the world's top planting designers, and interviewing many more working professionals. Whilst they all might have different styles, ideas, or start and end points, at a fundamental level they all approach their work in a similar way. This framework enables us to create innovative, imaginative plantings.

Successful planting designers may give different weight and importance to different aspects of their work, but a solid design framework allows time for the exploration, definition, and development of ideas. The steps of detailing and delivering planting designs will then flow naturally and efficiently. Whether you are a designer with a particular style for which you've become well known or enjoy working across a wide range of styles and with a diverse client base, the use of a framework process will give you the confidence that what you have created will successfully meet your objectives and help you find your design voice.

The next chapters focus on explaining this framework for creating planting design in the context of an ever-changing world where every project brings something potentially new. It will help you to develop your own approach, framed within a wider landscape context, because planting design is a creative, changing experiment where every design is unique. It will also give you context for various approaches to elements such as structure, aesthetics, and plant qualities.

It's a loose framework that will encourage your creativity and innovation but give you the flexibility to launch yourself in different directions as you develop your design voice. It will support you when you want the confidence to be innovative and imaginative in your planting design and to take on any scheme, whatever its size or location. It will also support you when you are up against a timescale and just need to get on with it.

It's important to note that the proposed framework is not designed to support the creation of a single style or archetype such as naturalistic, formal, ornamental, urban, country, native, or nonnative. It will deliver the outline of a process to work to for any style of design (those stylistic planting archetypes, however, are explained in Chapter 7). The case studies featured throughout this volume are from designers around the world, and there are examples of all these planting styles. These case studies also illustrate how contemporary design for different landscape types might emphasise different stages of the framework in their creation. All the case studies, though, have two things in common: first, the thoroughness of thought that has gone into the discovery and definition of each project and, second, they illustrate the importance of a strong narrative and

▲ Designer Colm Joseph uses hedges and birch trees to anchor a strong garden structure whilst informal planted beds create an immersive experience in this small rural garden in Suffolk, England.

atmosphere, whether purely functional or creatively conceptual in their delivery.

The framework approach to planting design will enable you to tackle any design regardless of scale, wherever you work and whatever challenges you face. It will encourage you to take time to explore what is required of your setting, whether you have an inspiring mandate or not, and to familiarise yourself with the regional climate; from there you will define your project brief, your objectives, and your rules to create a compelling narrative and atmosphere.

You will soon develop your own planting design voice, your own approach that will open a world of planting opportunity. It will help you stop being tempted to use the same stalwart plants every time and instead consistently develop a wider knowledge of what could be rather than what simply is. You'll discover how planting design can be a creative, changing experiment and how every design can be unique. The opportunities are endless, and this framework aims to keep those opportunities open for you for as long as and wherever you might be designing with plants.

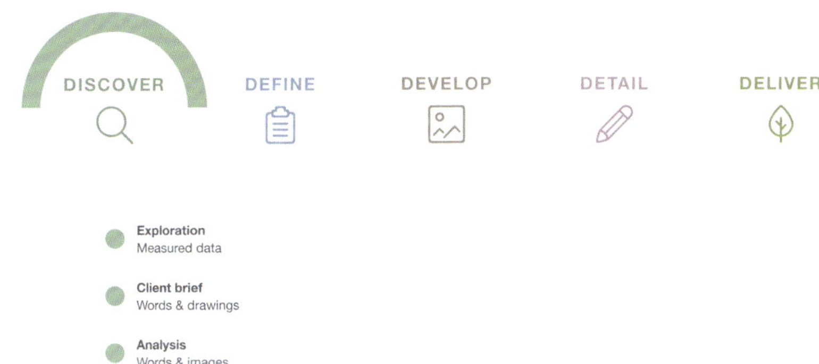

CHAPTER **3**

SOLVING THE RIGHT CHALLENGE

◂ To create engaging planting designs, we need to first start by discovering what we have and understanding what our challenge is before we can begin to make any design decisions. Here the designer Jo Wakelin evaluated existing conditions in terms of soil, moisture, and climate before creating planting that celebrates both the plants and their setting in a wider New Zealand landscape.

The practical, logical collection of information is our starting point for creating great planting designs. Design is a journey. We need to start somewhere, and we cannot make decisions about the planting we will use without collecting useful local data, digesting what that data means, and then ordering the information we have collected. We need to discover and define what the real challenge is before we can solve it.

There will be information we cannot change; this is survey data whose effect on our plans we might question, but is unequivocal. We always need to collect and consider objective data when designing with plants, such as aspect, nearby buildings, and measured size. We can seldom change these data points, but having this data at hand might allow us to consider how to ameliorate less-than-ideal conditions further into our design process. For example, we might create artificial conditions to host plants that wouldn't normally grow in that soil, climate zone, etc. say, a botanical display of acid-loving plants in a raised bed.

Then there are the more subjective factors that we need to consider: our feelings, tastes, and opinions. We will have innate subjective reactions to the setting, and so will our client. Both need to be revealed and understood. The project discovery stage, given to the collection and analysis of data and how you react to this objective and subjective information, will form the foundation of your planting design.

There is no denying that sometimes the information you need can be difficult to obtain, but it will clearly be an essential part of your design development. You should make time for this stage. Slow down and really analyse the information that you discover. It will give you the confidence to make decisions as you develop your planting design and help you to discover new and exciting possibilities with plants.

The systematic collection of survey data underpins the discovery phase of your design work. The most obvious part of the survey stage is the collection of data through a measured survey which will collect information such as overall dimensions, specific features, and level changes. The collection of survey data, to the planting designer, however, is more extensive than simply measuring a site's layout.

It is unlikely that we can change the undesirable conditions that we may discover within the survey phase unless we have a reasonable budget. For example, we might change the prevalence of shade within a garden by removing trees or formative pruning of shrubs; a new building might impact light levels, or conversely, we might discover a need to increase shade to satisfy the needs of the client. Similarly, we might change the soil when delivering our planting design through the addition of soil ameliorants, but only the most extreme client requests and budgets will lead to substantial changes such as importing new and different soil. And even then, we might try to change a client opinion about the

Where to Find Data

On heritage projects, the availability of historic images such as photos and postcards can be useful. When these are combined with a tree stump survey, they might reveal original tree species now lost that are good candidates for reintroduction.

Many resources can help you gather data:

- Environmental agencies
- Local and regional authorities
- State and federal government departments
- Independent institutions such as landscape, architecture, or heritage organisations
- Meteorological offices
- Online soil data maps, land surveys, historical societies, and heritage sites. But always be aware of provenance—who is giving you this information, and how reliable and up-to-date is it?
- Local libraries and regional museums, especially for historic data which has not been digitized
- The locality itself—key vegetation, geographic characteristics and indicator species, use and identification of local building materials

wisdom of doing so, especially if we are aiming for sustainable design and development with a low carbon footprint.

Much of the information we need will come from a site appraisal, but a large amount of information, especially data, can be collected in the office, online and through research.

ENVIRONMENTAL DATA

The primary elements in plant growth are water (moisture), air (carbon dioxide and oxygen), warmth, light, nutrients, and substrates. Without water, plants cannot absorb nutrients from soil or other substrates; these are also the physical support into which most plants will anchor themselves. And so, at a very basic level, discovering environmental data is about understanding moisture, soil, and light levels to analyse the likely performance of the plants you will eventually choose. It will help determine the nature and distribution of this planting beyond traditional design ideas of structure, pattern, and aesthetics.

Understanding what you have and where will help you meet the right challenge. Respect what you have rather than battling to change it. It will make it easier to create rich, biodiverse, and sustainable planting habitats. For example, understanding the size, usefulness, and ability of existing vegetation to adapt to a changing climate and that vegetation may be very useful if it has thrived in this place.

What environmental data is useful to collect? Weather (seasonal changes) and climate (long-term weather) should be considered through macro data like annual rainfall, but also consider the microclimate of the site; landscape features such as walls or windbreaks, buildings, and other vegetation might impact what will thrive. Soil type and pH are essential to our understanding for future planting, but don't forget to assess drainage and hydrology also.

Existing vegetation characteristics beyond aesthetics are important. If existing plants look healthy, incorporating them into your new design may be useful. Also consider how plants that may be beyond the planting site's boundaries, such as tall trees, might modify the growth of your plants by casting shade or creating copious leaf litter.

At a basic level, you should attempt to identify fauna, pests, and diseases that might be prevalent in the local landscape and determine how they are currently managed. Future proposals may require ecological surveys and a deeper understanding of the site, but locally available data and observation should help you identify immediate challenges and your understanding of local biodiversity.

The challenges created by air, water, and noise pollution may not be immediately obvious the first time you visit a site, but be aware of these and consider, for instance, the impact of nearby highways and watercourses on your design choices.

◂ Extremely detailed and realistic high-resolution 3D illustrations of planet Earth are readily available from several governmental agencies. This image, taken from space, is furnished by NASA.

▴ A tropical forest in Central America.

▴ Take fauna into account.

⏶ Flag square in downtown São Paulo, Brazil.

▲ Picturesque village Adlestrop in the Cotswolds, U.K.

Local or regional identity can have an impact on your eventual plant choices, so be open to identifying locally native flora as well as design styles that may be prevalent in the area that you are working in.

It's important that you spend the time to find out what could be vital information; the survey element of discovery can mean that you will need to collect a large amount of information. You might decide to use an aide-mémoire to ensure you collect all the survey data you need. This is a good way of gathering all the relevant data in one trip to a research facility so that when you return to the office you realise you haven't left something out.

Measured Data

Most measured data will be obtained by having a professional surveyor create a digital record of your project area. A planting designer will be likely to place different emphasis on data than, say, a landscape architect. For example, hydrology might have more importance on the selection of plants than the general layout of a park.

Your surveyor may not have the knowledge to identify trees and shrubs; they may have delivered locations and sizes of certain objects in their drawings, but you may need to add the detail. However, a professional tree surveyor will be easy to find and can provide you not only with the identification of trees but also an idea of their current health and future resilience. Always use a professional and always be sure of the provenance of your data. If an existing measured survey is supplied, ensure that it is up-to-date and accurate by checking some key dimensions; even digital surveys can lose accuracy when being converted into different types of files or in printing.

RECORDING MEASURED DATA ON OVERLAY SKETCHES

As well as measured dimensions and slope, you should consider capturing data such as the overall topography, aspect, and orientation, as well as the impact of existing structures, services, and vegetation on the garden. Sketches overlaid on a measured survey can be helpful to understanding and communicating your findings.

Also research and record relevant, practical data such as:

- Built environment. What hard materials will be retained and could have an impact on planting?
- Ownership. Who might control any changes to the landscape?
- Land use. Is this an existing landscape or a perceived planting strategy for the future?
- Architectural style, history, and heritage. Are there particular regional requirements in force, such as an effort to promote an endemic species?
- Legal restrictions. What local, regional, and state planning restrictions and constraints could have an impact on your design proposal?

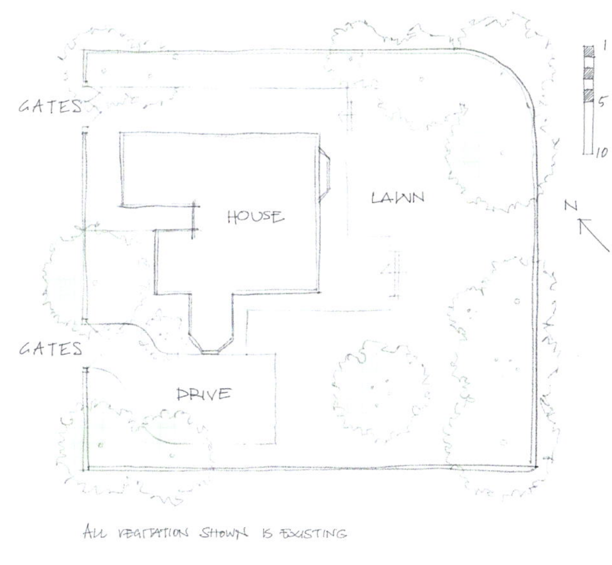

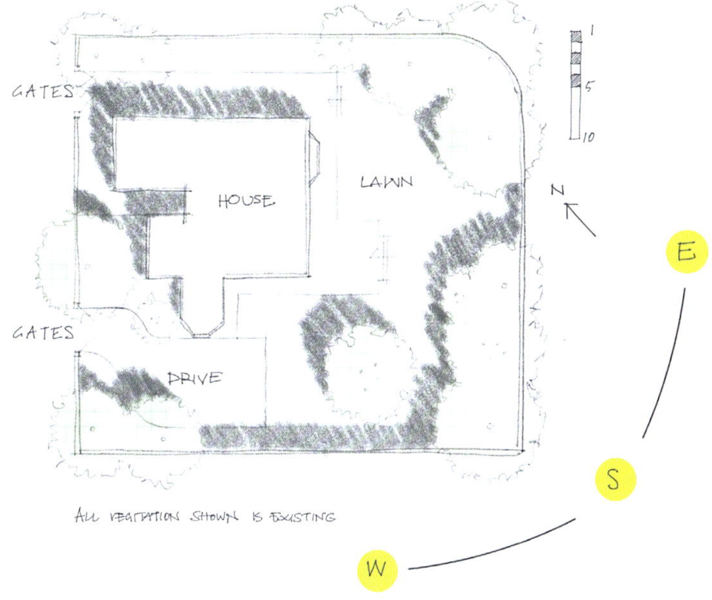

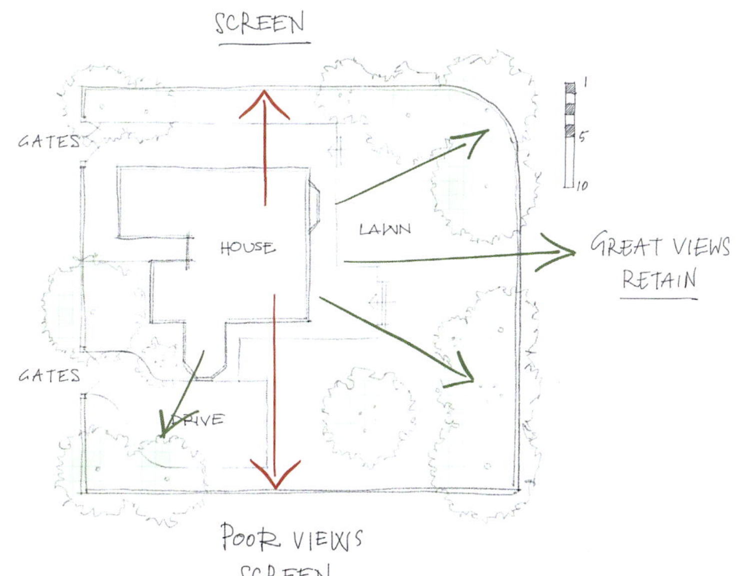

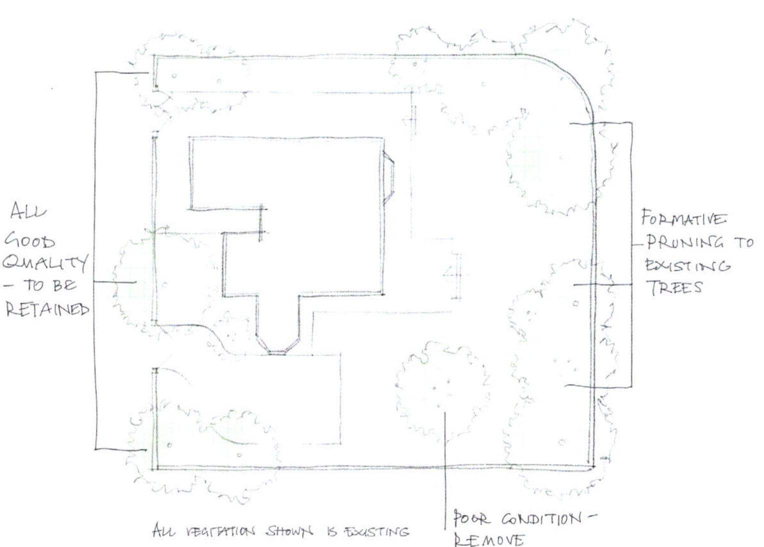

Consider using your original survey plan (top left) with an overlay of how the sun and shade on your landscape site changes through the day with the passage of the sun (top right). You could also use this tool to review how the sun and shade will change through the seasons.

Your survey plan might help you consider and illustrate access and egress, where views out of and into the site exist, and the quality of these views. Should they be 'borrowed' or do they need screening from view?

Existing vegetation that might be useful to retain for a site where sustainability is of importance should be recorded. Consider spatial and horticultural characteristics, especially the condition of existing vegetation.

DISCOVER

THE CLIENT BRIEF

Client opinions will be expressed in a client brief. Sometimes this is a written document, occasionally it's a series of visual images or a mood board, but this is most often simply a conversation between you and the client. It is very likely that you will be the one to write up the client brief, although your client may occasionally take that initiative or start to put something formal together. You should always consider that brief as valuable intelligence in determining a starting direction, but a client's wish list will likely contain insufficient data to inform your planting design in and of itself. Consider it one part of the picture that you need to build before progressing to design development.

Landscape and garden designers will naturally give some reverence to the brief that they receive from their clients, but client briefs are often not detailed when it comes to planting design. A client might have a strong idea of how they want a garden or landscape to function, but it is rare that they will have as strong a vision of the planting they want. It is not unusual for clients to approach us for help with their outdoor spaces because, whilst they know they want plants, they do not understand how plants work or how to include them within a design. Plants, of all garden design elements, hold an almost mystical level of intrigue for our clients. They quickly get caught up in the challenge of scientific names, the vast range of possible plant choices, not to mention zonal and climate constraints. This can be to the advantage of the professional planting designer, for it enables them to make a living from their services. After all, if everyone understood plants and how to use and grow them, there would be no role for us!

WHAT DO YOU ALREADY KNOW?

If you have already been involved at an early stage in the design development of a garden or landscape, you may already have a good understanding of your client's needs and what they want from their space. However, planting designers can often be brought into a project at a later stage, when the structural layout of planted areas has already been determined. This is especially true for public projects, but if you work regularly with a larger design team, request to be included early on in a project as the one with the planting expertise.

It is also possible that no earlier design stage exists, and your client is asking you to create new planted areas within an existing landscape or to replace existing planted areas. The busy lives people lead often mean that they want planting that requires less aftercare but do not understand what this means. They might even fear what 'maintenance' will entail. It's your job to reassure them. They may have heard that native plants are 'good' but don't understand why. They might ask for them without understanding the look they'll create. Or, a client may be replacing existing planting in hopes of a scheme that is aesthetically more engaging or will be more adaptive to a changing climate. Whatever the reason, we should uncover what is driving our clients' decisions and whilst your survey data provides objective facts that *you* can deal with, the client brief may reveal conflicting ideas. Open discussions around these will lead both them and you to make sound subjective decisions.

Remember that a client may not be visually creative and will understand that they won't have the planting vision that you have. They are employing you *for* that vision, your experience, and your ability to spot the opportunities that they cannot. If, on the other hand, they have a strong opinion about planting, ask them for examples of other gardens they admire. They might not understand the challenges inherent in executing a similar vision on their own property, nor, conversely, what other planting directions might be a good match for their space, but it's a good starting point.

Prompting a Client Response

The development of a client brief is often based on loose, somewhat relaxed research involving conversations with a client. Experience demonstrates that many clients are not able to articulate what they want easily and so the use of images to prompt a reaction can be very helpful. Those images might be of previous work you have created or might employ reference images of other landscapes. You might also use conceptual images to prompt a response—for example, the pattern of a woven fabric can be used to explain colour and tone. You might explain planting structure through simple sketches in elevation or perspective.

This piece of woven material by the artist Anni Albers, at right, could inspire a conversation about colour and layout, for example, if the expectation is for planting at a large scale.

Your role is to ask questions to determine what might work for your client. It is a useful skill to get a client to elucidate their ideas through words; not everyone is good at this, so showing a variety of images alongside what they tell you can be a great way to get a reaction. Indeed, this use of vision or mood boards to start a conversation on what planting might look like in terms of atmosphere is a useful tactic at this stage. Mood boards allow your client to understand the effect of planting on the character of a site and to voice an opinion about various styles, colours, and textures so you can consider what plants they might or might not like.

Showing your client images of existing planting alongside your words is a good way of getting a reaction. This perennial meadow style of planting in Maximilianpark in the Netherlands by Piet Oudolf, at right, would quickly provoke a reaction from the client to this naturalistic concept.

WHO ELSE MIGHT HAVE A PROFESSIONAL OPINION?

Other people in the design process will also have an opinion which can be fed into the client brief at this stage. The opinions of the principal garden or landscape designer or landscape architect will be important because they will have already spent time with the client and understand what they want. The project lead may even have already developed a narrative, certainly for the landscape but also for the overall style of planting that will be required. They can be your best source of subjective information. Others that may have a say in the client brief will be other build professionals such as architects and other landscape professionals such as hydrologists and sports surface designers. Existing gardeners, especially head gardeners, possess deep knowledge of the existing site and will look after the planting once delivered. They have a very useful role to play for your site discovery and the eventual long-term success of your planting design.

▾ Sometimes it's useful to get out and meet groups that have an interest and a say in the future of a landscape. You may get useful information by engaging with them in the landscape under consideration.

WHAT ABOUT PUBLIC OPINION?

Public perception of a site can be important and can reveal cultural significance that you might not have found on your own. For a publicly accessed landscape, you should consult this wider audience at this early stage, especially if there are groups involved in the landscape development, such as traditional custodians of the land, heritage societies, or volunteer gardening groups. In a public or communal space, they may be people who will use the landscape alongside your client. Indeed, your client may have already collected some data from them and be acting to develop the planted landscape as a way of providing a service to these groups.

You should certainly consider coordinating a response from these groups or individuals through surveys, interviews, and observation. Onsite events to gather opinions can be very useful. However, there is a likelihood that you will be collecting a large amount of conflicting information. Each invested party will expect you to respond to their individual desires, but of course your task is to meet the demands of a larger overall group. Ultimately you are unlikely to be able to fulfil everyone's demands and may have to disappoint some stakeholders if there's not one clear consensus.

In reality, it will be simpler to engage with a wider audience once you have at least an outline of your planting design narrative to present to them. You will develop this in the next phase of your work, where you can convey the narrative in words and a planting atmosphere through mood boards. You will more easily gauge a reaction to your proposed narrative for the planting knowing that you have already generated some ideas for how that design could be fulfilled. This focuses the wider audience's minds on the parameters set by the survey and your client's brief, and how it can translate into an outcome that they will benefit from.

By developing a client brief, even if the client is relatively inexperienced about plants, you will form a foundation of information to add to the survey data. You are likely to get some sense of the narrative you might be able to employ for the planting. Client conversations will give you hints of what inspires them, whether it's a favoured holiday destination, an artist, or a preference for formality or looseness. Therefore, it will always pay to spend time discovering more about your clients and their interests and inspirations, as well as researching the survey data that forms the objective facts about their landscape or garden space.

USING THE SCIENTIFIC DATA YOU HAVE COLLECTED

Before moving forward to defining your project in terms of narrative and design quality, it is appropriate at this phase of the process to consider the horticultural or scientific qualities of plants and landscape. Design qualities of plants are described in more depth later in this book, as you start to detail plant choices, but for now simply be aware that they will play an important part in your role as a planting designer and in producing successful designs. Here we are looking at the horticultural knowledge that underpins your design, as planting designers have an obligation to promote good horticulture as much as to create engaging designs.

ECOLOGY AND OUR ROLE

The relationship between plants and people is based on the underpinning science of ecology, for we are all part of nature and ecological processes. Ecological principles are very much in play when we design a new planted landscape. These principles are often presented in different ways but will interact with each other and are in a complex state of change due to time, location, intervention, and plant species. Plants can interact spontaneously where we have no control, but they can also interact in a designed way, as we will discover when exploring the composition of plants and the level of control that can be exerted over plants within different design approaches.

Soil and Other Substrates

The main function of soil is to provide an environment for plants to grow in, supplying nutrients through water within the soil, and anchoring the plant in its place. Soil is the most biodiverse material on our planet, though it covers only a small part of the land mass. Only about 7.5 percent of the earth's surface provides the arable soil we rely on for food. Depth is a fundamental property of soils; most soils are less than 3 metres deep, but actual depths vary significantly for different soil types. The relationship between soil structure and plants is also complex and ever-changing.

There is an uncertainty about defining soils objectively that we can only begin to discuss in this book, but in modern times a planting designer might consider the benefits of soil structure in terms of supporting biodiversity, conserving water, absorbing runoff, and mitigating climate change.

There is also now much experimentation around soils and substrates, especially artificial and manufactured soils; the professional planting designer might look for solutions ranging from the preservation of naturally occurring soils to the creative use of substrates such as construction waste when faced with challenging sites. The latter is often discussed in terms of wildlife value as much as a soil for planting, helping to increase biodiversity.

▲ Soils will vary even within short distances from each other and will help define rules for your planting project.

◄ Plants can provide an opportunity to improve our well-being, as seen here through a community planting project.

Delivery: Mapping Your Data

- A lot of the practical and environmental data that is critical for designers may only be of passing interest to a client. For example, they know which views they want to retain and which to screen, but not how those choices will impact the design.
- Satellite images can be useful for exploring the wider landscape beyond your site boundaries, especially for large sites. You might discover a wide diversity of habitat within a short distance of your own project landscape.

- It is useful to map your data for a public presentation, especially if you might not be present, to create some context. This could be in the form of satellite maps or basic data overlaid on a survey plan so that members of the public understand the data you are dealing with. It also helps establish your professional standing. Generally, this will be collected information that will inform later design phases and so it will also be important information that will be used internally.

Manufactured soils are created from organic waste such as green waste (from household waste, bark, and other sources) mixed with inorganic materials such as sand or crushed rock. Naturally occurring soil will tend towards being a dynamic product with a naturally supportive microbial diversity. Consider this a good environment for planting but one that may also be damaged—especially from interaction with humans. In modern times, imported soils will often be manufactured soils; these may be a bespoke mixture with the aim of supporting the planting that is intended for a specific project. If you can protect and retain as much naturally occurring soil as possible on your project, you will be well placed to create a good environment for your plants. But it's just not always possible. New urban landscapes might therefore often include a range of soils—both naturally occurring and new manufactured soils.

Moisture

The primary elements in plant growth are moisture (water), air (carbon dioxide and oxygen), warmth, light, nutrients, and substrates. Without water plants cannot absorb nutrients from soil or other substrates which are also the physical support into which most plants will anchor themselves. All these elements interact and are essential to plant growth.

The impact of moisture availability on your planting design will vary wherever you are located and from project to

▾ Moisture availability is a key element in plant choice.

A changing climate requires planting designers to constantly test their ideas about plant choices.

project. Close attention to the behaviour of soils and growth of plants at the survey stage will help you determine some of the potential challenges you may encounter. For example, you may witness a need to improve drainage after prolonged periods of rain or recognise signs of heavy clay soils during periods of drought.

Moisture issues are relatively common, and a knowledge of horticultural techniques will help you address them as well as give you the ability to develop creative solutions. For example, drainage can be improved with the addition of organic matter over time, but you might consider the use of rain gardens (discussed later) to collect and filter excess water as a more immediate remedy. The latter is a particularly useful solution as we are generally experiencing more severe downpours because of a changing climate. The inverse to this is the need to improve soil moisture retention. Amending soils with organic material will build water-holding capacity overall, and waterwise techniques such as regular removal of weeds and mulching will also help.

Climate

Whilst we are experiencing a wide range of effects from a changing climate, several specific factors will impact the planting designer's work. These can best be summarised as:

- Hotter temperatures and therefore heat stress
- Increased drought, restrictions on water for irrigation, and increased risk of fires and forest mortality
- Changes in seasonality
- More severe storms that can lead to localised flooding
- Loss of species and biodiversity
- Habitable region of pests and diseases expanding

This is just part of the overall picture, but outlines some of the key challenges to creating resilient planting schemes. Sustainable solutions are discussed later in this book.

Microclimates

Larger changes in climate are only part of the story for planting design. Microclimates will also have an impact within an individual landscape. Factors that create microclimates are easily assessed at the survey stage, and strategies aimed at working with opportunities or countering challenges can be worked into your design rules for the project brief (discussed in the next chapter).

- Topography: the higher the landscape above sea level the cooler it will be, and, possibly more exposed. Hills can intercept rainfall, dips and hollows within the topography of a site will collect cooler air with the chance of frost pockets, which in turn will increase the chance of harmful late frosts and shorten the available growing season.
- Aspect considers the amount of light and warmth on the landscape. South-facing (in the northern hemisphere), or north-facing (in the southern hemisphere) aspects are lighter and warmer. Slopes might enhance this. Walls that warm during the day might release warmth through the night.
- Exposure to the desiccating effects of wind can be stressful to plants and, with more extreme storms, cause plant damage. But plants can be part of the solution when used to slow down rather than block wind. Whilst a simple fence will create more air turbulence for plants and likely give them a short life, a planted hedge will be considerably more resilient and provide biodiversity benefit.
- Shade should always be considered an opportunity, especially in warmer climates, and it also offers a chance to grow shade-loving plants. Indeed, some approaches to planting composition (discussed later) will adapt themselves well to a design where there is an existing canopy of trees and shrubs. In some regions there is a move towards planting shade gardens to contribute to a reduction in the incidence of skin cancers.
- Plants will influence microclimate, the obvious factors being creating shade and moisture demand. Over time, they might also modify a microclimate further and affect other factors such as soil conditions. For example, deciduous tree leaf litter can initially make a soil nutrient poor and moorland grasses can gradually acidify the soil they are planted in.

An understanding of microclimates can lead to more creative choices in your designs.

▲ An understanding of plant growth habits and interactions is essential to planting design success.

Plant Growth Patterns

The characteristics of how plants grow and change over time and then interact with other plants will have a direct impact on the way that you design with plants. A naturalistic planting approach will select communities of plants that grow in the same conditions or habitat and will engage with the dynamic nature of plants as a relatively simple way of controlling how plants will grow together.

The very fact that we place plants to grow alongside each other means that there will be a natural interaction between them that can, over time, lead to changes in the way that your chosen plants will grow as they begin to form their own dynamic community. A good example would be the self-seeding of plants that might not be so welcome in a formal ornamental planting as in a wilding project. Even naturalistic planting requires some human interaction to ensure that no single species dominates. The level of human interaction with plants will be an individual choice. Increasingly, for example, a changing climate has encouraged people to plant more trees; but this is not a panacea, can't be applied to every site, and the impetus to plant trees is often dependent on cultural preservation or heritage.

▸ *Armillaria mellea*, the honey fungus, is impacted by the surrounding environment and a changing climate.

Pests and Diseases

The rapidly changing climate is having a major impact on the spread of pests and diseases, as is global trade. Milder winters, rising temperatures, and changing seasonal patterns, matched with drought stress, flooding, and storm damage increase the susceptibility of plants to pest and disease damage. As planting designers, we need to be aware of how plant performance is changing in relation to these threats and to follow adaptive strategies where we are working. Knowledge is our friend, so consider following plant scientists, horticultural institutions, and government environmental information through social media as much as through professional bodies to keep up with the latest research and regulations.

Human Impacts

Whether we actively or passively interact with nature and landscape, humans have the greatest impact on plants. In an urban setting we can choose to ignore issues such as pollution, water management, and noise, or we can use our plant knowledge to alleviate these challenges. Developers might ignore and damage trees but increasingly at their own cost, as local government authorities often impose fines for careless behaviour. In the countryside, we can witness big agriculture degrading irreplaceable soils but also increasingly better managing the land, including the planting of large areas of trees and different management of hedges as a way of supporting a more biodiverse landscape. Our clients will expect their needs and desires to come first when we create a new planting, so whatever we design will implicitly include a human impact to consider. How we promote that complex balance between nature and humans, work to improve biodiversity, and protect existing ecosystems will be vital for the future (and sometimes, with a client that is uninterested, we might do it anyway, by stealth).

▲ Humans have an outsize impact on plant life, but we can choose to make this a positive experience for both sides.

▶ You should analyse the quality of the site you will design. In this garden in Provence, France, for example, you might put a high value on the expansive distant view of the French countryside, which may lead you to borrow the view in your final planting design.

ANALYSING AND UNDERSTANDING YOUR DATA

Merely collecting data and information will not help you analyse a site, you must synthesize it. Before you complete this phase in the development of your planting design, you should consider the information you have gathered, or it will be left behind and forgotten when you begin to develop your design and make plant choices.

Analysis is the final element of discovery that brings together the information you have gathered. Looking at data with a critical eye will lead to the formation of a complete project brief and vision for your planting design in the next phase of the planting design framework. By analysing the information collected, you are encouraged to react to what you have learned. You will consider the existing quality and character of the landscape that you have been presented with to make decisions on the future quality and character of the planting that you will design.

Your analysis gives a value to the objective survey data and the subjective client information you have collected. You should ask yourself about what you have discovered. What is your reaction to the site? How does it make you feel? What is your reaction to the data you have in hand?

Analysis is about valuing the information you have discovered. For example, that there is a view out of a garden to a larger landscape is objective analysis, while questioning whether it is a great or poor view is subjective analysis. By placing a value on that view, you will understand what you are dealing with and begin to make judgements that will support you in your project development, such as whether you frame or screen that view.

At this stage, you will be starting to form some opinions about the project. Analysis of your data will essentially start you thinking about the opportunities presented and will set you on a path to a strong narrative. You may also start to grasp some subjective challenges that you have no control over, such as how a garden is overlooked by a neighbour, but you might also know there may be a planted solution. You may also identify objective challenges that you have no control over, such as aspect and the way that the sun travels across the landscape. By analysing this, however, you will be able to create a planted solution to compensate for difficult conditions—for example, by creating more shade.

Your analysis about the character of the landscape will, in the next phase of your planting design development, form part of your project brief. In this next phase you will create rules that will deal with challenges and support your planting decisions as you develop your actual detailed planting design. For now, you should assess all this survey information using some simple rules:

- Narrow down the field of information to what is essential and important.
- Acknowledge that objective assessments cannot be changed, and accept them.
- Decide which subjective assessments also cannot be changed, such as a client's firm opinions, and accept them.
- Know when to stop analysing and start doing.

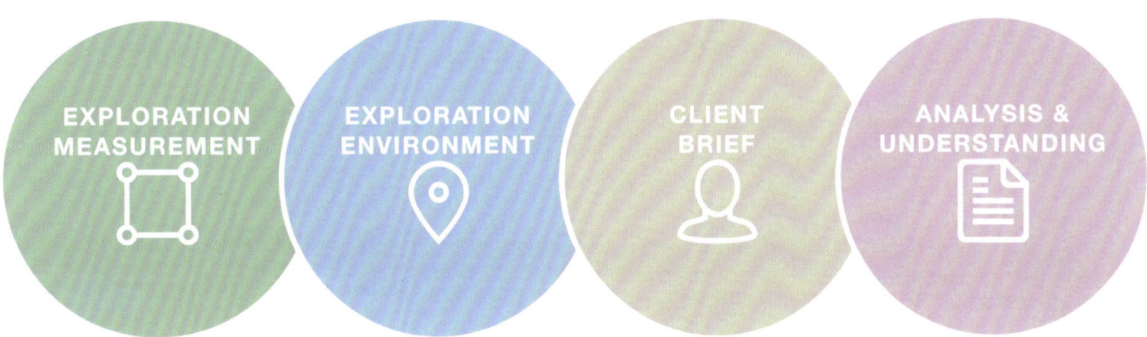

The value in your analysis and synthesis of the data you have collected lies especially in how it brings together your exploration of the measured and environmental data with your client brief to bring meaning to the information collected.

How to Identify Plants

Identifying plants can sometimes seem a daunting task when you first start to design, but many types of resources exist to help you build up your own plant knowledge.

The diversity of the plant world is extensive and sometimes it seems we'll never find the name of a plant we've discovered in a garden or park. There are plenty of books that list and illustrate plants, but how do you know where to start?

You will find a wealth of knowledge amongst your professional community. Befriending a few colleagues will help make your plant identification easier. A support group like this can be invaluable in identifying not just plant names but also pests and diseases when you've exhausted your own knowledge and research hasn't helped you make an ID.

Fortunately for us, technology has greatly improved our ability to identify plants at the press of a button. Search engines like Google Lens can be very handy and there are plant identification apps that have varying degrees of accuracy. Search on your app shop for 'plant identifier' and lots will come up. Check the reviews to see if others have found them useful, then test them out. They will often show you several options for a plant; several searches will tell you if it's consistently telling you the same plant name. Start by choosing a plant whose name you know with certainty to see if it's working!

SUMMARY: DISCOVERING THE TRUE VALUE IN YOUR NEW LANDSCAPE

The importance of the discovery phase lies in the information you find through a complete survey, using it to craft a meaningful client brief, and the value that you place upon the data you've gathered in your analysis. Don't rush to a planting master plan and try to design planting straightaway. Give yourself time to consider the parameters and challenges that you are working towards, and especially what will inspire and be acceptable to your client. This means that instead of attempting to select plants based solely on your existing plant knowledge, you should place equal emphasis on your newly acquired *project* knowledge. You will start to see unexpected opportunities. This will eventually lead you to new planting design ideas and a much deeper plant knowledge, broadening your practice overall.

This is your true role as a planting designer: to spot the challenges and opportunities that your client doesn't see and deliver ideas for connection, innovation, complexity, and resilience through your design.

▾ Spending time to discover what assets you already have in your new landscape will lead to identifying unexpected opportunities and uncovering innovative ideas.

CASE STUDY

ANNIKA ZETTERMAN

Inner Stockholm Archipelago, Sweden
Private Residence

Climate: Humid continental (Dfb) south/southwest facing
Rainfall: 540mm (21.2") per annum
Temperature: Minimum -20 degrees Celsius (-4 degrees F)
Maximum +25 degrees Celsius (77 degrees F)
Soil: Varies, including sand

A coastal design that resolves its challenges of climate, exposure, and cold winters with a characteristic lightness of touch.

PLANTING DEVELOPMENT

The designer's approach for this private garden was to create seasonal planting interest that also advocates biodiversity of plants and wildlife. The front garden faces north but is protected from strong winds by a large property whereas the rear coast-facing garden is exposed to both sun and sometimes strong winds. This garden is large, with several very different planting areas within the site.

As the client spends time in the garden mainly in summer and on the coast-facing side, the structure here is less of importance in winter, but all-year interest is more important in the front garden, as people traverse it every day as they come and go. Lighting helps emphasise trees and focal points during the darkest time of the year.

PLANT DETAIL

It is unusual for a garden to have a sandy private beach, as here, with some planting soil depth (often this is rockbed in the Stockholm region) and so the designer put extra thought into creating a 'beach garden' with a different look and feel than the rest of the space. As this garden is situated some distance from the main house (or any other houses) the visitor can be truly connected to the water, waves, and views in this space. The movement of ornamental grasses and perennials, such as *Molinia arundinacea* 'Skyracer', *Scabiosa caucasica* 'Perfecta Blue', and *Agastache* 'Black Adder' along with soft decking, paths, sand, and boulders create a natural, loose arrangement by the sea.

Overall, the atmosphere aims for a light expression of colours, textures, and patterns. The designer describes the front garden as having lush, happy green tones in warm contrast to the grey slate paving. Anchor plants have light foliage colours, such as *Acer platanoides* 'Drummondii' or interesting detail such as the characteristic seedpods of the *Koelreuteria paniculata* and cones of *Rhus typhina*. Most perennials carry flowers in blue tones for a calm, coherent palette that complements the surrounding coastal colours. The design also includes plants that benefit wildlife, and native and indigenous plants with historic value, including species such as the heritage apple tree *Malus* 'Signe Tillisch'.

CHAPTER **4**

DEFINE—THE PROJECT BRIEF

In the discovery phase, you explored a project in depth and in doing so you may have collected a large amount of data. It is important that you make the time to explore that data and decide what points are critical to your planting design, which are less useful, and what can be discarded. However, the quantity of information that you have gathered can be challenging to synthesise. You can only move forward by bringing together this wealth of information into a concise and understandable presentation of knowledge which will likely reveal potential opportunities and problems and ultimately help solve the right challenge.

◂ The highly sculptural form offered by succulents is softened with texture from native shrubs and evergreens, while a tone-on-tone palette unites the composition in this poolside garden by Terremoto in California, United States.

Moving from the discovery phase into the definition phase means that you can evaluate your collected information and define exactly what the project needs. Handling and prioritising this information are achieved by creating a project brief that brings together the different strands of your knowledge to date: the survey data, the client brief (which you may have written), and your analysis.

The purpose of the project brief is to define the parameters to which you are working within a concise workable document. It allows you to bring together the information that you have found, to explore that information further, and prioritise what is important to your project. The project brief is your strategic tool for generating each individual planting design project.

THE PROJECT BRIEF: STRATEGY AND NARRATIVE

Whilst you may have considered the ramifications of your data and your client's needs as you discovered them, it is often useful to explore this information even further to define a comprehensive project brief that will lead the development of your planting design. Not everything that you have learned will have equal importance to the development of your planting design. For example, improving biodiversity around a commercial warehouse might be at the top of your priorities for a landscape where there is little human activity, whereas resilient, low-aftercare planting might be a priority for a residential garden where the primary client requirement is for a garden for entertaining.

▾ In this large country garden designed by Jo Thompson, a strong narrative has helped the designer to stay true to the vision of a wildlife haven through careful master planning and wildlife-friendly detailing. These improve biodiversity whilst keeping aftercare to a minimum.

Whilst nearly all the information you have collected will have some use, further exploration will help you evaluate and define focused objectives for your planting design. When you later develop your planting design, make design decisions and plant choices, it will also enable you to return to your project brief to audit your ideas against your objectives and to ensure you are continuing to work within the rules you have set for the design.

The first part of your project brief will therefore help you prioritise practical requirements. Detail the information that you gathered in the discovery phase that is of most relevance to your project through a series of objectives and rules. It is, if you like, a strategy for the planting design.

The second part of the project brief will be to find a compelling narrative or story for your planting design. Your exploration should open your mind to new ideas and opportunities. For example, a Swedish client who has told you that they love to spend long summer evenings in their garden might inspire a narrative around using the colours present at a midsummer sunset in the Swedish archipelago. As you explore your project further, make a note of these ideas for the next stage, when you will decide upon a design narrative and atmosphere for planting your client's landscape.

THE VALUE OF A PROJECT BRIEF

Every one of your clients will have a unique response to planting, but all of them will want you to employ your imagination to create the best possible planting design that meets their individual needs. You might take a traditional approach to ornamental planting, such as a formal layout of hedges interplanted with seasonal perennials, or take a contemporary approach that requires complex, large-scale areas of native plants to create a meadow. Using your imagination and creativity will help you create innovative planting that will make your work stand out and give you the satisfaction of knowing you've created something new and unique. This process of developing a detailed project brief helps you achieve this, firstly by writing down and illustrating the parameters and priorities of your project, and then by creating a compelling narrative.

EVALUATION THROUGH FURTHER EXPLORATION

The first part of your project brief will be a summary of the three strands of the discovery stage—survey, client brief and analysis—but it should also reflect your exploration of these areas. It isn't just a collection of all the information you have discovered. Through your further exploration, you will have found the key factors that you decide will drive your design. It is your experience and opinion that matters here. What do you believe are the important factors that will help you to create an impactful planting design? How will you prioritise these factors?

Much of your project brief will be presented as text, but you might also illustrate some of your findings. Some of the types of illustrations you might employ were detailed in the last chapter and are relevant to the survey of the site, such as the impact of the sun on areas of shade and semi-shade across the landscape. You could also illustrate objective factors, such as circulation around the site through plan diagrams, or the history of the landscape with collected images. Subjective responses can also be illustrated; for example, if you got a positive reaction to examples of other completed planting designs then these could be helpful within the project brief.

Your client's opinion is important, but you must also articulate your own opinion to support an imaginative approach to the design. The project brief, by organising and prioritising your thoughts, will help you do this.

▲ In this country garden, the project objective was to increase the diversity of wildlife at the site. The design rules for this garden can be even more specific; for example, a rule could be to use plants that provide winter sources of food and shelter for migratory birds arriving late in the season, in this case through the provision of seed heads and evergreen trees.

CREATING YOUR PROJECT BRIEF

The project brief is a living document that you will want to revisit periodically as your planting design develops. It will help you to audit your design decisions and, as you begin to make decisions on planting locations, plant composition, and other elements such as colour, you might also find you need to adjust it.

Include the elements from the client brief that you feel are important, key survey data presented as both text and illustration as appropriate, the initial rules you have made for your design, and any constraints you have discovered. You might also add other key images that have been helpful, such as that of a specific plant the client would like. The key to a good project brief is that it is easily read and used. It shouldn't be very long. It is not an essay but a report, and text can be bullet points. Illustrations and images should be kept to the essential but can be just as helpful to your imagination as your words are.

PROJECT OBJECTIVES AND RULES

Part of the value of this process is that it will prompt you to further explore your thoughts about the eventual design outcome before committing to a design narrative. You can decide upon some eventual outcomes that you want to achieve. These will be your project objectives for your planting design. Clear objectives will define what your challenge is in a positive light.

Objectives are the goals that you need to reach, whereas design rules are the factors that determine how you can achieve them. For example, you will inevitably find some environmental landscape characteristics, such as soil moisture and availability of light, that will have an impact on the plants you should use. These characteristics can become planting rules. So, whilst objectives give you inspiration for developing your planting design ideas, such as how you compose plant structures, your rules will help you narrow down your plant choices as you begin to make detailed design decisions.

HOW MANY OBJECTIVES AND RULES DO YOU NEED?

As you start to develop your planting design you will learn to consider the larger surrounding landscape first before focussing down to a detailed level. Your planting rules can be structured in the same way to focus your choices. So, at this stage of the project brief rely on creating just a few rules that will cover the larger landscape.

Project rules can be as simple as stating the aspect of a garden or defining the areas of shade. For example, you might make a design rule for a woodland garden that says, *All plants within the woodland area should be tolerant of seasonal shade and, in some areas, semi-shade.* By setting this rule you have automatically discounted a large range of plants that cannot tolerate shade or semi-shade, and therefore you have reduced the number of plants you need to consider. You've quickly given yourself a smaller palette of plants to choose from.

You might also set some rules which have come from your conversations with your client. Whilst a client request to include roses in the planting design may lead you to an obvious rule, your analysis of the landscape and further exploration of the survey will help you write a more accurate, defining rule, such as *Use fragrant roses in places where they will be easily accessible to the client.* Define location for more detailed rules but always start by looking at the larger scale first before you focus on individual areas.

Setting planting rules should not be onerous. They should aim to support your design by focusing on what is required in the project brief. There is no point in creating long lists of rules unless they are helpful as a way of auditing your plant choices later, when you start to detail your planting. Keep your plant rules simple and relevant and they'll keep you on track.

◂ Constraints tend to be outside forces that will have an impact on your eventual planting decisions.

Site specific planning requirements

State or federal planning guidelines

Environmental requirements

Heritage designations

Client led constraints

Budgets

WHAT MIGHT LIMIT YOUR PROJECT?

We've determined that the development of a project brief will enable you to identify key factors that will drive your design. Objectives and rules should be written in a positive way. However, at some point you will likely discover some constraints that will have an impact on how you can develop your planting design. There will seldom be a project with no constraints, and it as well to consider them early in a project instead of after you have put time and effort into the planting design development and detail.

The earlier example of creating a rule for a shaded, woodland garden could in some ways be seen as a constraint in that you won't be able to use sun-loving summer flowering plants but, as a designer, you can pivot to approach this challenge in a positive way by turning your mind to finding a very wide range of plants that *will* thrive in this type of setting. In this example, other factors may also come into play, but the requirement to work with a shaded woodland is an opportunity to enjoy stretching your plant vocabulary.

Planning regulations can have a major impact on design, but are often there to protect existing environmental conditions—such as tree protection measures. Equally, heritage designations will often protect more than just buildings and may extend to the surrounding landscape. Client-led constraints may be to retain treasured plants. The available budget can have a large impact on what will be possible. Remember you can grow a planting design; it doesn't have to be planted with mature, containerised plants immediately.

The availability of a budget is often a leading factor in the development of a new landscape. The planting of a landscape is often the very last thing to happen in a wider development project, and this can lead to the planting budget coming under pressure if the wider project budget is already strained. By being part of early conversations with the initial design team, it is possible to get client support for ring-fencing planting budgets as a key element of a development, especially if planting is a requirement of planning control.

On paper, plants can appear as a very small part of an overall project budget, but it's worthwhile to point out that they have one of the greatest impacts; remind your clients of this when developing your project brief. Indeed, contemporary methods of planting can even enable us to grow a landscape in situ from seed, which can significantly reduce cost but still provide rich, engaging planting.

Your role as a planting designer should be to convince a client of the importance of well-designed planting as an element of their new landscape. By engaging with that client to create a great project brief that identifies clear objectives, you will be able to help them recognise the benefit of spending money on planting within the wider remit of a large development project.

SUMMARY: THE PROJECT BRIEF AS LIVING DOCUMENT

The development of a project brief can be used not just for the planting design element of a project but also for the overall landscape design. If you are working as part of a team, others may have already developed some form of project brief that will help you build an associated planting design brief. At this stage in your project, you are creating a document that will guide your planting. It is a living document to support, not hinder, your work with the objective to move your work forward.

You can always return to your project brief if you want to make changes as you develop your ideas. It is only part of the process of defining the project and should always give room for your imagination to create an innovative and unique planting design for your client. The second part of the definition stage will be to create an imaginative narrative for your planting, and in deciding on a narrative for your planting design you may want to revisit your project brief and update the rules to reflect that chosen narrative.

The project brief will help when you become stuck and hesitate to move forward. It will support you when you decide how to compose your planting, to research possible plants to meet your brief, and make final choices. By regularly revisiting the project brief you will remind yourself of what your objectives are and continue to move forward. Like any strategic document, the project brief is no good if it's left in a file. Use the brief as your personal strategic document for each planting design that you create; it will always give you the confidence to focus your thoughts and inspire you to create the best possible design.

CASE STUDY

COLWELL SHELOR LANDSCAPE ARCHITECTURE

Cloud Song, Scottsdale Community College Business School and Indigenous Cultural Center
Scottsdale, Arizona, United States

This design mitigates extreme environmental conditions—incorporating green infrastructure and other sustainable design elements while serving to educate and promote understanding of Indigenous culture.

Climate:	Hot desert (BWh)
Rainfall:	260mm (10") per annum
Temperature:	Minimum +16 degrees Celsius (61 degrees F) Maximum +29 degrees Celsius (84 degrees F)
Soil:	Varies across landscape

PLANTING DEVELOPMENT

Cloud Song is an 8-acre development created to house the Indigenous Scholars Institute and Cultural Center and Business School on the Scottsdale Community College campus in Scottsdale, Arizona. Scottsdale Community College is the only public community college located on Native American land. The Indigenous Cultural Center is the realization of a longstanding commitment by the College to provide a cultural center for the Salt River Pima–Maricopa Indian Community (SRPMIC), to deliver programs that provide academic and personal support for a successful and enriched college experience for the American Indian student. The contemporary exterior spaces of Cloud Song celebrate and commemorate Native American culture, environmental teachings, and craft.

The landscape design was derived by collaborative process through an Indigenous lens. The community engagement process was explicitly inclusive and thrived from the cultural context and lived experiences of tribal stakeholders. Efforts to fully engage with the

community ensured meaningful and just participation—leading to a better understanding of interconnectedness, identity, culture, nature, and sustainability. The outdoor learning environments enable the Center to provide training and host classes and cultural events to enhance awareness of the diverse culture of the SRPMIC and other Indigenous peoples. The design is distinctly contemporary, reflecting forms and shapes of Native American basketry, rugs, and pottery with a modern twist. The transformation creates a rich pedestrian experience from the initial arrival through the mesquite bosque to more formal and inviting building entries, stormwater gardens, and ceremonial spaces.

PLANT DETAIL

The landscape takes it cue from regional washes. All condensate, surface, and roof runoff are captured and held onsite to irrigate the Indigenous plant palette. Many of these species are adapted to thrive on rainwater alone, withstand extreme heat, require no fertilizer, and still provide a vibrant habitat for pollinators and wildlife.

The west entry to the building is based on a riparian river bed, with a grove of native mesquites and a series of bioswales planted with native riparian plants interconnecting throughout the space. An edible garden produces native herbs, fruits, and vegetables, harvested by the Culinary College to educate students on Indigenous foods, creating cross-cultural empathy, awareness, and open-mindedness.

CASE STUDY

SURFACEDESIGN

Private Residence
Woodside, California, United States

Climate: Cold summer Mediterranean (Csc)
Rainfall: 600mm (24") per annum
Temperature: Minimum +10 degrees Celsius (50 degrees F)
Maximum +18 degrees Celsius (64.5 degrees F)
Soil: Varies across landscape

A challenging soil and site that allowed for an innovative planting design responsive to the climate and newly graded topography.

PLANTING DEVELOPMENT

Each design is a reflection of the site, client, and often a larger narrative. Here, the movement and wildness of the meadow are a counterbalance to the structure of the grove of ancient olive trees, the vineyard, the bands of lavender, and the sculptural cactus garden at the entry. The pool acts as a threshold that divides the garden's structured and nonstructured planting areas.

The site had been used as horse paddock for many years, which meant that the soil was degraded and heavily compacted. The soil was rebuilt and regraded, with the topography featuring as an abstraction of the adjacent foothills. Depressions between the rolling hills transfer water runoff to both treat the water as it moves through the depressions and simultaneously create a safe route for the water, diverting it away from the buildings. The engineered path also slows down water flow, allowing it to infiltrate back into the water table. The designers' idea was to use plant selection and soil remediation to treat and slow down runoff.

The designers' main approach was focused on creating a planting design that worked to rebuild a degraded site and connect it to the regional landscape by selecting drought-tolerant species and a mix of native and adapted plants.

PLANT DETAIL

The plant palette in the upland and lowland elevations on the site reflect and celebrate the movement of water across it. It is immersive year-round, achieved through a series of flowering types and durations, as well as structural and ornamental seed heads. The garden holds visual interest throughout every season.

Plant choice was based on each species' preferred location on the slopes. The designers created a topographic map and then reinforced those edges with plant material where they would naturally take hold. Because they were shaping the mounds, there wasn't a painterly approach to the composition. The composition and form were used to come up with the structure of the meadow. Where the plants were placed was based on where they would naturally like to be.

Plants were chosen that would naturalize easily on the site—through maintenance, they have also encouraged reseeding. The other key component of this design is celebrating the life cycle of each plant within the garden, by planning around when plants would leaf out, what the seed heads would look like, how the colour would evolve.

Plants that could survive when they were suddenly but temporarily swamped out were chosen for the riparian corridor. The designers took a transect around the world, looking at regions with the same climate and at the same latitude to understand how native plants from around the globe might function here. The majority of included plants are native to California, but plants from other Mediterranean climates are also incorporated, and this greatly expanded the ability to incorporate a variety of plants from similar regions.

The client gave the designers somewhat of a free hand, so they were able to challenge themselves with the notion of finding a palette and a medium that would respect and honour the climate conditions and the passage of water rather than try to adapt the site to the cultural norms of residential gardens. The result impressed the client thoroughly. Through Covid, she would walk the garden with a cup of coffee in the morning and a glass of wine at night. She was able to connect with nature daily in an explosive, colourful way and to appreciate the subtle changes of seasons. Her extended family also uses the garden regularly now as a place to connect with one another.

CHAPTER **5**

FINDING YOUR NARRATIVE: TELLING STORIES WITH PLANTS

◂ The Meadow at the Old Chicago Post Office, by Hoerr Schaudt, transformed a heritage building into a modern workplace based on a narrative that the rooftop should be designed with sustainability and energy efficiency in mind.

Design is about creating experiences, telling stories. The importance of storytelling and narrative in all creative disciplines is well-documented. It helps us understand ideas and people. Storytelling is used in every culture and explains how we can understand, persuade, and engage each other. The power of a planting design lies not in an individual plant or even a combination of a few different species of plants, but in the story that can be told through those plants.

▾ In the Hokongo-in Temple in Kyoto, Japan, a very simple combination of hydrangea and evergreen shrubs, consistently repeated, creates the sense of calm that is called for in a sacred space. The rhythmic simplicity of this planting works beautifully in this setting; the alternative, a use of many plant combinations, may have resulted in a design that would not feel relaxing.

A narrative will help you to better understand your own objectives and allow your imagination to begin to conceive of a design. A compelling narrative will also engage your client emotionally with your design, making them more accepting of your proposals. This will be especially beneficial if they seem confused or worried about the planting of a landscape project. A narrative will make it considerably easier for them to comprehend what you have designed and why; it aims to invoke a reaction and helps a client to see that the design will be about creating an experience. A narrative helps them connect the mechanics of planting to a mood, a feeling.

LET YOUR IMAGINATION FLY

Narrative is important for the planting designer because the development of a new narrative for each new project will help stretch your imagination and therefore give you a better chance of creating a truly innovative planting design. Your client will also get something unique and exciting.

You likely already have a vocabulary of plants, however large or small; these are the plants that you are familiar with, find useful, and may have already used. You will also have an experience of planting design, which might have come from the work you have already completed or from just being surrounded by landscapes where you have spent time observing how plants have grown together. This is most often an experience of absorbing 'plant combinations' in both designed planting and in nature. We all carry these internal, sometimes subconscious impressions; they can be useful but are not distinct enough to rely on when attempting to create a cohesive design for a client.

Your personal experience with planting design can be difficult to unsee when starting out on a new project. It is easy to defer to something you've done before when you're up against a deadline or not feeling especially inspired by a site, and it can limit the possibilities for the new project you are working on. By placing the creation of a narrative into your design process, you force yourself to step back, slow down, and consider the story you want to tell through plants on any given project. Each new narrative will help you visualise a planting atmosphere for each new project. It will encourage you to use your imagination in a different way each time, to be innovative in your approach. You may still draw upon your personal experience and core knowledge of plants, but the narrative will push you to try new designs and engage you to research new plant genera, species, and cultivars—in turn, this will widen your knowledge and understanding of plants and benefit your overall practice and career.

▲ New residential developments will often have a requirement for substantial green space where planting design will play an important role. Large developments also involve a whole team of design professionals. The architect may have already created a narrative around green living and well-being to make this a place where people want to live.

FIND YOUR INSPIRATION

The value of narrative in supporting your creative process may be clear, but where does the narrative come from and how can you develop it? For some people, finding a narrative can be a challenge but placing it here, at a point where you have just spent time exploring the project, gathering information, and especially, talking with your client is the best time to help shape your concept before you delve into any more planting details.

Within other creative professions the co-creation of narrative between designer and client can be important, and you may find this useful as well. If you have listened to what your client has told you, it is likely that you will have discovered elements of a story that will engage them. For example, a client who travels often may have told you about a special place to them, a memory that they have of a country, a garden they visited that left an impression. These are all events that can be used to help develop a planting narrative.

Collaboration with other professionals can also be a good way of discovering a narrative for your planting design. The design team might create a narrative that ties everything together, not just the planting but also the landscape structure, buildings, and way of working. For example, a new eco house with a narrative about sustainable use of materials, construction, and maintenance would comfortably engage a narrative for your planting design focused on sustainability.

You might also use some questions to challenge yourself to find a narrative. Here are some ideas.

- What is unique about this project?
- What element of this garden or landscape is completely new and unfamiliar to you?
- What are the main challenges with this garden, and how do they relate to each other?
- How might the garden change your clients' lives?
- How does this project differ from others you have undertaken?

▲ Even for commercial landscapes, such as this modern industrial and warehousing district in the U.S., designers are increasingly setting buildings within green perimeters that can provide outdoor resources for employees and benefit the local community by reducing pollution from highways' increased traffic. A planting design narrative that focuses on staff and community and includes positive sustainability initiatives are more likely to be accepted by planning authorities.

Imagine the position your clients are in and try to see their needs from their viewpoint. What is it that they are trying to solve, and how complex is the challenge? For example, a commercial client may be struggling to attract staff and think that installing some outside spaces where employees can relax during lunch breaks will help, but perhaps they have a small budget for landscaping and maintenance. Imagining yourself in their shoes will help you empathise with their situation and might encourage you to conceive an imaginative solution. A conceptual narrative of the 'one-hour landscape' where staff experience small areas of a larger planted landscape in warm seasons will give you direction for planting decisions based upon when the landscape will be used and what plants attract people most in that context.

Challenging sites will push your creativity. Don't shy away from them—lean in. For example, you might have discovered that your project site has poor drainage, and whilst the climate is quite dry and droughts are frequent, when it rains the rainfall can be heavy and short-lived. Challenges like this will lead you to become more innovative in your planting design and, in this case, might naturally lead you to a practical narrative of climate-resilient planting, maybe even to create a bioswale or a rain garden with new ground contouring that can accommodate excessive rainfall runoff and is planted with plants that can withstand waterlogging for up to forty-eight hours whilst stormwater gradually seeps away. A strong narrative like this for a challenging site can take your career in new directions.

▲ This bioswale at Bishan-Ang Mo Kio Park in Singapore is an important landscape element. Similar features could form part of a climate-led narrative for any public landscape. Pointing out how a bioswale will concentrate and convey stormwater whilst removing debris and pollution, and showing how planting can be beneficial to ground stabilisation and recharging groundwater will resonate with authorities.

▲ Often the setting of a garden can inspire a strong narrative. In this beachside weekend garden designed by Jo Thompson there is a practical requirement for salt-tolerant, resilient planting that would inspire a practical narrative, but the larger landscape could also inspire a conceptual narrative reflecting seasonal tides and coastal nature.

CONCEPTUAL NARRATIVES

Practical narratives that react to the conditions you are presented with are often the simplest to use and in the example above they resolve a key challenge. But practical narratives won't always push your creativity as a designer. Part of the fun of your job is to develop new ideas that engage you as much as your client. These might be ideas that are more conceptual in their nature that could be based upon something that your client said or the sense of atmosphere that you discovered when you visited the site.

For example, your project might be located on the coast. This is your client's weekend bolt hole, out of the city, that they visit throughout the year, often spending holiday weekends here. The house is small, simply decorated with a coastal motif and very much an informal family retreat. It would be easy to create a practical narrative that is a reaction to your client wanting to relax as soon as they arrive at their weekend home and the need for salt-tolerant plants. This might lead you towards a practical narrative of *the beachside retreat—a garden for weekend relaxation*. This would inspire easy, self-reliant and salt-tolerant plant choices with low demand on your client's time for maintenance. It could be a planting design which is as easy as their need to lock up and drive away at the end of each stay.

But you could also take a more conceptual approach and create a narrative such as *seasonal tides—a garden of changing moods*. This narrative might inspire an interesting structural layout of plants based on the patterns created by waves on a sandy beach and, within that, planting choices that will peak in their flowering at different times of the year. You still need to select salt-tolerant plants. It's the same garden but with a different, and more conceptual, narrative that leads to a very different planting design. Neither is necessarily better than the other—the important thing is that each narrative will push your imagination and innovation. Both would make it easy to win your client's support for your idea.

Developing Your Narrative Writing Skills

Writing great narratives for your planting designs is a skill that needs to be developed like any other. It doesn't come easily to many, and if it does then perhaps you are taking too simple a route! We all need to be challenged in our design work to develop our ideas further, but there are some simple things that help us push our boundaries:

- **Remove distractions**
  Being creative takes focus, and that means giving yourself the best chance at innovative thought by removing distractions. If you're hungry, feed yourself; if the neighbours are noisy, put some headphones on and remove yourself to another world. Some people find mindful exercise helpful to calm the body. Whatever works for you, just try to distance yourself from outside interference and get into a flow state.
- **Make a connection**
  An emotional connection with your chosen narrative will encourage participation. That's why it is so important to listen to your client when you are generating their brief as part of your overall project brief. Our clients are not always great at articulating what they want in design terms, but you can find out likes and dislikes by taking time to listen to them and then asking questions that might reveal their true interests.
- **Be specific and focussed**
  You should be able to tell any planting design narrative in just a few sentences. As in the example given of the 'Sky Garden' at right, you might elaborate on it later, with more words, but your narrative should be short, sweet, and encapsulate your aims clearly. A straightforward mission statement will engage your client, and you, when you start to compose a design and select plants.

PRESENTING YOUR NARRATIVE

You want your client to understand your narrative immediately upon encountering it for the first time. When you are developing your presentation, consider what they will read, hear, and see. The first two are about words, how you write and verbally present your narrative; the third is about how you visually present your narrative through images. Each method enables you to present your planting design story in different, complementary ways that will engage your client.

Your written narrative can best be presented in three simple ways, each building upon the information given before.

As an example, consider a chosen narrative for a new large-scale planted landscape for the headquarters of an aviation company. It might be titled:

> **'The Sky Garden'**

This is the **headline** description, the first way that you explain your narrative. The title immediately conjures up images of what the planting might be like. If accompanied by an atmospheric mood board so that your client can see your proposed cloudlike plantings of grasses and flowers across a large open space, this *might* be all that is needed for your client to grasp the narrative.

Next, elaborate on this headline with a simple **strapline** explanation of your planting design in a few sentences like this:

> **'The Sky Garden'**
>
> 'The planting of the Sky Garden will evoke the feeling of flying through wide-open spaces and give a sense of never-ending views. The planting will reflect the skies above and the views through breaks in the clouds to the water below.'

You can then develop this simple explanation further with a few, more detailed **outline** paragraphs, like this:

> **'The Sky Garden'**
>
> 'The planting of the Sky Garden will evoke the feeling of flying through wide-open spaces and give a sense of never-ending views. The planting will reflect the skies above and the views through breaks in the clouds to the water below.'
>
> 'The space will be formed of two principal layers of plants. The ground layer will be formed of large swathes of individual species of grasses and perennials.

These will interact with each other informally, and will be limited in their range of heights so that they peak at between 600mm/24" and 1200mm/48". Informal paths will be laid through the planting so that the visitor can be at once immersed within the planting but also see distant views across the planting.'

'The second layer of planting will be a tree layer with small clusters of low growing trees up to 10 metres high, formed in glades so that visitors can walk into them, lie back on lawns in the centre of the open glades, and gaze up at the sky. These glades will feel like private spaces where they can sense the sky and a feeling of complete escape.'

Each way of presenting your narrative is useful and builds upon the concept presented in the headline. For some clients, this might be enough to garner approval. Even if that happens, the more detailed explanation will support your own design development, by explaining your story and presenting detailed planting rules. Indeed, in this example, the measurements mentioned in the outline could easily be added into your project brief as planting design rules.

This written description will support you in making a verbal presentation; it's how you read and hear the narrative. The third visual method, an atmospheric mood board, will be helpful to your client, who might not have the visual imagination that you have, to see what you are proposing.

▾ An atmospheric design board will help you explain your narrative in words and images, in this case conjuring up the idea of views to the sky, layered planting, woodland paths, and even colour inspiration from an array of Røros blankets.

THE SKY GARDEN

The planting of the sky garden will evoke the feeling of flying through wide open spaces and a sense of never-ending views. The planting will reflect the skies above and the views through breaks in the clouds to the water below.

The space will be formed of two principal layers of plants of which the ground layer will be formed of large swathes of individual species of grasses and perennials. These will informally interact with each other and will be limited in their range of heights so that they peak at between 600mm/24" and 1200mm/48". Informal paths will be laid through the planting so that the visitor can be at once within the planting but also see distant views across the planting.

The second layer of planting will be a tree layer with small clusters of low growing trees up to 10metres high formed in glades so that visitors can walk into them, lie back on lawns in the centre of the open glades and gaze up at the sky. These glades will feel like private spaces where they can sense the sky and a feeling of complete escape.

◂ Consider who your client is and where their interests lie. The members of a country club might be more interested in the golf than your ideas for meadow planting. You might win the approval of the golf committee by telling them how it will enhance the landscape that they play within, rather than the environmental benefit, which might be of more interest to the members who are gardening enthusiasts.

Telling Your Story Effectively

You will nearly always have to pitch what you are aiming for to your audience. Not every client will want to listen to a long story about their garden and how you have reacted to it. Others *will* be interested in the process and how you have come to make plant choices based upon a compelling narrative. It's up to you to read your client and to decide how far you'll need go to state the case for your design.

- **Keep it simple.**
  Brevity is a skill. Try to be as specific as you can in presenting your narrative and, if your client's concentration is short, give them one single idea that they can take away. It could be in a simple narrative headline that gives your client the ability to tell someone else what your planting design is based upon. For example, if you are going to create planting for a Mediterranean climate based on a fond memory of a past holiday then the title could simply be 'Capri in Springtime'. Ultimately, your narrative will be clearer and have more impact if focussed around a single big idea.
- **Does it connect?**
  Think carefully about the words you use and the usual emotions that they evoke. Will they resonate with *your* client? Do they create an emotional connection *for them*? One of the attributes of successful planting design is that it demands a reaction, engages people with planting, creates a connection. This makes the narrative as important as the final plant choices. You might present a new planting design for a golf course in a straightforward, practical way because the club members are simply more interested in playing golf than in your planting. But if the club has a garden group there may be more time and more interest from those members for your idea.
- **Is it believable?**
  Your narrative must be able to be readily understood and believable. Test your narrative by speaking it out loud, even to a friend or relative. Are you able to present it in a way that makes them grasp the concept immediately? If you work with others, present your narrative to them as it develops and see what reaction you get.
- **Use images.**
  You are trying to persuade your client to think openly and emotionally, not analytically. This can often be achieved through images even better than with words. You are also working in a very visual way, which your client may react to more easily, so use images as well as words—your clients may appreciate this form of communication. Images of individual plants might not be especially useful at this stage unless you are creating a specific design, such as a rose garden. Try to use atmospheric images to explain your overall ideas. These images might be literal, such as pictures of existing landscapes, or conceptual if your narrative is aiming to establish mood or atmosphere. Use sketches and drawings as well as photos if needed.

EXPLORING YOUR NARRATIVE THROUGH A LANDSCAPE ATMOSPHERE

Some clients and even your colleagues may find it difficult to grasp the quality of planting that you are aiming for through a written or verbal narrative. One of the main reasons that clients come to us in the first place is because, whilst they might be able to appreciate a space, they cannot visualise the atmosphere that you will create through planting.

Clients can also start out with an auditory approach to articulating desires; it's a common way of trying to describe a space if they don't have an actual or strong *vision* of what they want. Of course words are important, but gardens are sensory experiences and a visual description of your planting narrative through an atmospheric mood board can also be very helpful in finding common ground.

Consider what the client will experience when walking through your planting. Think about what they will see, feel, hear? What is the sensory experience? What emotions will they feel? What is the atmosphere you will create? For example, if you are planting in a woodland, a narrative will help you describe the *quality* of the shade it casts, whilst images will demonstrate the *atmosphere* of that shade.

▸ Both images and words about the planting atmosphere you are imagining will help your client understand the narrative you are promoting. You might describe in words what the client will experience as they walk through your new planting and at the same time support the text with images that show the quality of the planting you are aiming for. In this design by James Alexander-Sinclair, that experience will be a walk through a planted perennial meadow that retains views of the countryside beyond the garden borders.

The narrative you are aiming to tell should fully describe the atmosphere you want to create; one of the simplest ways to present atmosphere is to research the words you are using and how they might be represented in images. A simple digital image search using those keywords will likely present many visual options as you begin to explore your own ideas and to illustrate what you are aiming to convey through images. You can refine the search as you progress if necessary to sharpen the concept.

Later, as you make detailed decisions you will see how, even with a clear idea of the spatial qualities of your planting, you will want to return to your narrative and consider the quality of atmosphere that you are creating through your planting. For some projects this might be obvious, as in the woodland example. For other projects, you might be keen to explore a more conceptual atmosphere where a landscape transports the viewer to another time and place away from their day-to-day lives, and to an entirely different setting.

The presentation of your design narrative through planting atmosphere is a useful tool for any designer in exploring ideas and in presenting to clients. It will give you a much deeper understanding of the feelings and emotions you can create with plants than a simple written narrative ever can, and it is very likely that your clients will more readily understand and accept your narrative.

Using Images to Explain Your Narrative

A design mood board will help you to convey your ideas to your client but will also help *you* to put down on paper what is in your head. It will be helpful to include images of planting composition, less so of individual plants and more so the communities of plants that you might use but, it can also include non-plant images for colour inspiration and other influences on your planting. Remember that at this point you have made no decisions on plants that you will use; these design mood boards are just to communicate your initial ideas, narrative, and the atmosphere you are aiming for.

This image of colourful tiles conceptually delivers an idea of both the colours you might create in a large-scale planting design as well as their distribution. There are no plants shown here, just a matrix of colour that delivers a conceptual idea of your proposed narrative.

A single, simple image of planting can often best present to your client the planting atmosphere that you want to create. This image of a woodland in spring instantly communicates a vision. It's a practical image that allows your client to quickly grasp your proposal and agree to it, or not.

DEFINE

SUMMARY: HAVE CONFIDENCE IN YOUR IDEAS

The real value of creating a narrative and describing the atmosphere for each of your projects through words and images is in the focus that it will give you to move forward and develop your planting design. The narrative will give you confidence as much as your client. A practical narrative will immediately refine and reduce the range of plants that you might be able to use in the next phase of planting design development. This is useful, as there are so many possible plants that you could use. A conceptual narrative will not always rule out any specific plant, but it will narrow down your choices and allow you to focus on the plants that are good candidates for creating the desired atmosphere.

Inexperienced designers will normally pick up a 2D plan and pencil and start jotting down plant ideas, whereas a process of project exploration, defining your objectives and ideas through a project brief, and then creating a narrative and atmosphere will give your work considerably more focus at an early stage. You will find yourself making choices that you can easily explain to yourself, that your client will understand, and that will lead you to make inspiring and engaging planting designs, expanding your plant and planting design knowledge with confidence.

CASE STUDY

FISHER TOMLIN & BOWYER

Veitch Heritage Garden, Warren House
Coombe Wood, Surrey, United Kingdom

Climate: Temperate
Rainfall: 615mm (24")
Temperature: Minimum 3 degrees Celsius (37 F)
Maximum 24 degrees Celsius (75 F)
Soil: Existing sandy loam, improved with compost produced on site

A planting design that celebrates the important plant heritage attached to its location, recognising the role of the gardeners who made the garden and the plant collectors who discovered its plants and brought them back from distant regions to be cultivated.

PLANTING DEVELOPMENT

During the Victorian Era, Coombe Wood was famous as the home of the Veitch Nurseries, one of the most prolific breeders of plants sent back from all parts of the world by its famous plant hunters such as William Lobb and E.H. Wilson. Warren House adjoined the nurseries and, for a short while, expanded its gardens when the nursery closed in 1914 to include the Japanese water gardens built by the Veitch family. They are all that remains of the nursery, but the house, now a hotel, and its gardens have strong ties to horticultural history and this garden celebrates that heritage and story.

The Veitch Heritage Garden is within the house's original walled kitchen garden. The planting design narrative celebrates the head gardeners who have worked at the house since its construction in 1865 and the plants that were brought back from around the world by plant explorers to be introduced to Europe by the Veitch Nurseries. An objective of the planting is also to provide a long period of seasonal, successional interest so that the garden can serve as a backdrop to outdoor events.

PLANTING DETAIL

Working with historic records, plants were chosen that were essential to the Veitch Nurseries' history and used as focal points for the structure as well as within a wider relaxed ornamental planting of beds. Species such as the handkerchief tree, *Davidia involucrata*, a collection of magnolia species, and a grove of fifty paperbark maples, *Acer griseum*, form anchors within the planting. Perennial plants and rose cultivars are used to create waves of romantic planting as a suitable backdrop—for wedding photography in particular.

To maximise the benefit for events, the planting is then extended forward with a bulb meadow of large flowering low-bulb species such as *Scilla siberica*, *Muscari latifolium*, and *Chiondoxa luciliae* to provide early food for pollinators and bridge spring into early summer. At the other end of the season, there is a strong element of autumnal colour. Some plants also contribute edible flowers to the hotel's kitchen and bar.

Sustainable practices were incorporated into this design. Planting was designed with as low-maintenance-as-possible aftercare in mind, and the bulb meadow means that grass cutting starts late. Planting is regularly mulched, and with that, no artificial irrigation is required.

CASE STUDY

HASHIUCHI LANDSCAPE DESIGN

Private Residence
Hitachinaka Prefecture, Ibaraki, Japan

Harmony and balance in a small, year-round planting design that respects cultural significance as much as visual and horticultural needs.

Climate: Humid subtropical, no dry season (Cfa) south/southwest facing

Rainfall: 440mm (17.3") per annum

Temperature: Minimum +3 degrees Celsius (37.5 degrees F)
Maximum +29 degrees Celsius (84 degrees F)

Soil: Varies, including sand

PLANTING DEVELOPMENT

For this private residence, achieving the optimal balance between hardscape and plants was crucial to creating a harmonious and functional landscape. The designer worked with some key principles that placed the planting first in the design, including:

Proportion: Ensuring that hardscape elements are proportionate to the overall garden space and do not overwhelm the planting areas.

Contrast: Using hardscape materials that complement the plant palette, providing contrast in texture and color while maintaining a cohesive aesthetic.

Functionality: Ensuring that hardscape features serve practical purposes, such as providing seating, defining spaces, or improving accessibility, while also enhancing the visual appeal of the garden.

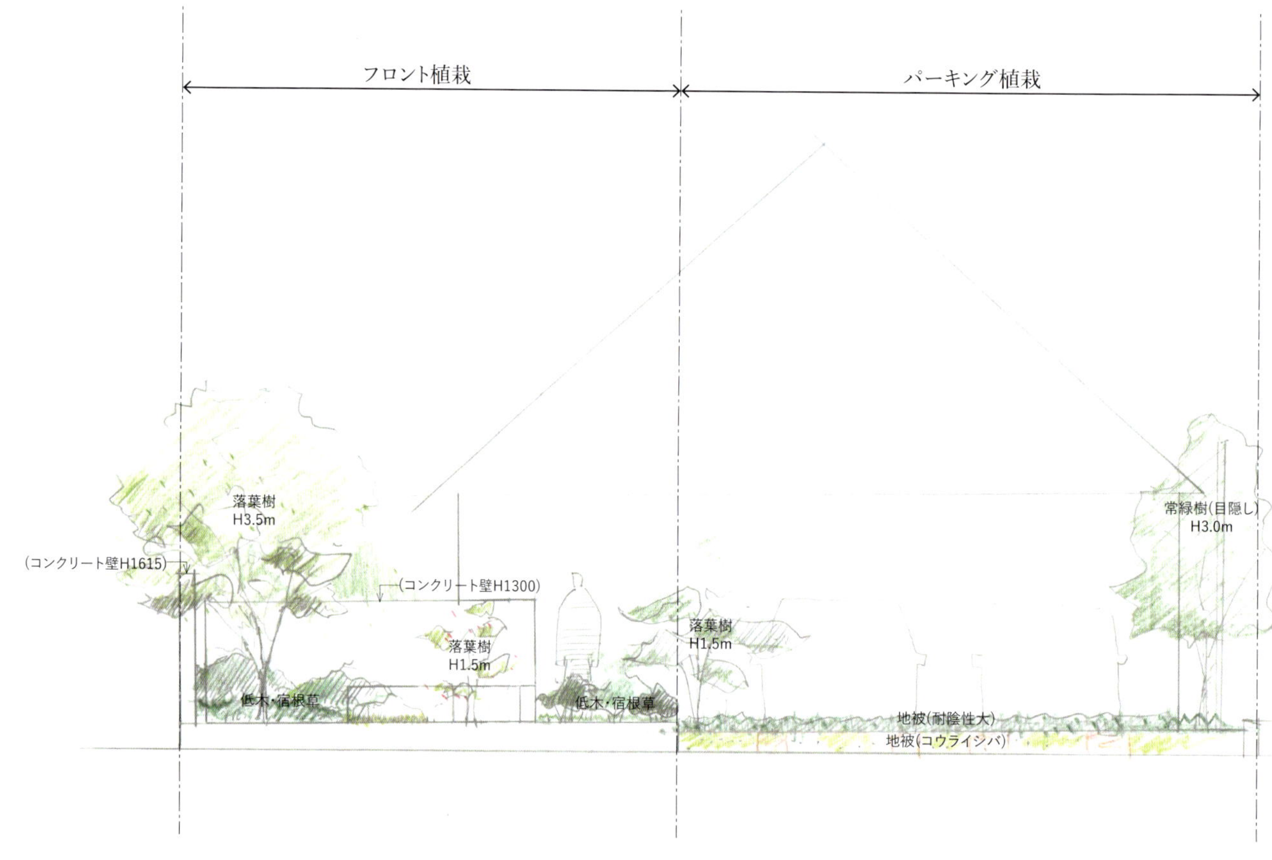

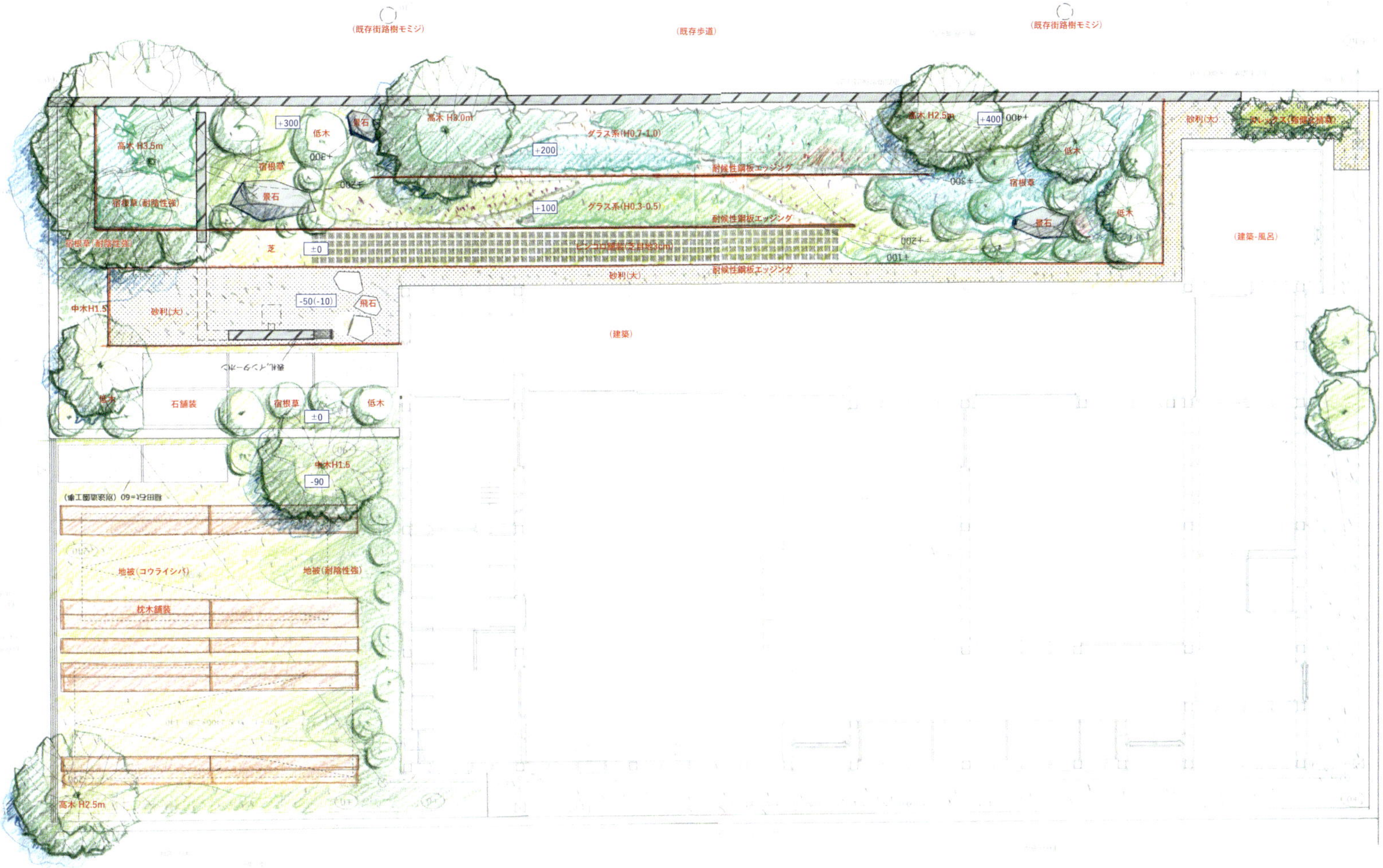

As the images show, this is a year-round planting picture. Since it's always visible from inside the house, and even acts as living wallpaper, the planting design carefully considers seasonal changes to ensure that each season offers a distinct and memorable experience for the client. Japanese native plants are intermingled with exotic and horticultural varieties of ornamental grasses and perennials, aiming to create a garden that is both ecologically sensitive and visually appealing. This approach enhances biodiversity, ensures year-round interest, and provides a variety of textures, colors, and forms.

PLANTING DETAIL

The planting design features a thoughtful blend of native Japanese plants and ornamental grasses in a balanced composition that highlights the beauty of both plant types. Key considerations included:

Cultural Significance: Native Japanese plants, such as *Acer palmatum* (Japanese maple) and *Camellia hiemalis* (kantsubaki), are chosen for their cultural significance and aesthetic value. These plants reflect the rich botanical heritage of Japan and create a sense of place.

Visual Contrast: Ornamental grasses such as *Miscanthus sinensis* (Japanese silver grass) and *Hakonechloa macra* (hakone grass), are introduced to provide visual contrast and texture. Their graceful, flowing forms complement the more structured appearance of the other included native plants, adding depth and overall interest to the garden.

Seasonal Interest: The combination of native plants and ornamental grasses ensures year-round interest, with different plants taking the spotlight in each season.

Balancing native Japanese plants with ornamental grasses required careful consideration by the designer to maintain a cohesive aesthetic. The challenge was to create a seamless blend that felt natural and harmonious. By selecting plants with complementary colors, textures, and growth habits, he was able to create a visually appealing composition that highlights the strengths of both plant types while ensuring they work well together.

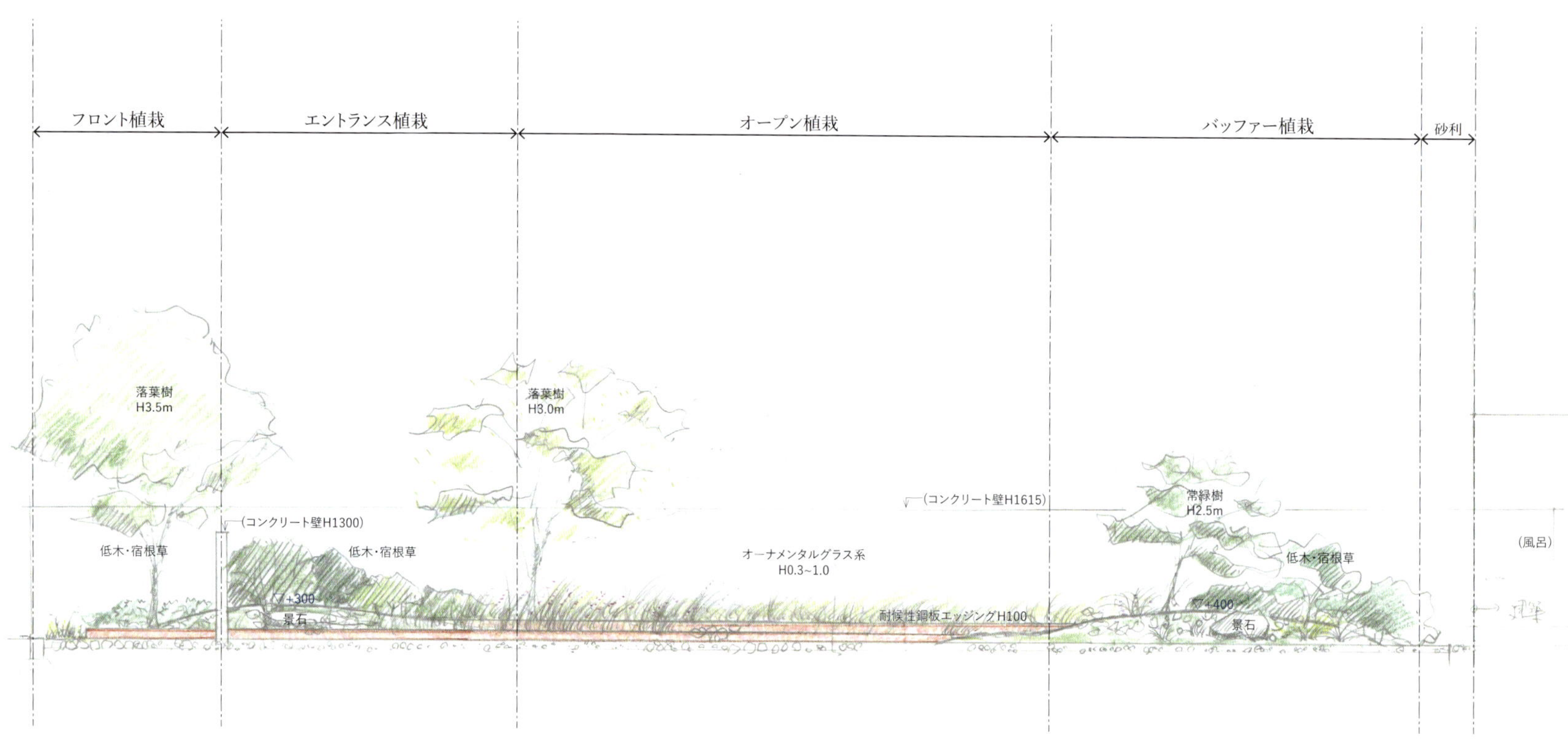

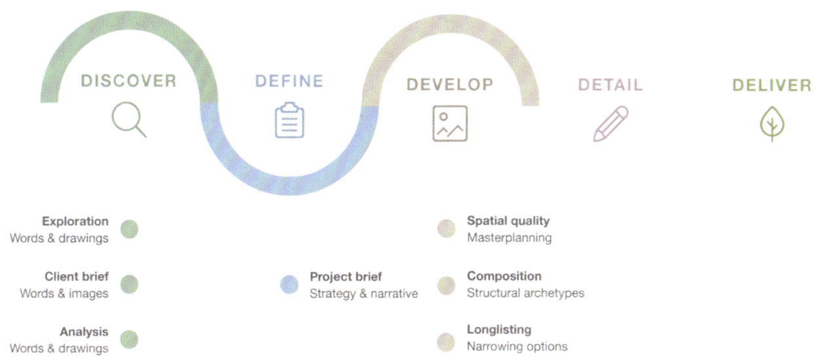

CHAPTER **6**

DEVELOPING YOUR PLANTING STRUCTURE

The framework for planting design that has already helped you to define your project brief and narrative now moves into the development phase. This is where you will start to see your planting design structure take shape, to make decisions on the underlying spatial qualities of your planting and how they are designed together. It will likely also be where you start to recognise the approaches that other designers have taken towards their work, whether as a purely ornamental approach or an attempt at reflecting a naturalistic, informal approach.

◂ The famous Abbey Gardens at Tresco, Isles of Scilly, United Kingdom, are master planned to take advantage of a unique microclimate.

Having completed a comprehensive strategic project brief and created your engaging narrative, you can now start to design your planting, master-planning the layout and composing structure. But how do you now organise your design so that you can start to choose plants? Your early development work will focus on the creation of a layout first at a large scale as a master plan and then at a smaller scale to give each area of planting character. This chapter considers the larger spatial qualities that will drive your layout and how to organise planting structure in 2 dimensions (2D) and 3 dimensions (3D). A range of useful contemporary approaches to planting design are helpful to show how to tackle structuring your design; these are described in the following chapter. Their differences are often focussed on the level of control wanted, and your desired aesthetic and the choice of approach will often be driven by the atmosphere you decided upon earlier.

This development work includes the use of sketching techniques to explore relative scale and space. These techniques will help refine the character and structure of the planting before you move on to make detailed design decisions on the qualities of the plants themselves, such as colour and fragrance. We start first by exploring how you can explore and organise your planting design and how to start to record ideas for the plants that you might use.

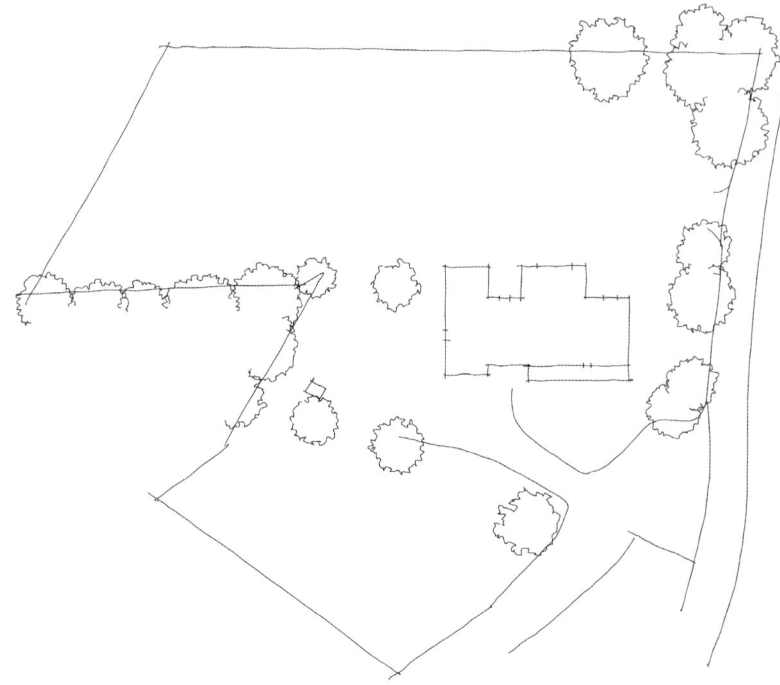

▲ Figure 1. Underlying measured survey.

SPATIAL QUALITY IN PLANTING DESIGN

Earlier we recognised that the attributes of great planting design will rely on us creating connections between plants and people, being imaginative and innovative, having an ecological approach, and aiming for a resilient outcome. This will always be a balancing act. Some attributes will be more important than others for any given project. Every design is different, but by using an overarching framework for planting design, we can create a successful solution that engages our client and fulfils each of these attributes in various measure.

Having created a foundation of knowledge about the site to be planted, identified project objectives and design rules, refined your narrative, and decided on the atmosphere you want to achieve, it's now time to start making some decisions about the physical, structural elements of your planting design through spatial design decisions.

Spatial design is a relatively new concept that brings together a wide range of disciplines and principles into a single project. Whilst it considers space and people, it operates on another level as well, by introducing sustainability and experiential design—using emotional experience as a guiding principle—into the design process. A good example would be designing planting that is immersive for the viewer. For a spatial designer, every project brings a new opportunity to engage people and innovate in the interpretation of each project through the interaction between the client, plants, and materials that will be used. This experience helps explain the importance of narrative and atmosphere in planting design and will also encourage creativity and innovation. In spatial design terms, the atmosphere that we create through planting, whether passive or active, simplistic, ponderous, immersive, absorbing, multi-dimensional or characterful, will engage with the viewer and directly impact their experience of your planting.

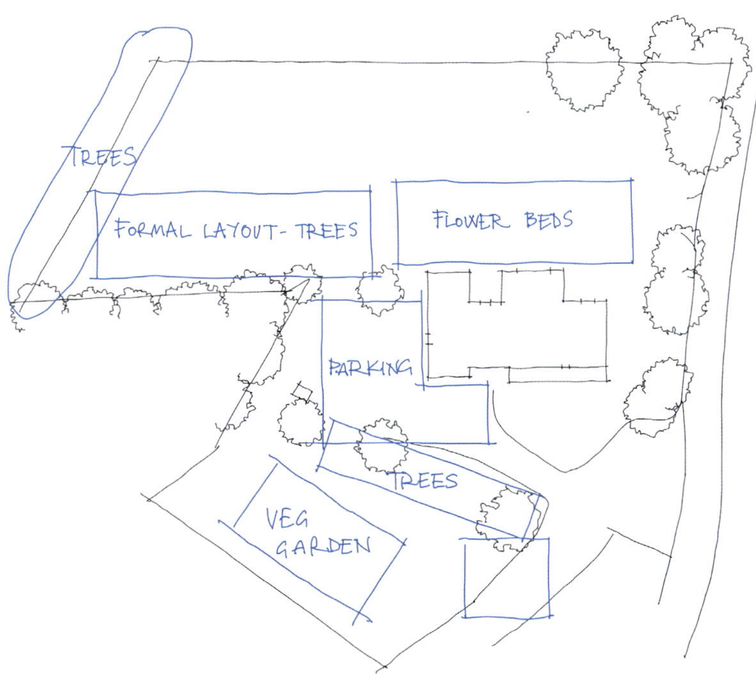

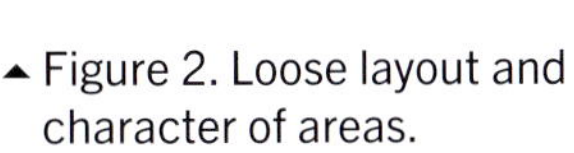
▲ Figure 2. Loose layout and character of areas.

▲ Figure 3. Final master plan in 2D.

▲ To make a master plan for your planting design, start by taking your measured survey (Figure 1) and overlay this with the layout and character of different areas (Figure 2). You can experiment loosely and quickly with how you will organise the space before moving towards a final detailed location of planting areas and the character of each planting area for your master plan (Figure 3).

MASTER-PLANNING: DESIGN IN 2D

There is only so much complex information we can process in our heads but this can be substantially relieved by using graphic techniques to record our ideas visually. For example, you might already have some ideas of the character of tree planting needed, shaped during your narrative development, and by setting this down on paper your structural ideas, whether for woodland, orchard, or tropical forest, can start to take shape. This leaves thinking space for you to decide about what should make up the height, mix, and range of that tree planting in a usable format.

Using both 2D layouts and elevation drawings, you can quickly start to make decisions about the spatial quality of your landscape and move on to decide which approach you will then take to compose your plants within that structure. The organisation of planting structure in a 2D layout is also referred to as master-planning. If you have been involved with the overall structural design of the landscape project from an early stage, you will already be familiar with the underlying 2D structure of your planting design, and the character of different planted areas may already have been determined within this. If you are approaching the project for the first time and are working on a team with other professionals who have already designed a layout, then you will need to explore the requirements of this master-planned landscape a little more to understand the design objectives.

Master-planning is a key step for any landscape design. You can work at a larger scale and loosely allocate ideas about the spatial layout of a landscape through a simple and loose sketch diagram. This will give you time to explore different opportunities in layout form before moving towards a more precise and accurate decision on where and what type of planting will be located. A scale of 1:50 for a smaller residential garden or landscape will work well; for a larger landscape you might work at 1:100 or 1:200. Using transparency paper over a master copy of your landscape plan will help you produce those drawings without having to redraw the original.

EXPLORING CHARACTER THROUGH SKETCHING

The purpose of this sketching process is speed and exploration. Generating quick drawings will enable you to get your ideas about potential 2D spatial planting layouts onto paper in an efficient way, and to try out different layouts. You can define areas by different functions and concepts for planting and start to see how they interconnect on the ground. Loose characterisations of planting such as 'screening' and 'edibles' at this larger scale enable you to work quickly before thinking about the more detailed planting character and choices that will follow later.

These are practical structural descriptions that focus on a specific planting solution and have narrowed down your plant palette from a general to more specific groups of plants. Character descriptions can still be conceptual in nature at this stage—such as 'welcome' for the entrance to a landscape, or it might be about activity such as 'play' and 'entertaining'—and might be supported by your earlier atmosphere mood boards. Whilst the use of these descriptions and the organisation of planting through them is quite loose at this stage, the value in using this technique is that you will be able to handle a lot of information on paper and have time to explore more than one possible solution through quick 2D drawings to scale.

USING ELEVATIONS: DESIGN IN 2D

The use of elevation drawing is a natural progression from the organisation of your planting design using a 2D master plan. It will encourage you to consider shape, area, location, and direction in your planting layout. Organising planting in 2D and elevation at the same time can seem complex, but if you move between the two formats, you will be able to explore your ideas and make decisions on the spatial quality of your planting before moving into more detail. The challenge of spatial design is that you are juggling different ideas and thoughts; it is considerably easier if you download and organise those thoughts onto paper at a true scale.

Help yourself explore the structure of planting in relation to other elements by imagining your planting as a mass, such as large drifts of low grasses, single or groups of trees. Consider the mass of planting by exploring this in an elevation, imagining that you are looking at the space from a ground-level viewpoint. The spaces between plants will be voids that give meaning to the plant mass, but there will also likely be other landscape elements, such as buildings, hardscape or gravel surfaces, and water features to consider as mass and void on your elevations.

▸ By sketching simple 2D elevations of the same landscape, you can quickly explore the structural opportunities for your planting in the same location. Here the designer has considered formal and informal planting (Figures 1 and 2) as well as a combination of both (Figure 3). These sketches can be produced in overlays—use transparency paper for hand drawings or, as here, on separate layers when using a digital tablet and pencil.

▲ Figure 1. Formal planting in elevation.

▲ Figure 2. Informal planting in elevation.

▲ Figure 3. A combination of informal planting with more formal details in elevation.

Elevation Drawings and Sketches

An elevation is a flat representation of a vertical view. It will illustrate plant shapes in relation to a fixed point, usually ground level based upon the viewpoint of a human. Although your elevation is effectively a flat 2D view, it can be a very useful technique that allows you to explore your ideas about plant composition quickly and discover how different approaches might work.

By taking one of your defined planting areas and sketching a composition of plants, you will reveal the mass and void that your plants could create in your design. You will get a sense of proportion through the scale of different plants in relation to each other, and be able to see what structural compositions will work best for your planting.

Remember that you have already decided on a planting narrative and atmosphere. A narrative such as 'an urban jungle' will give you a structural lead that is very different from a narrative of 'a Mediterranean meadow', but in each case the narrative will give you a sense of the structural composition that you want to achieve.

Looking at several elevations of the same planting structure together can also be useful for exploring the changing nature of your plant ideas across seasons; for example, the change in plants within a large border starting with spring bulbs, moving into early lower perennials and then a tall late-summer mix of flowering perennials and grasses at their peak before they die back to reveal a structure of just a few shrubs and trees in winter. This technique is especially useful for exploring successional planting.

Elevation drawing will help you quickly lay out detailed planting plans. It's worthwhile to practice this technique when exploring your ideas to compose planting at almost any scale, from small courtyards to large open spaces.

Other illustration techniques can help you better understand what you are designing.

▲ Elevation sketches will help you explore your narrative and get a sense of what will work for your design, vertically. Here a narrative of 'a tropical paradise' is explored using different layers of planting. The second sketch shows how taller and larger specimen plants work in the elevation.

▸ Consider relative scale in your elevations; there is a big difference between a small yard and a large, open landscape. It can help to add in a sketch of a person at scale to give immediate context. You could also add a height scale vertically next to the elevation, to explore the impact of different heights of planting.

▸ Sometimes your planting design will borrow the view of the landscape beyond the boundaries of a site. The mass of this borrowed land-scape will have an impact on your design—even a single tree on a neighbouring property may need to be considered as part of the 'design' of your own plan. In this drawing, colour has also been used to enhance the impact of different elements of the elevation.

REFINING YOUR MASTER PLAN

Once you have decided upon a loose definition of how your planting design will be laid out in 2D, you can create a definitive layout of planting areas and their character descriptions. These will become your final planting layout. Working to scale and defining character for specific areas are useful tools to help your design progress.

SCALE

Your plan should be at a scale that lets you accurately define where one area of planting gives way to another. For smaller landscapes and residential gardens this is likely to be at a scale of 1:50, an ideal scale for when you start to detail the plants you have decided upon. For larger residential and public landscapes you might use a larger scale of 1:100 or 1:200, so long as it allows you to accurately define planting types and where they change.

CHARACTER DESCRIPTIONS

At this stage, you are still not deciding on the exact plant choices that you will eventually need to make, but as part of creating your definitive master plan you should start to be more detailed in the description of the character of planting for each distinct area of the garden. For example, you might have sketched in an area dominated by trees within your landscape at one of the earlier planning stages. At this stage, you should define that area more clearly, so what was just a vague idea about including an area of trees becomes, for example, 'woodland tree and edge planting', 'tree screening', or 'specimen trees'.

If you have a good idea of what you want in a particular area, define it now. Descriptors such as 'ornamental planting', 'avenue', or 'mixed native hedge' will help you start to organise your ideas. It gives you capacity to detail the plants later rather than trying to keep everything in your head now.

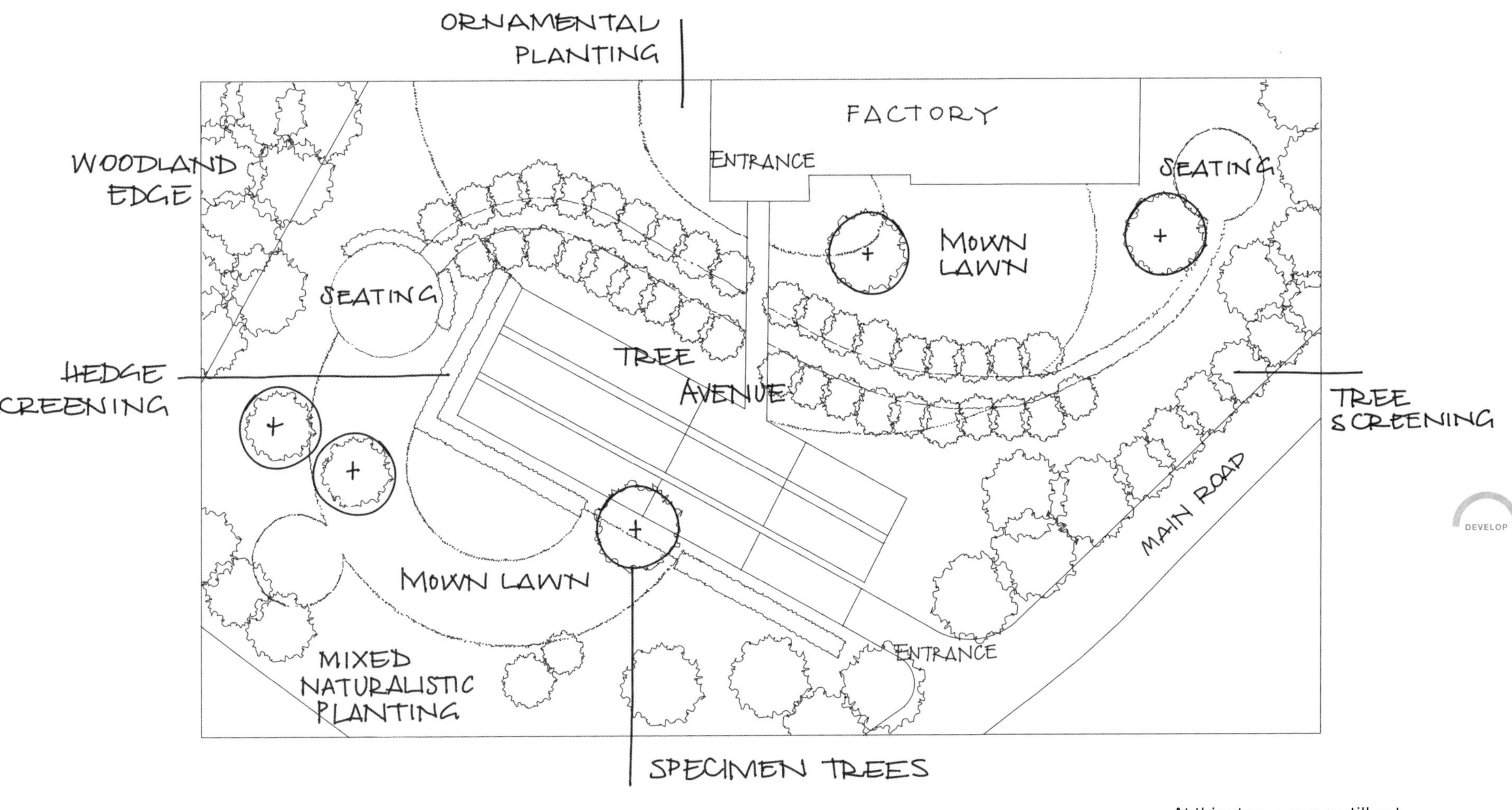

▲ At this stage you are still not making detailed plant decisions but you *are* deciding on the character of specific areas, (e.g., the avenue of trees that your client has requested), or how some planting will function to serve a purpose, (e.g., to screen the factory from the main road).

USING PERSPECTIVE DRAWINGS: DESIGN IN 3D

You can only develop your planting ideas so far using a flat 2D layout plan and elevations. Your eventual plant choices won't exist in 2D, and it is difficult to visualise detail in 2D unless you have experience with a wide range of plants. While a key attribute of good planting design is to innovate through the exploration of new plants and ideas, it is likely that you will more accurately be able to visualise and understand how new plant choices will look and interact through perspective as well as elevation sketches.

The exploration of the spatial qualities of planting in 3D through perspective drawings will help you make better, faster decisions on how you compose plants for the different compositional approaches you might take. You will experience your planting design in a more realistic and understandable way and find it easier to reflect the atmosphere that you illustrated earlier in the project brief. For simple perspective sketches, use transparency paper over your photos of the site to experiment with mass and volume, then draw your perspective in detail when you have agreed on your detailed master plan.

A perspective drawing will more closely represent how we really experience a view because it gives a clearer definition of depth within a drawing. It can be technically more difficult to draw quickly in perspective when exploring ideas for plant structure, nonetheless perspective drawings, effectively a three-dimensional representation of the two-dimensional elevation, are worth employing when you have a clear idea of what you want your planting to achieve. It will help both you and your client understand how your planting might appear.

▾ Creating a simple perspective drawing of even one key feature of your master plan will make the design come alive for your client and help them understand your ideas. Here, a perspective of the all-important welcome to the factory shown in the commercial master plan earlier is sketched in simple graphite pencil to show planting structure at the entrance.

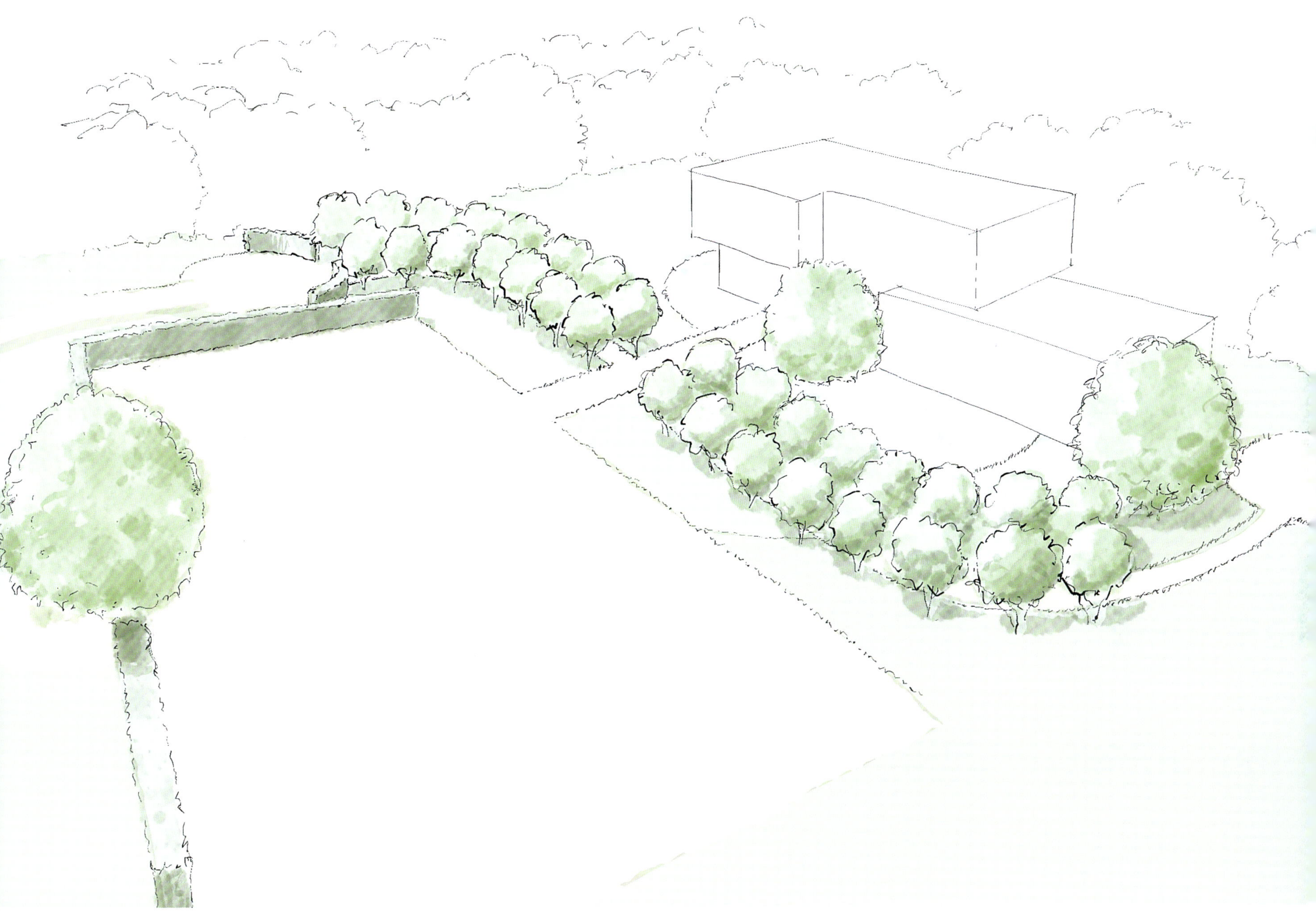

▲ The commercial landscape that was shown in master plan earlier is shown here in a large-scale, bird's-eye view with simple lines and colour added to enhance the drawing. You could create this in a CAD programme, but you may find that you can impress your clients equally with hand-drawing skills.

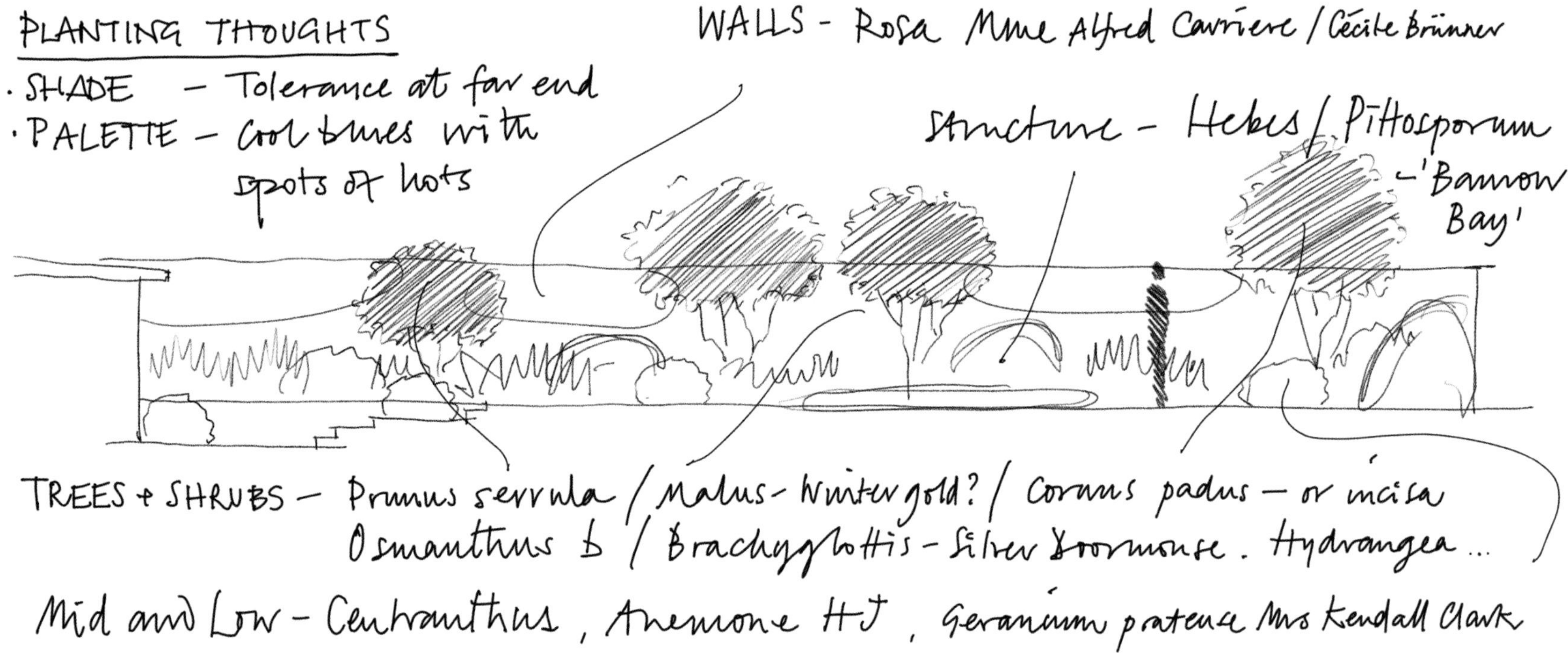

▲ Long-listing usually takes the form of a handwritten list of plants under distinct headings such as 'trees, shrubs and perennials', but a more useful way to long-list is to write your ideas alongside your elevation. In this example, you could also add in a few project rules to remind you of your original concepts and key ideas.

LONG-LISTING PLANTS

It's almost impossible for the plant professional to approach a new planting design without getting some immediate ideas about what plants might fulfil the project brief and spatial design. We all have our go-to plants, and any recently acquired knowledge about new plants that we want to try out can make us race to conclusions on plant selection. Remember to slow down and aim to give your client a unique design, not a repeat of what you've done before. Sure, you can use plants you know, even some combinations of plants that you've tried, tested, and love, but consider whether that's right for a particular project and its circumstances. You are more likely to innovate and inspire confidence in your design if you come at it with an open mind.

By this stage, you are juggling a lot of information from your project brief and development work. Starting a long list of potential plant species and cultivars and getting this information down onto paper will free up your mind to explore your design and innovate even further. If you get an idea for a plant that might fulfil your objectives and help create the planting atmosphere you desire, then start a planting long list, drop yourself a quick note, and move on with the larger task at hand. You might even make some notes as an overlay to your underlying plan, but return to your long list later as you start to select plants. Look at the qualities those plant ideas have while researching others that might be new to you and could fulfil those same objectives and rules that you set yourself much better.

Model-Making as a Tool

Another method for exploring spatial quality in your design is to experiment with overlaying your plan with a 3D model. Some designers find this a fun and practical tool for organising planting mass and void. They often use cuttings of plants, such as dried hydrangea flower heads, to stand in as trees and readily available materials, such as dried moss, to show large-scale areas of herbaceous planting. It is a great way of working in a team because planting elements can be moved around spontaneously as colleagues work to reach consensus on a master plan.

As you begin to see the value of model-making, also consider using 3D printing as a foundation to support your ideas—this will rely on your being able to supply CAD models of the underlying design layout. The model above, made from 3D-printed buildings, paving, and rocks, uses new technology to support the goals of traditional model-making: to explore the spatial layout of trees and other planting.

SUMMARY: DEVELOP YOUR MASTER PLANNING SKILLS

Master-planning in 2D and 3D is an essential stage in the development of your planting design. By introducing 2D elevations and 3D perspective sketches into your process, you will find that when laying out your planting plan you will already have arrived at a level of confidence about your conclusions, allowing you to use the remainder of your time more efficiently. The process of illustrating your ideas in elevation and perspective will also help you to audit your structural ideas against your narrative, chosen atmosphere, and the rules that you created as part of the project brief.

You will have the confidence in the structure of the planting that you are designing before having to meet other project objectives and rules that you may have set for your design, such as year-round interest, shade tolerance, or using sun-loving plants. Your master plan and the decided character for individual areas will already have narrowed down the plants that you might use before you start looking for them, allowing you to move quickly into making decisions about composition and the plants that you should use.

CASE STUDY

GAVIN MCWILLIAM AND ANDREW WILSON

Private Residence
Quinta do Lago, Almancil, Portugal

Planting to return a garden space into a natural wilderness aesthetic where sustainable motives are to the fore.

Climate:	Warm Mediterranean (Csa), cooler and wetter in winter, drier and hotter in summer
Rainfall:	500mm (19.7") per annum
Temperature:	Minimum 11 degrees Celsius (52 degrees F) Maximum 28 degrees Celsius (82 degrees F)
Soil:	Alkaline limestone

PLANTING DEVELOPMENT

This design concept is of *região selvagem,* or wilderness. The entire garden is devoted to a return to a wilder experience. To achieve that, the designers use a range of native or close-native species that aim to produce a sustainable landscape. Sharply defined terraces, decks, and screening walls contrast dramatically with the planted landscape to deliver a play of light that changes throughout the day as sun and shadows move across the garden. The textured foliage planting—including grasses, creeping groundcovers, herbs, gnarled shrubs and trees, and tall pines—provide a rich contrast to the clean and monumental architecture of the house, raised terraces, and refreshing pools.

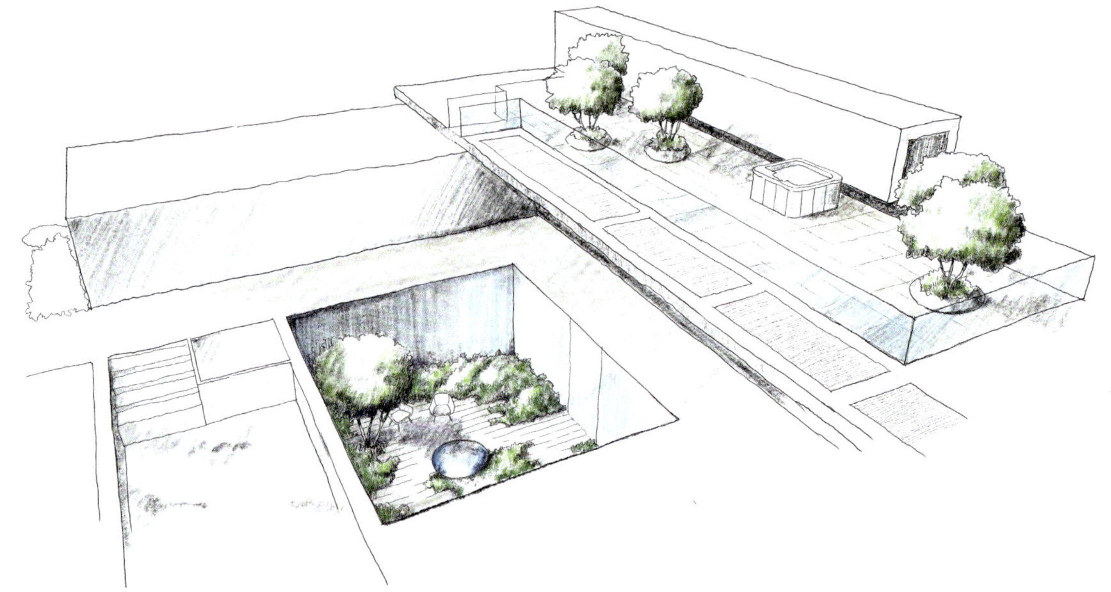

PLANTING DETAIL

The planting design strategy delivers a foil to the architecture with dry gravel and naturalistic planting inspired by the local native landscapes and habitats. Tall *Cupressus sempervirens* deliver vertical emphasis and punctuation while multi-stemmed *Quercus suber* and *Arbutus unedo* are planted throughout the design to link the site to its history and past.

Inspired by the dry-streambed landscapes of the local area and the wider *maquis* or *garrigue*, the design turns its back on the high-input, water-thirsty gardens typical of the surrounding area to offer a new aesthetic of naturalistic and native planting that does not require irrigation beyond the establishment period. The planting will also dramatically increase biodiversity. Existing pines were retained where possible, given the dramatic increase in the scale of the new property and its impact on the sloping site.

The planting uses both ornamental and naturalistic approaches to planting. Trees and key shrubs are set out individually, positioned and oriented to feel as natural as possible. The planting around the house and through the dry river garden is designed to feel naturalistic but is in reality carefully orchestrated—each plant or group of plants is positioned in a specific, predetermined location. Towards the boundary, a matrix of grasses and perennials is used.

Sourcing plants, particularly the trees and large shrubs, was a major challenge. Palms and olives are ubiquitous throughout the Algarve, but tracking down native trees or more unusual specimens proved very difficult, so the majority were sourced from Italy. For the perennials, local nurseries along with observation of surrounding gardens, public spaces, or plants growing wild in the landscape provided a starting point for plant development. The landscape contractor had a very keen interest in more naturalistic planting and delivering something different in the region, which proved of great benefit in helping source plants.

CASE STUDY

SURFACEDESIGN

Pierpont Lane Privately Owned Public Space
San Francisco, California, United States

Climate: Cold-summer Mediterranean (Csc)
Rainfall: 600mm (24") per annum
Temperature: Minimum +10 degrees Celsius (50 degrees F)
Maximum +17 degrees Celsius (63 degrees F)
Soil: New manufactured soil

A respite and a garden oasis within an urban environment celebrating seasonality through a series of intimate spaces.

PLANTING DEVELOPMENT

Mission Bay is a rapidly developing part of San Francisco, dominated by new office buildings and housing that has an anonymous character. The designers wanted to bring in intimate-but-informal garden spaces as well as to celebrate wildness with native and adapted plants. The project is intended to be a respite, a garden oasis within the Mission Bay neighbourhood. It celebrates seasonality in Northern California, which is unusual because people from outside the state tend to think that California doesn't experience distinct seasons; there is actually a lot of fall colour here.

Planting inspiration came from Pina Bausch's performance art *Nelken* (Carnations) and paintings about the void by Robert Motherwell, an American Abstract Expressionist.

The atmosphere creates intimate spaces reminiscent of a lush garden where you're absolutely surrounded by plants. The designers intended this to be a little surprising—the technical term for that is *disruptive*—because they arrived at it in an atypical way. This project creates something very sensual and immersive for an unexpected, urban context. The compositional desire was to frame visual connections to the city while simultaneously shielding and hiding the user from that city. The suggestion is that plants can achieve that.

Buildings (both existing and new) surround the entire planted area, so significant parts of the landscape are in shade. This was a driving force in the development of the plant list. There is also a uniquely urban condition present—the sun rays bounce off the glass windows and can burn some of the trees. They were not looking for a purely native planting scheme, but they embraced adapted plants. This is not a restoration project, it is in an urban garden in a temperate zone, so the design integrates native plants with plants that are adapted.

PLANTING DETAIL

The planting composition relates to individual garden spaces and the experiential qualities of those spaces as well as the habit, form, and texture of the plant material. A significant percentage of the plantings were planned as bioretention, i.e., stormwater management. Another major organizing principle was around colour, specifically whites and pinks or purples. Colour is muted in response to the refined strength and boldness of the architecture. The ground plane also responds to that; there is the sense that the buildings rise directly out of an existing ground. Planting is also used to highlight the monolithic stone blocks placed throughout.

The open-space planting recalls a perennial meadow. It is the people's garden, a place of serenity and respite from the surrounding urban pressures. With the seasonal transformation and floriferous display of the upland slopes and the lawn bowl framing the sky through a ring of cajeput paperbark trees, this portion of the campus planting includes the most diverse palette of trees, shrubs, groundcovers, grasses, and perennials in the project. Integrated seating alcoves complete the tree ring, dappled with flowering perennial plants amid shrubs and trees for structure. Cracks between eruptive stone blocks are planted, calling on the serendipitous feats of nature.

The boundaries of Pierpoint Lane are intentionally obscured to expand the open-space experience. The plant palette is conceived to focus on overwhelming green. The defined forms of flowering shrubs and creeping groundcovers create a sense of rhythm and cohesion through the lane. Canopy trees provide shade while understory trees present colour, form, and density. Columnar trees provide emphasis at the project crossroads below the architectural sky bridges and Third Street frontage.

The site is on landfill, so the designers had to be thoughtful about how the land will settle; this had an impact on composition, materiality, and plant choice. Differential settlement was a major issue as they explored how the site would change over time

Lightweight foam was used to mitigate settlement of over-excavated soil. New soil material was designed and blended to add to the project. Biological amendments were implemented to promote the biological growth and fungi in the soil, which will in turn support the larger ecosystem in addition to the health of the plants onsite today.

Sculpted topography includes landforms and depressions that act as bioretention treatment for runoff; their performative function is also reflected in the planting selection.

CHAPTER **7**

CONTEMPORARY APPROACHES TO PLANTING COMPOSITION

The professional planting designer will have to meet the needs of a wide range of clients and landscapes. Different projects will require different creative approaches to planting design, so no two projects will ever be the same. This will always make for an interesting workload with ample opportunities to widen your design and planting knowledge, but it can also create challenges in framing your work. Whatever the landscape you are working on, by referencing the planting design framework stages set out here, you will be able to get started, explore and develop your ideas and, at this stage in your planting design, develop a detailed planting structure for your project.

◂ *Anthriscus sylvestris* flowering with a mix of annuals and perennials in early summer in an informal cottage garden at Great Dixter, in the United Kingdom.

ARCHETYPE	CONTROL	FORM	APPROACHES
Ornamental e.g. traditional mixed border	High	Structured or formal	Incremental layers Canopy layers
Naturalistic e.g. urban public space	Medium	Dynamic and informal	Matrix Vertical layers
Wild e.g. seeded wildflower meadow	Low	Spontaneous	Seed mixes

◂ Contemporary approaches to planting design structure. These compositional archetypes will be recognisable in different measure in every planting designer's work.

There are many different structural, stylistic and aesthetic approaches that a planting designer might take, and each approach will be specific to the individual and to each project and its own nuances unique to the location. For example, take the 'naturalistic' aesthetic, which has seen a surge in popularity over the past several decades. This is a very broad stylistic approach that can be achieved in a variety of ways, from carefully positioning plants to create a 'natural' aesthetic to carefully mixing seed with a thorough understanding of how each plant will behave in a community and then randomly broadcasting it over a planting area. The approach you take will depend on factors such as scale, soil type, moisture, client expectations, aftercare protocols, and experience. However, there are few clients who will agree to a planting aesthetic merely because it is fashionable—they will more likely describe what they want in terms of colour, aftercare, resilience, and other factors that give a character and atmosphere to their landscape, and a practical solution. That choice may well include a naturalistic atmosphere but could equally be created with a more formal controlled composition of hedges and topiary, which still have many fans in contemporary garden design.

COMPOSITIONAL ARCHETYPES

The composition of planting is a major element of the planting designer's work. Composition at this stage is about developing spatial quality and can sometimes be referred to as the 'structure' of a planting scheme, but as this term can also be used in other ways within planting design it is useful here to refer to the different structural approaches as compositional archetypes. Broad definitions of different compositional archetypes will help you decide upon the spatial quality of your proposed planting and enable you to transfer an archetype into a planting layout. This chapter will help you understand the range of modern approaches to designing with plants for each of these archetypes.

It is important to understand that compositional archetypes are not about small plant combinations, which will more often focus on a few different species that work together aesthetically and horticulturally. Compositional archetypes are about creating planting structure at scale that, along with the narrative that you have chosen, will help you achieve a compelling design solution. Each archetype will encourage you to use individual plants in different ways, but the detailed selection of plants comes after you have master-planned and then decided on the overall structural composition you are aiming for.

◂ In this large-scale planting design by Jo Wakelin at Mount Pisa in New Zealand, the designer has created an informal character for the planting; although the individual plants were carefully placed, the end impression is that of a naturalistic atmosphere.

BUILDING A CONTEMPORARY PLANTING DESIGN

In this book we start at a different point than most other design books because, as the chart opposite shows, we are not advocating a single approach but comparing different approaches led by the different outcomes that you are aiming for within the context of a compositional archetype. Rather than focusing on a single approach that might give you the same outcome from project to project, this asks first what type of structural planting outcome you want to achieve and then suggests different ways of achieving it. It will also give you context for the different approaches taken in planting that you may have studied as well as a way forward to design the underlying structure of *your* planting design.

This chapter focuses on the most common contemporary planting archetypes of the twenty-first century, most of which have their roots in earlier planting design movements. For example, the nineteenth-century enthusiasm for picturesque landscapes that favoured nonnative plants in natural groups, inspired by the arrangement of plants in landscape painting, is a planting design archetype. A similar enthusiasm for organising plants according to what appears in nature has led in recent decades to a relaxed, informal aesthetic now usually referred to as 'naturalistic' planting. It differs from earlier archetypes in that it might use only native or regional plants and near-native cultivars, but it can also accommodate nonnative plants that thrive in similar habitats. The underlying enthusiasm for ordering plants in a natural way remains unchanged.

Each archetype is defined first by the level of control and planting form that will affect your planting aesthetic and therefore the approach that you should consider. For example, matrix planting is a methodology for achieving a naturalistic aesthetic. In this case, it's a sophisticated approach that relies on an understanding of phytosociology; this is best described as studying how a community of plants that are usually found together in nature will interact with each other in a cultivated setting. Plants are likely to be set out onsite by a designer or by a landscaper using instructions from the designer. It is this human intervention that can make elements of the planting appear more defined or organised within a naturalistic planting. Equally, matrix planting on a larger scale may use several plant mixes that are laid out in a more randomised way to create a wilder and more spontaneous-seeming aesthetic. The control in each project is maintained via the selection of plants and the method of distributing the plants in the design phase, and then how they are set out onsite.

▲ For this contemporary parterre, designer Nina Baxter has chosen to retain a traditional structure whilst incorporating a sustainable narrative by selecting nontraditional *Myrtus communis* as a resilient hedging solution and drought-tolerant planting.

KNOWING WHICH APPROACH TO TAKE

The desired atmosphere or outcome of the planting design will most likely affect which approach you take and thus the earlier development of your planting design narrative and the atmosphere that you are aiming to achieve is crucial in deciding your approach. For example, the planting of the entrance to a historic home might call for a formal atmosphere using woody plants such as topiary and clipped hedging. This will naturally push the designer towards an ornamental, incremental approach. Conversely, a more informal atmosphere created with swathes of grasses and perennial plants might be achieved through a naturalistic planting approach. This will become clearer as you study the different approaches.

DEVELOPING YOUR SKILLS

The remainder of this chapter explores contemporary compositional approaches for different planting archetypes in use today. Few planting designers will want to specialise in just one planting archetype, although their practice may receive more commissions for one particular approach as their career develops and they become 'known' for one style over another. Indeed, it is possible that a single large landscape may call for different approaches to be used simultaneously, each according to its location within the site. You will certainly work with a range of different clients, and so a flexible process that allows for different approaches to be used should reward you with the skills to enjoy and achieve a wide range of design outcomes, whether a client is requesting a traditional mixed border, rewilded landscape, or something in between. Crucially, by keeping an open mind about all planting archetypes you will start to develop your own distinct approach to composition.

The description of these approaches is also, of necessity, presented only in outline; it is recommended that you investigate the reading list at the end of this book to add depth to your understanding of the nuances of each approach.

◀ This planting design for a walled garden in Worcestershire, England, is very typical of what we think of when we consider ornamental composition, but this contemporary approach uses modern cultivars of shrubs and perennials to provide a long-lasting display.

ARCHETYPE: ORNAMENTAL COMPOSITION

Ornamental planting is a style that we are generally very familiar with, as it appears regularly in residential gardens and public spaces. Whilst often thought of as a traditional style, it is still extremely popular because it includes a strong element of control resulting from a combination of thoughtful design and regular aftercare. The mixed herbaceous border is a good example of ornamental planting and can be found in very large landscapes as well as in smaller gardens.

The composition of an ornamental planting is more structured and formal than other planting archetypes and, whilst it gives the designer more control over plants, it will also likely demand a fair amount of attention in aftercare to retain the desired effect of every plant thriving in the right place as specified from the outset by the designer.

ORNAMENTAL COMPOSITION: INCREMENTAL LAYERS, THE TRADITIONAL APPROACH

The incremental development approach to design will comfortably build upon your earlier exploration of planting design quality or atmosphere. Led by the exploration of planting structure in elevation, this approach will enable you to translate your chosen structural idea into a 2D plan quickly and efficiently.

With this, plants are placed in different plant categories to build a planting composition by stages. It is especially useful for smaller-scale landscapes, home gardens, and individual borders, etc. It's a simple approach that works; indeed many well-known designers such as John Brookes have proposed variations on this theme because the systematic use of plant categories such as focal, structural, and decorative plants promote a level of spatial control that is reassuring to the planting designer and garden enthusiast alike.

The approach uses a system that allows you to select plants in each category, starting with the focal points and then building on your composition through a series of stages, down to groundcover and seasonal additions. The categorisation that follows is the author's own, but most forms of incremental planting have similar group descriptors and follow this order.

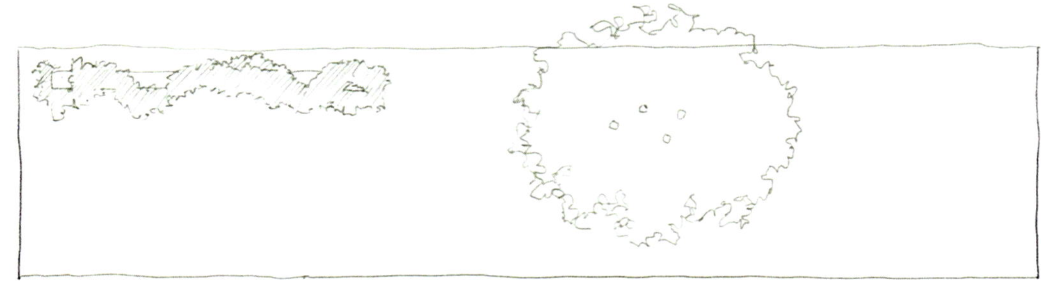

▲ Figure 1. Focal points.

A. Focal Points

The first choices to be made are the focal points, sometimes referred to as the star performers or specimen plants. These are the plants that will capture our attention. They might have a seasonal peak but must have year-round presence that will lead our eye through the landscape. Specimen trees are often used as focal points, but this category can also include large shrubs that catch our eye.

B. Structural Plants

This is the predominantly green backbone of the planting. It will most often use shrubs to create a skeleton of plants to provide a year-round backdrop. Evergreens naturally fulfil this structural function, as do structural shapes such as topiary and hedges. This category includes deciduous plants that, whilst they may have seasonal climaxes of flowers, such as with viburnum cultivars, their primary function is always to provide structure to a planting design.

Climbers will often provide structural definition within this category, often in support of hard elements that are already doing this, e.g., fences and arches, and so you can also treat climbers as a structural green backdrop.

▲ Figure 2. Structural plants.

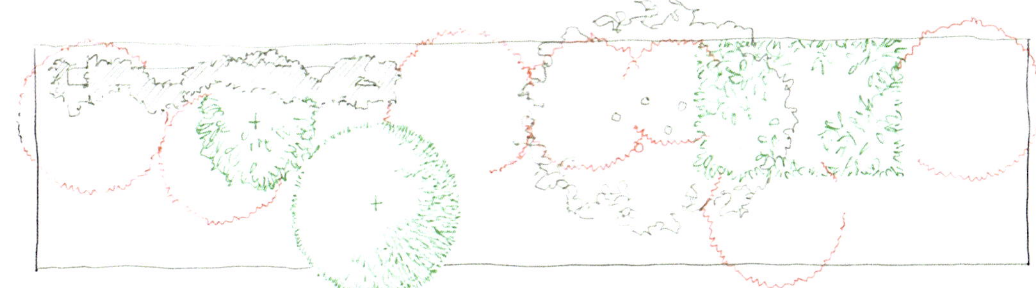

C. Decorative Plants

Decorative plants can still provide structure, but their primary use is for decoration in the form of flowers and foliage. They can be shrubs or perennials or even small multistem trees such as a *Hamamelis* spp. or *Amelanchier* spp., used to provide interest across seasons. Long-flowering shrubs such as hydrangeas, roses, and lavenders and long-flowering perennials such as hardy *Geranium*, *Salvia*, and *Callistemon* are found in this decorative stage, providing a long continuous period of interest, often bridging seasons and giving great value.

▲ Figure 3. Decorative plants.

DEVELOP

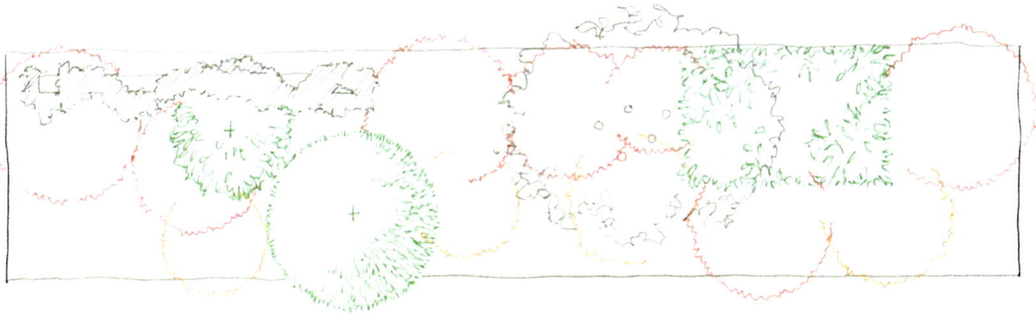

D. Seasonal Flowers and Foliage

These are the plants that provide bursts of ephemeral interest for a shorter season than the decorative plants. They are often perennials that demand our attention, if only for a few weeks or less. *Paeonia* cultivars are a great example that the designer often chooses only if there is space because they flower briefly, if spectacularly. Other seasonal flowers such as *Stachys*, *Actaea* and *Helleborus* and many grass species will provide peaks of flowering interest, but also useful foliage interest at other times.

▲ Figure 4. Seasonal flowers and foliage.

E. Groundcover

Sometimes regarded as infill, groundcover can be an essential backdrop planting to help other plants shine. For example, a low-growing epimedium spread beneath a grove of specimen *Acer griseum* (paperbark maple) trees. It may have a fleeting flowering moment, but its main function is to provide a simple frame to the trees that grow within it. Grasses can provide a similar supporting role to other decorative and seasonal plants, infilling amongst other plants and providing a foliage backdrop.

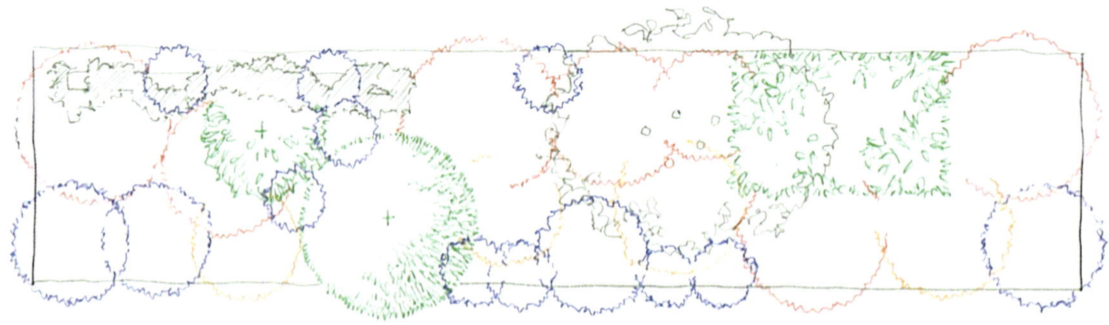

F. Seasonal Jewels

These are the plants that add extra seasonal interest before dying back either for another year or to be replaced the following year. Many bulbs will fall into this category, providing some jewel-like seasonal colour only to disappear once it has rejuvenated its bulb and to let other plants, such as ferns and grasses, grow around it. Plants such as *Lilium* spp. are often used in pots to briefly fill empty spots in an herbaceous border. Annuals are also good for temporarily filling spaces and can be especially useful for the first few years of a new planting design, until shrubs and trees that were planted as small specimens begin to achieve their mature size.

▲ Figure 5. Groundcovers and seasonal jewels.

Delivering an Incremental Planting Plan

The real value in sketching your ideas becomes apparent when you start to lay out a structure utlising the plants that you want to include. Very simply, by sketching planting in elevation at this stage, articulating the style or atmosphere that you want to create through those sketches will allow you to move quickly between elevation and plan views and towards a more detailed level of 2D planting layout.

Whilst ideal for ornamental planting, you can also use this technique in other planting design approaches, illustrating your idea in elevation and then transferring it to a plan, moving between the two to create your final design.

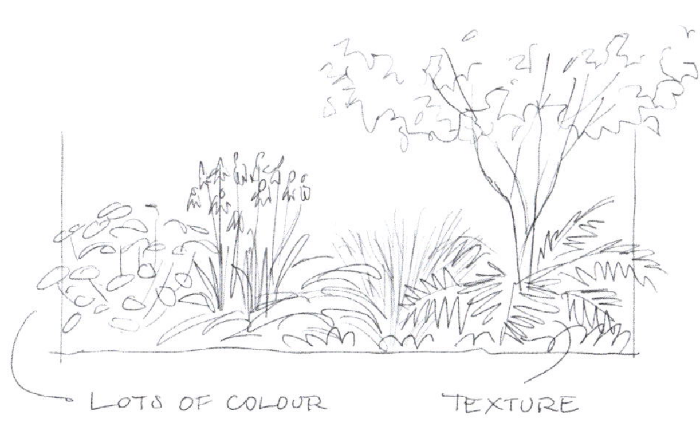

▲ Figure 1. A sketch elevation for a short border 7m (21') wide and 3m (15') deep for the rear of a courtyard garden. By sketching first in elevation, the designer has been able to move from a rough sketch of an idea down to a basic 2D layout very quickly.

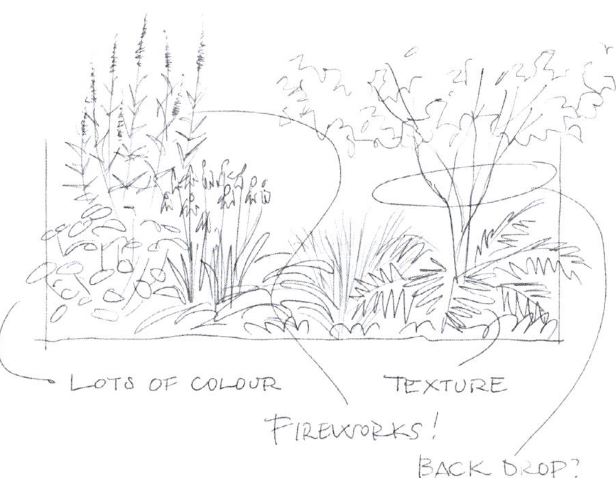

◀ Figure 2. It also allows them to move between plan and elevation, especially when their elevation view hasn't given the full coverage of a planted area that they desire. So, they can fill and expand the planting into the whole depth of the border. They can also explore whether that expansion of planting should be with a completely new plant or by repeating a plant already included in the elevation.

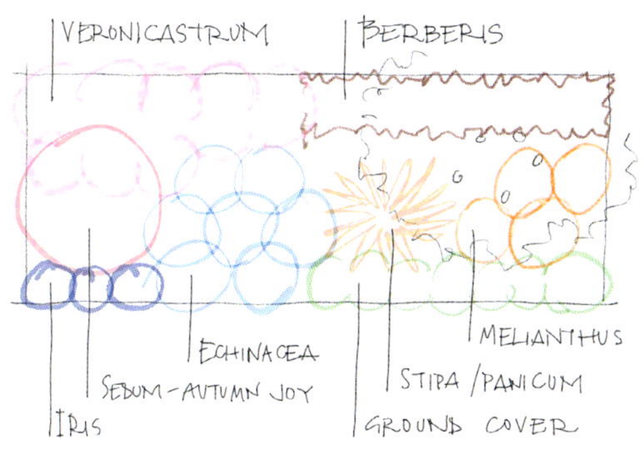

◀ Figure 3. And finally, with both the draft layout of plants and the sketch elevation of the plants in hand, the designer can quickly start to find plants that will fulfil their visual criteria for height and spread. They might even at this stage consider adding some colour to the sketch, based upon their chosen narrative, if that helps them move the planting design forward.

Traditionally, mixed ornamental borders included trees and shrubs as well as perennials. The contemporary ornamental border has been influenced by a more extensive use of perennials that in themselves can produce different peaks of interest through the growing year. Relying on perennials for seasonal interest often requires large areas of planting space, so the balance between hard and soft landscape features has moved in favour of plants in the twenty-first century.

DEVELOP

The benefit of this incremental approach is that it provides creative opportunities whilst controlling the buildup of your planting design. Using the technique of starting with an elevation of your planting allows you to clearly understand the structure of your planting and then, with an understanding of horticultural requirements such as soil and moisture, you can begin to make planting decisions.

The approach also allows you to place plants within a genus in any category, for example a single *Viburnum mariesii* could be regarded as a focal point in one scheme, a group of *Viburnum tinus* could form a structural backdrop, and a *Viburnum* x *carlcephalum* might serve as a decorative element in another.

It is always useful to have a wide knowledge of different plants, but this approach will enable you to research plant possibilities as you develop your ornamental planting scheme, creating a long list of possible plants that you know and discovering new plants that you could also use before you make a final decision. Many designers find this an excellent approach for building their plant knowledge and understanding how a plant could be used.

Whilst this approach is familiar for smaller spaces, if you look closely, you will see that planting designers will also use these same principles for larger-scale planting, especially large mixed borders, to provide focal points with trees, shrubs, topiary, and massed blooms of a single species. Likewise, a naturalistic prairie-style planting takes some ideas from incremental planting to provide those focal points that will lead our eye through a landscape with trees that anchor the planted space.

This large-scale planting design for the water gardens at Longstock Park in Hampshire, England, uses the availability of light to direct planting in three layers: tree canopy, shrubs, and perennials. This approach is discussed on the following pages.

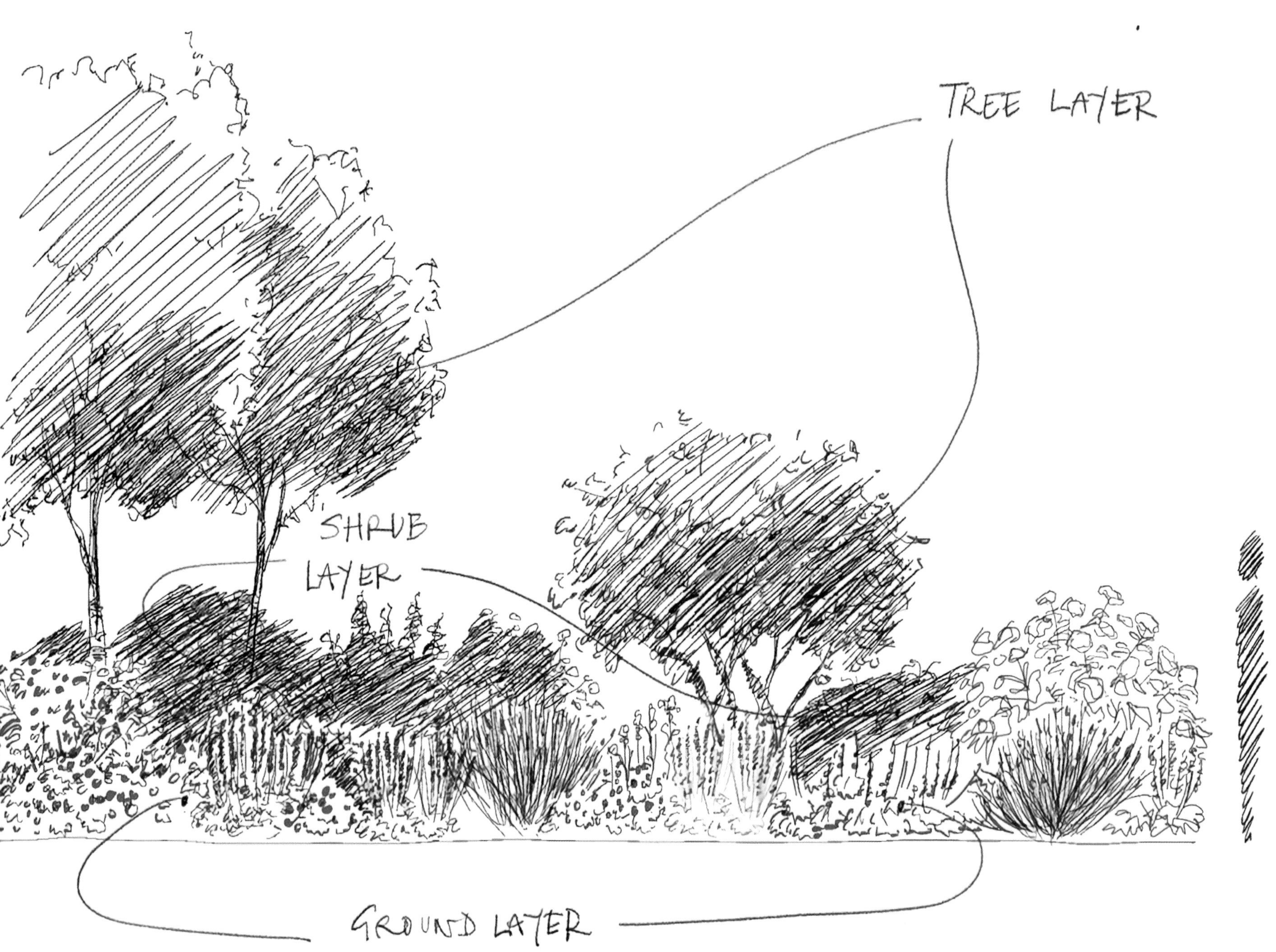
TREE LAYER
SHRUB LAYER
GROUND LAYER

Tree Layer
An open canopy of trees and large shrubs allows space for light to permeate to lower levels. There can be substantial open areas in the shrub layer below as well, similar to the formation of glades in a natural woodland.

Shrub Layer
Choose plants that can establish in areas where light permeates indirectly or are relatively shade tolerant, especially when the tree canopy is at maximum density. Many woody shrubs will thrive in these conditions, including *Weigela*, *Rosa*, *Leycesteria*, *Mahonia*, *Callistemon,* and *Physocarpus*.

Ground Layer
Beneath the shrub layer, and especially under more open forms of shrubs that let light permeate to the ground, there is an opportunity for a shade-tolerant lower layer of planting such as spreading shrubs and perennials. This layer infills the gaps and spreads and suppresses weeds, but can still add height. Examples include *Hemerocallis*, *Iris*, *Hosta*, *Helleborus,* and other plants that might not supress weeds but will still add visual interest.

ORNAMENTAL COMPOSITION: CANOPY LAYERS, DESIGNING WITH LIGHT

The use of plant layers to develop a planting design makes use of the seasonal changes in planting, particularly foliage to provide seasonal layers of *both* flower and foliage. Many layered approaches for planting composition have been developed by planting designers and scientists. Many are linked to naturalistic or wilder planting design and will be covered in the next section. A canopy layer approach essentially looks at where light is available to create layers of planting interest below. It is an approach to creating ornamental planting that found favour in the twentieth century but lost traction when incremental planting approaches were promoted. It has proved popular again in the twenty-first century, especially within larger-scale public spaces and with more informal planting schemes.

In ecology, the term 'canopy' most often refers to the uppermost layers of a forest or woodland, whereas in ornamental planting composition a 'canopy layer' refers to each of a scheme's planting layers, whether or not they are trees, starting with the highest layer of vegetation and introducing further 'canopy layers' by successive height, down to the groundcover. In nature, woodlands fill in with plants based on available light from above and seasonal changes, particularly with deciduous plants. In a canopy layer approach to design, the planting layers are decided in a similar way.

With this approach, plants will often take advantage of seasonality to produce single-species blankets of flowers when higher layers are not in leaf and the light permeates to the ground layer.

A canopy layer approach is very simple and effective for large areas and especially where aftercare might be variable, meaning plants need to look after themselves. It does require a very sound knowledge of plant habit and is often best used when you already have experience with a wide range of plants and how they might grow together in these conditions.

Delivering Ornamental Planting Borders with the Ribbon Layout Technique

Whilst there are distinct advantages in using an elevation-and-plan approach to laying out plants, designers might also use a system based on sweeping groups of individual plants that sits partway between the steady buildup of a diverse mix of plants for an ornamental planting and the more spontaneous, randomised laying out of a naturalistic planting. Large sweeps of plants can be especially effective in large-scale spaces like traditional planted borders and will provide visual impact. This is a familiar approach used by leading plant experts and dates to earlier centuries and heritage gardens.

Traditionally, this method began with blocks being drawn out on a plan or even be laid out onsite using lines of sand, then infilled with each group of plants. But creating the right scale of planting lines and groups can be challenging. Fortunately, there is an easier way of laying plants out using directional, curving lines, or 'ribbons' that create rhythm through a space and also function as anchors to sweeps of plants. Even if you have not yet decided on a final plant selection, this method can help you visualise your plants on the ground. Ribbons interact through the space and, by switching between this detail on plan and elevation sketches, you can quickly build up a detailed scheme.

HOW TO USE THE RIBBON LAYOUT TECHNIQUE

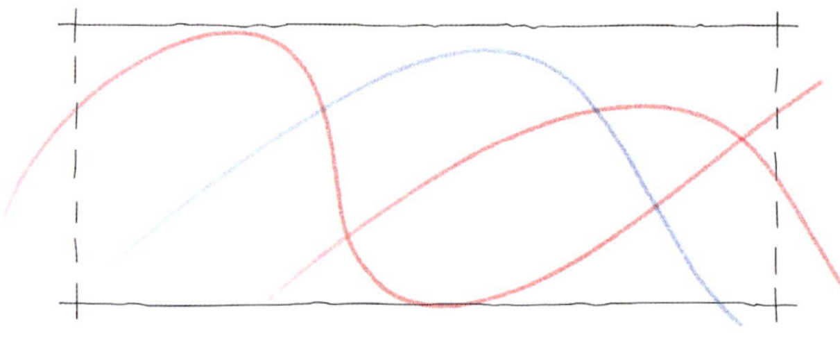

◀ Start by laying quick, sweeping lines across your border plan. These should have direction but can be completely random. You shouldn't think about the journey but rather the end-point for each 'ribbon'.

▶ Part of a double ornamental border that stretches for 60 metres (65 yards), designed by Jo Thompson for maximum impact. Species and cultivars wind their way through the borders, creating subtle rhythm. Large-scale topiary acts as an anchor at the end of this border.

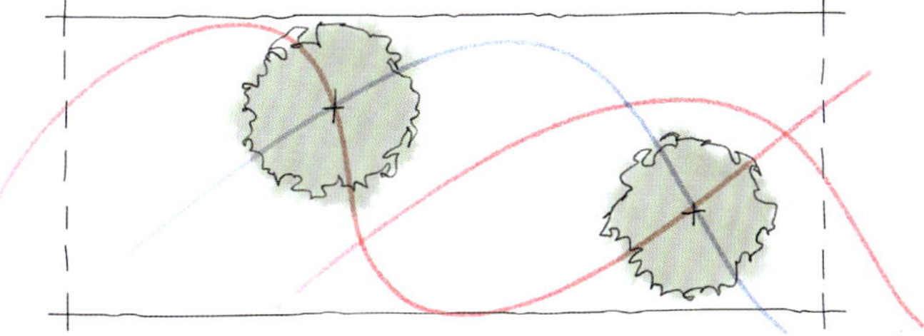

▲ 1. Once you have some overlapping lines, place some focal points. These will often be large shrubs or specimen trees. They could be positioned where the lines intersect, as shown, or along the lines.

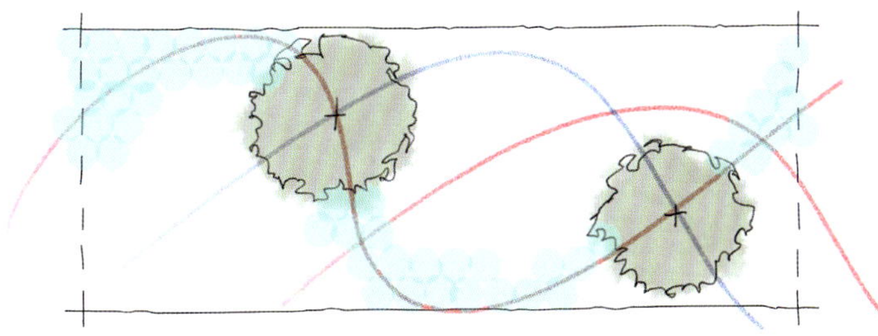

▲ 2. Follow one line to guide your layout of an individual plant group.

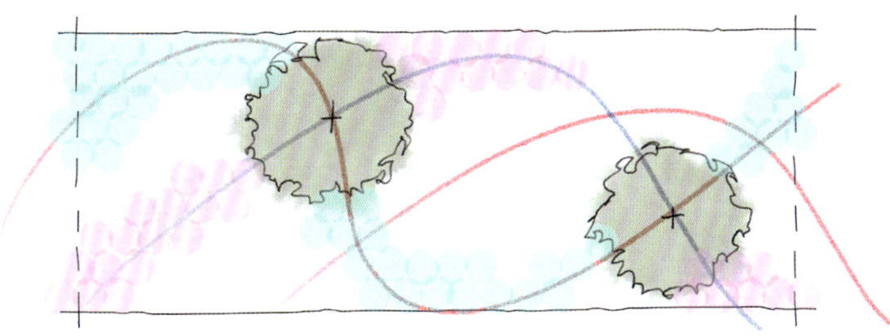

▲ 3. Place additional groups of plants along other available lines. Think about how they'll interact with others. For example, which group will be dominant and sweep visually 'through' the other?

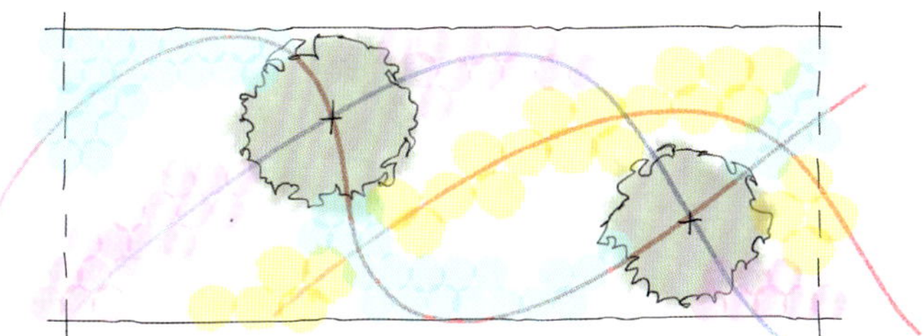

▲ 4. Continue laying out further groups of plant species until all the lines have been claimed.

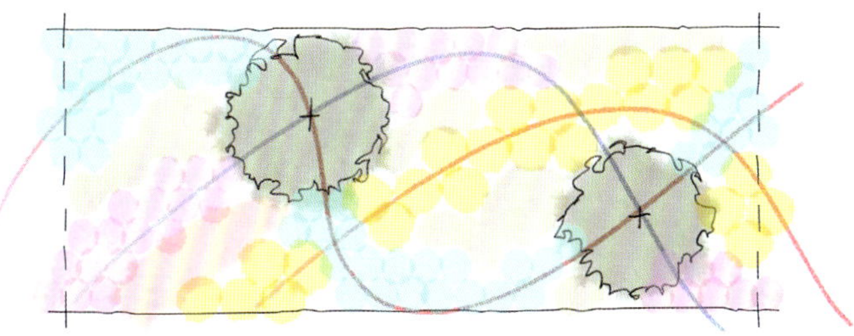

▲ 5. Fill in between sweeps of plants with other plant groups to complete coverage of the border's ground plane.

▲ 6. Finish by erasing your ribbon lines. Now, start to make plant choices. Consider translating this layout into an elevation as you develop your ribbon planting to assess vertical impact.

ARCHETYPE: NATURALISTIC COMPOSITION

Naturalistic planting has become a common and popular planting archetype in the twenty-first century. The idea of creating a planting composition and atmosphere that will, to some extent, recall a natural or wild landscape allows for the use of a wide range of plants, both native and nonnative. It's a contemporary iteration of the tradition of designing nature artificially, where both nature and the perceptible artistry of the human hand are united and the combination is held in high esteem. This is not a new idea, and can be seen in earlier approaches to planting that created relaxed, informal planting compositions that engage people in nature and provide a way of improving ecology, particularly in cities.

Compared to more traditional planted landscapes, many forms of naturalistic planting tend to give greater opportunities to boost habitat and biodiversity with reductions in human inputs such as fertiliser, artificial irrigation, and aftercare. These factors make this approach especially attractive for public spaces.

Proponents of naturalistic planting in public spaces, particularly the earlier Dutch and German adopters of this approach, emphasise the beneficial functions that a naturalistic archetype might bring to a landscape, especially flood alleviation, heat and pollution reduction, and low inputs of aftercare and resources. Other designers, such as Nigel Dunnett and James Hitchmough, prioritise the archetype's aesthetics and the enjoyment planting offers people.

▲ Naturalistic planting is often referred to as 'meadow planting' and sometimes 'prairie planting'. Whilst it is not what we would recognise as a traditional prairie, this term does show an attempt to reflect how the use of plants in designed communities can thrive together. In this public park in Utrecht, the Netherlands, a large-scale planting designed by Piet Oudolf displays the immersive nature of a naturalistic meadow.

Different landscapes might have different priorities and approaches to achieving a planting design. For Dunnett, this archetype places a useful emphasis on engaging people through colour and plant succession. Indeed, the idea of a 'pictorial meadow', coined as a term by him, is a designed urban meadow that first and foremost provides an enhanced experience of plants. It draws people in by eliciting an emotional response to the planting. Colour is a big part of the attraction.

Whilst this approach allows nature to do some of the work for you, naturalistic planting will still necessarily reflect the skill of the planting designer. It sits between the more controlled ornamental planting described earlier, and the random spontaneity of a seeded, 'wild' planting approach. It is not a halfway house, however, and considerable research has been undertaken on different naturalistic approaches and their impact on people and places. It can also be attractive to your clients, especially for public spaces, where the naturalistic design allows for a reduced maintenance regime and only occasional intervention rather than regular aftercare. Indeed, proponents of this approach such as Roy Diblik promote the aftercare of naturalistic planting as a way of gardening *with* nature.

Naturalistic planting design has become an extremely popular archetype for contemporary planting, and there are many different approaches promoted by different practitioners that this book can only begin to cover. This chapter concentrates on two approaches: first a matrix system, and second a vertical layered system. Both prioritise people and are driven by aesthetics. As you develop your skills in naturalistic planting design you might want to explore the more individualistic approaches and strategies put forth by these leading designers, including those that emphasise ecology over people, whilst developing your own approach. A list for further reading is included at the end of this book.

▾ The concept of naturalistic planting design covers a wide range of aesthetics and settings. Some designs may be quite restricted in their diversity of species, especially where containerised plants have been used, whilst others might be much more informal and encompass a wide range of species, as seen in this seeded naturalistic meadow in Scotland.

Is a Naturalistic Approach Sustainable?

Whilst naturalistic planting might go some way towards addressing concerns about wildlife and climate change, you shouldn't automatically assume that this approach will automatically meet sustainable project objectives. Naturalistic approaches *can be* sustainable, but it is important to recognise that just because a design has the look of a contemporary, naturalistic planting it won't arbitrarily meet the sustainability objectives you might have set for your planting design. For example, if your design requires high embodied carbon (a carbon footprint) for its establishment and aftercare and then with the regular replacement of plants, the sustainability of your design will likely be low because of the level of carbon emissions. Conversely, a more traditional, formally laid-out ornamental planting might achieve a good level of sustainability if low aftercare is planned, biodiversity created, and wildlife-friendly plants are selected.

▲ Recent planting at the Barbican Centre in London, United Kingdom, designed by Nigel Dunnett using a matrix planting technique that allows for waves of planting to peak through a long growing season.

▶ Naturalistic planting allows a visitor total immersion within the plants. The grass paths in this design by Fisher Tomlin & Bowyer are relatively narrow so that the viewer can get up close to the plants.

NATURALISTIC COMPOSITION: MATRIX DESIGN, A PEOPLE-FIRST APPROACH

In the twenty-first century the matrix planting approach has been used to completely transform public spaces, delivering large-scale, naturalistic planting. It has become a popular way of engaging people with nature, especially in nontraditional city spaces such as pocket parks, on vertical walls, and green roofs where planting can also have a positive impact on overheated urban spaces, pollution, and flooding.

By focusing on re-creating communities of plants that would naturally thrive together, matrix planting is often promoted as an ecological approach to planting design. The approach has also been described as formulaic, however, and accused of removing the creativity from planting design (compared to ornamental planting design), but just as any planting design approach might be described as formulaic, there are plenty of opportunities for the designer to innovate creatively on different projects.

Matrix planting originated in European parks, particularly in Germany and the Netherlands. It uses plant sequences that are primarily made up of habitat-appropriate perennials and grasses, although the use of trees and other woody plants within matrix planting is becoming more widespread as designers experiment with new ideas and aim for a more biodiverse mix of flora. The approach aims to create an immersive experience which engages the visitor with dynamic planting that's perceptibly complex in layout and changes over time, both across seasons and over years.

The dynamism of matrix planting still relies on the traditional principle of right plant, right place. Gardeners have worked with this concept throughout history, but with naturalistic planting it is a key principle that matching plants in designed communities to enjoy the same soil, moisture, and climate will succeed. Plants that enjoy the same habitat, whether native or nonnative, should in theory be comfortable together if organised according to how they grow.

With matrix planting, designers aim to create plant communities that successfully balance the requirements of the individual landscape and that of the client. Their plant choices might vary, but there is an underlying principle of bringing plants together in natural communities so that they will support each other and develop resilience through density. The long-established method of waterwise planting, developed in the southern hemisphere, is in some ways a precursor to matrix planting due to its emphasis on designing densely planted communities of plants with similar water requirements that should coexist happily over long periods by thriving in the same soil and climate.

We already know that it is important not to make assumptions about an individual landscape based on something you have experienced before. Time, our evolving climate, and underlying environmental factors will create different conditions for every site. Climate creates a particular challenge to designing these communities, as do the different landscapes and ecologies that you may come across. So this approach, like any, requires the planting designer to monitor the success of their decisions over time. This builds knowledge and understanding of the extremes and the unpredictability of the climates that we are working in.

The discovery and exploration stages of the overall planting design framework will also give the planting designer confidence and understanding and then, by developing a narrative, will direct thoughts and design to generating a matrix of plants that will be successful. As with other planting archetypes, matrix planting also considers plant structure and function before moving on to individual plant selection. Therefore, elevation and perspective drawings are also useful tools for matrix designs. The first step, the setting out of trees and woody plants that form a backbone or anchor to planting, will especially be supported by elevation drawings before laying out other plants according to either dominance or seasonal peak.

The Development of a Matrix Planting Design

Although the results may look natural, matrix planting still has a strong element of organisation in its creation. Soils are cleared and, in the case of new urban developments often new, clean soil imported, to enable the planting designer to start with a blank canvas—the principle being that the only plants that should appear are those that you select. And just like in previous approaches, matrix planting has developed a series of stages that you can follow to achieve an ultimate design. The categories of plants that form each matrix stage may seem familiar, but this more informal layout of plants differs from ornamental planting, and is illustrated on the following pages.

▲ Figure 1. Structural plants. These are the dominant first plants that create a structure other plants can be built up around.

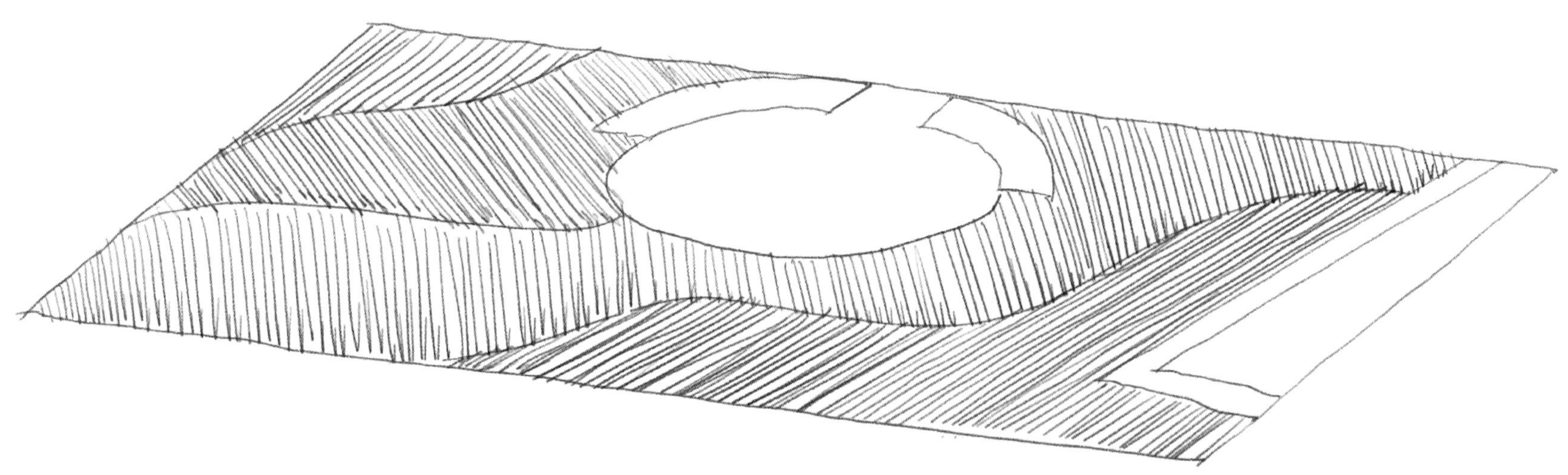

▲ Figure 2. Seasonal plants. These have no strong structural quality but offer seasonal peaks and aesthetics.

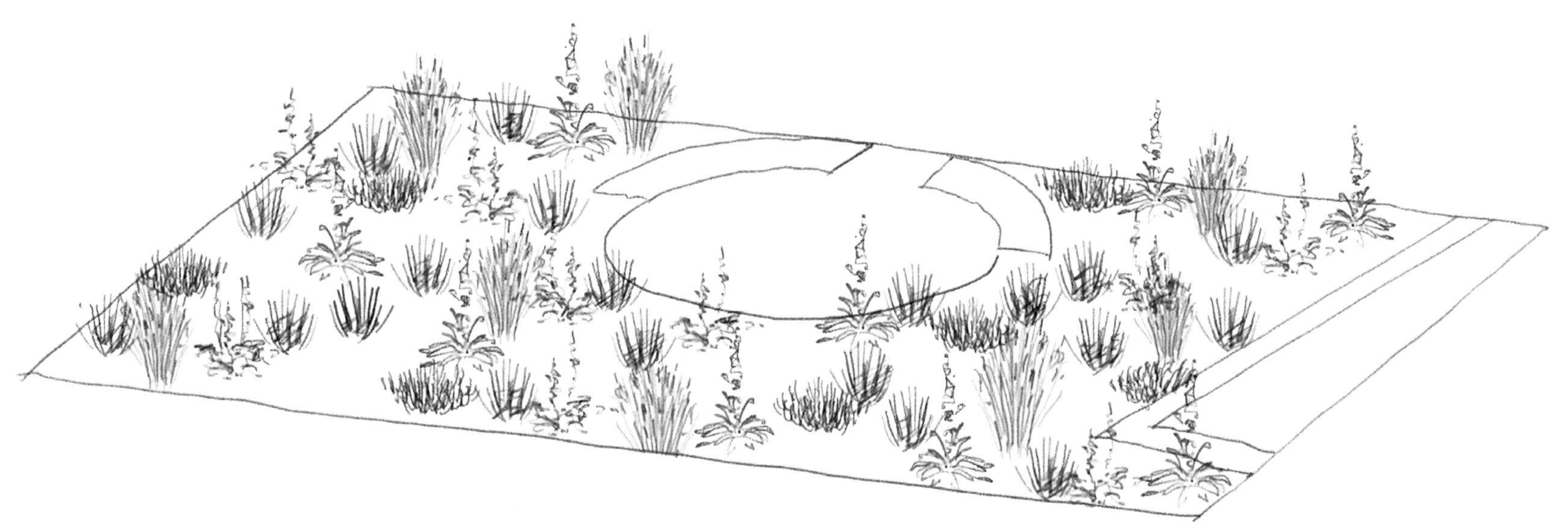

▲ Figure 3. Groundcover perennials. These plants create seasonal interest in late autumn and winter and early spring, often outside the main times of peak interest.

DEVELOP

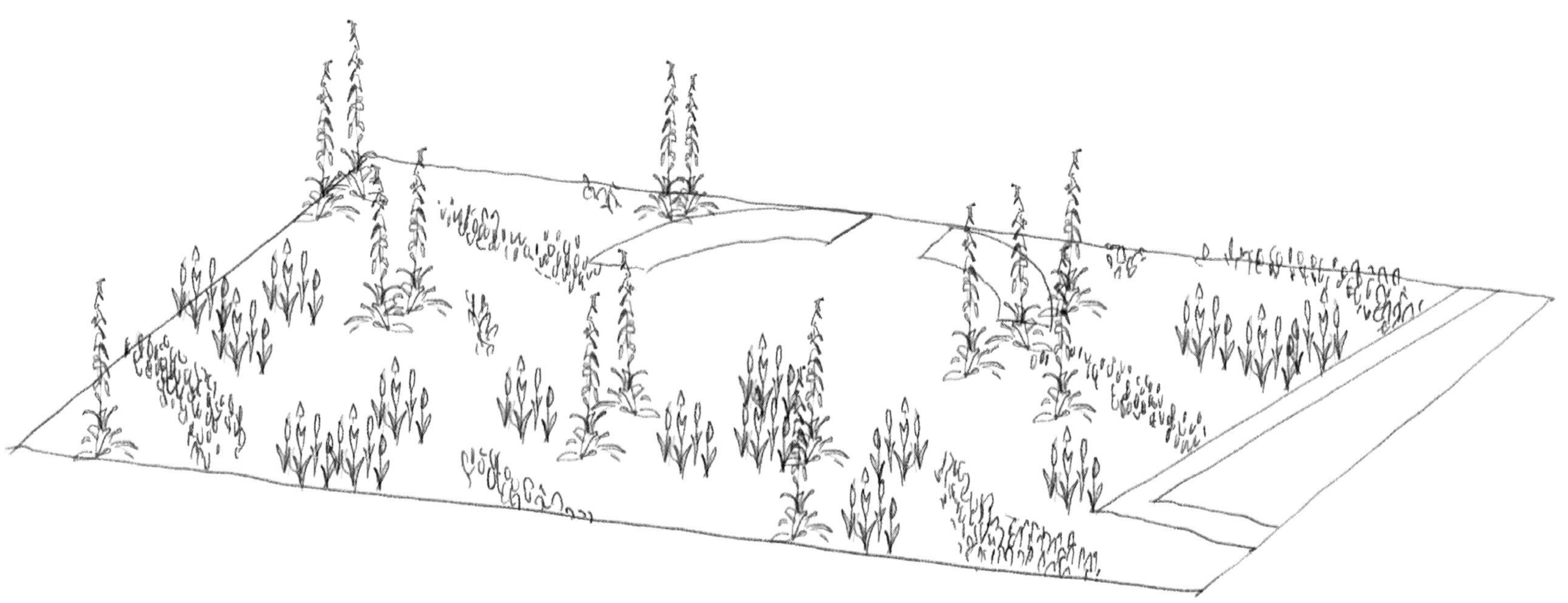

▲ Figure 4. Filler plants, bulbs, and geophytes. These short-lived perennials, biennials, and annuals fill gaps. They may die out, or bulbs and geophytes might naturalise.

The delivery of structure in a matrix planting design relies on the development of planting across five categories. The dominant plants, placed first, create a structure that other plants can be built up around.

Category 1: Structural Plants

Variously referred to as anchor, dominant, or skeleton plants, these are the first used to create a structure that other plants can be built up around. In colder climates they might be plants that give long periods of interest such as *Euphorbia*, large grasses such as *Miscanthus* spp., *Agrostis* spp., and in warmer climates, restios *Elegia* spp. and *Rhodocoma* spp. They are typically placed as individual specimens within the larger matrix.

Increasingly, designers of naturalistic planting are also recognising the usefulness of woody shrubs and small trees, especially for large-scale sites, where they act as structural anchors within a matrix planting scheme.

Category 2: Seasonal Plants

These are sometimes referred to as seasonal-theme perennials or companion perennials. They are plants that have no strong structural quality but offer a broad range of successive seasonal colour or bloom and aesthetics that are valuable to planting. They appeal to the viewer by building upon the immersive experience that the structural plants have started. They provide the drama and extended-season planting interest that you will find in a mixed border and, whilst they might add no real structural quality to the planting, they will engage the viewer with their flowers and seed heads.

Whilst many grasses might be used as structural plants within this approach, there are also grass species that can fulfil a seasonal role—especially when they provide autumn flowering interest. Plants that give longer interest through foliage outside of their flowering period are especially valuable. Take for example *Actaea* spp.

You might also create larger 'blooms' of single species across a large area of a planting. For example, a structural grass might be used across most of a space, and then large-scale use might be made of very few species that mimic the way that meadows can be dominated by just a few species of plants that bloom in seasonal peaks.

Category 3: Groundcover Perennials

This category of plants is quite wide-ranging because, rather than following the traditional definition of low groundcover and spreading plants, these create seasonal interest in late autumn and winter and early spring, often outside of the main peaks of interest. These plants form the base layer of the matrix from which the structural and seasonal plants emerge. In some ways, the principle of groundcover planting is the same as in more traditional planting, but their use in this category allows for a wider range of plants to be used. A useful rule might be that the plants used tend to grow to heights of up to 600mm/24" and no more.

This category of groundcover perennials must be shade tolerant because they are growing in the lowest level of available light. They work in a similar way to canopy layer planting in that they make use of the light at times of the year when higher layers of deciduous plants, such as grasses, are not in leaf but will create shade later. Designers often refer to these plants as 'visually quiet' species. They include small evergreens and semievergreens such as *Hakonechloa* spp., *Epimedium* spp., *Euphorbia* spp. and perennials such as *Artemisia*, *Saponaria*, *Geranium*, *Anaphalis*, *Aster*, and *Primula*. By contrast, I would propose that some of these plants might be deemed 'quietly flamboyant' instead, proving that the beauty in and function of plants that you might choose is very subjective and that you need to reference your narrative to decide whether they are contributing what you want to your design.

Category 4: Filler Plants

These are used to create immediate impact and are short-lived perennials, biennials, and annuals that, quite simply, fill gaps. The intention is that they disappear over time, often as structural and seasonal plants that may have been planted as small specimens begin to establish and mature. They might self-seed, but you don't want them to be long-lived as they can require a lot of maintenance to control.

Examples of good filler plants would be *Aquilegia*, *Campanula*, *Lychnis*, *Gaura*, and *Oenothera*.

▲ In this retrofit of an existing street scene designed by the Sheffield City Council in the United Kingdom with Robert Bray Associates and with planting design by Zac Tudor and Nigel Dunnett, spaces were reallocated to allow for extensive areas of rain gardens and bioswales. More pedestrian space is included, as part of a wider strategy to reduce water runoff reaching the River Don.

DEVELOP

▲ In this naturalistic planting design by Fisher Tomlin & Bowyer, seasonal perennials play an important role. The tree, shrub, and grass layers have already been selected; these plants are not restricted to flower in a single peak but have been chosen so that waves of colour interest will appear throughout the main growing season.

Category 5: Bulbs and Geophytes

These are useful for early interest, before the later seasonal plants develop and peak. They include the traditional spring-flowering bulbs we see in other types of planting, scattered through other categories of plants. Some, such as Alliums, might push through developing layers of perennials and grasses later in the growing season. They bloom at a similar time to filler plants, but they are intended to form an integral part of the planting and won't gradually disappear; indeed, some may need replanting at frequent intervals.

Low-growing bulbs within predominantly low grasses might give early support to early pollinators and so those with open flower heads, such as *Tulipa bakeri*, *Scilla siberica*, *Muscari latifolium*, *Crocus* vars., *Chinodoxa luciliae,* and early *Narcissus* spp. can be useful in this category.

Delivering a Matrix Planting Design

The dynamic nature of matrix planting means that every project will be different, and it will make it very difficult to draw your planting design as a traditional 2D plan, especially if you are aiming for a spontaneous planting atmosphere.

A typical matrix planting will be developed as a mix of plant species. Show a spreadsheet of included species alongside your elevation sketches. The plants will be set out directly onsite, whether by the designer or under written instructions from the designer that allows for a uniqueness to each planting layout. As the designer, you will have an understanding as to how the chosen plants will eventually interact as a community. If you get the mix right and set them out onsite yourself, you will be successful.

There is a place for some outline drawings, though. Master plans can be used that set out where the larger woody plants and trees will be located; everything else is designated as a single mix. If you decide to use several mixes, you might clearly indicate on your master plan where those mixes will be used.

▾ Mixes are usually specified with a calculation of how many plants will be used of a species as a percentage of the total planted area. Coupled with an indication of how many plants are to be used per square metre, this allows for calculating quantities needed. Accompanying instructions must provide an order for laying out whilst maintaining a degree of randomness.

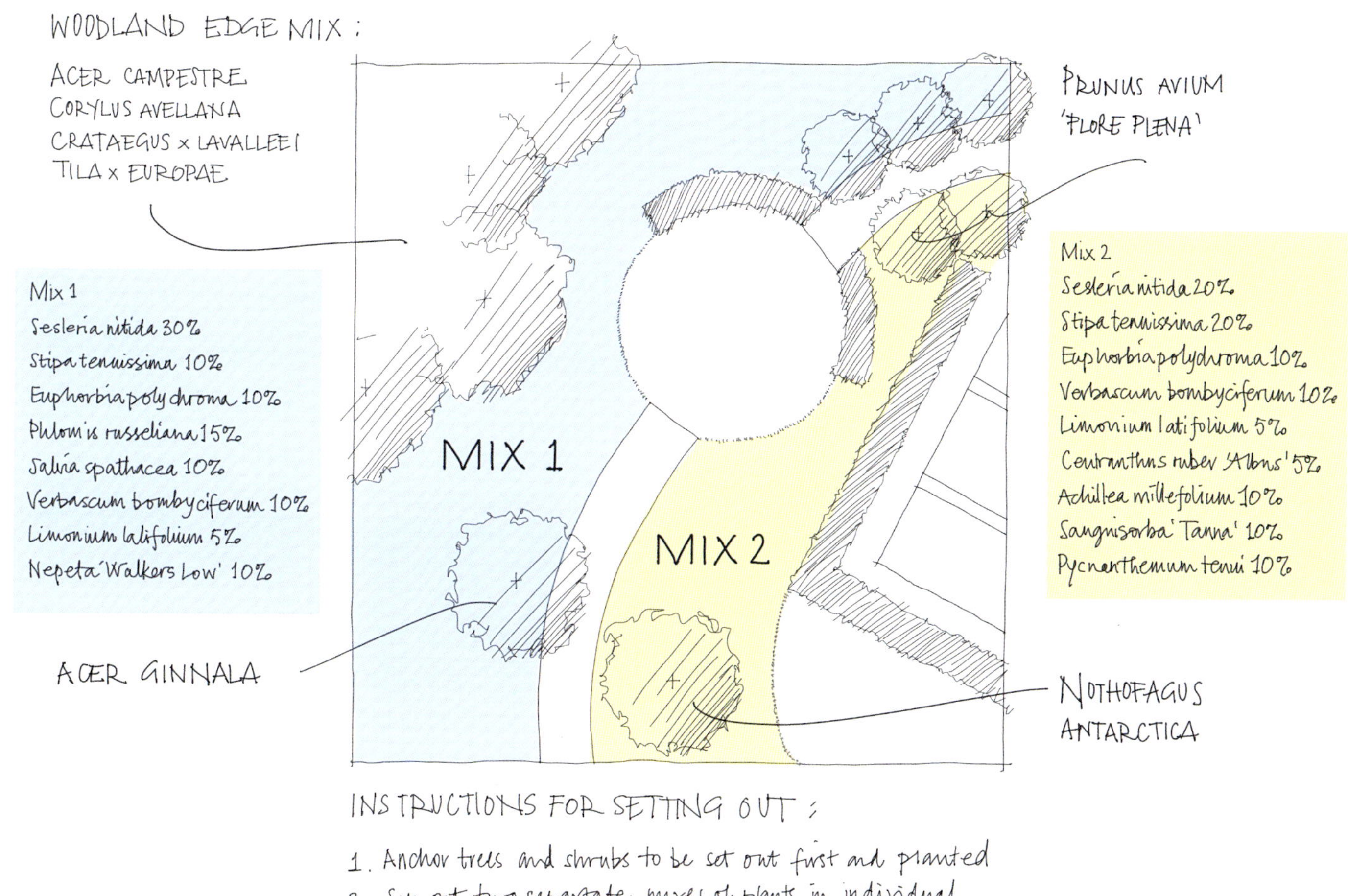

Key Considerations for Matrix Plantings

The underlying principle of sequencing plants for interest through the seasons is what makes matrix planting so attractive and allows for an immersive experience over long periods of time. It is successional planting on a grand scale, but it requires a good understanding of individual plants to make the right choices for your mix. Understanding each plant and what it will bring to the mix is essential, but there are some additional considerations to make:

- **Identify similar plant communities.**
  Your understanding of environmental conditions such as soil, moisture, and especially climate will help you identify communities of plants that will work together in the same conditions. For example, a Mediterranean climate with its mild, wet winters and warm, dry summers might allow you to choose and use plants that thrive in those conditions—whether they are native to the Mediterranean basin or native to coastal California, South Australia, central Chile, or the Western Cape of South Africa, which all share similar climates.

- **Simple but diverse.**
  Structure at a higher scale will provide year-round interest with a simple repetition of trees, large shrubs, and grasses. Repeated species are typical within a naturalistic planting design, but you should be mindful of keeping your planting diverse enough across the growing season to reduce the likelihood of plants becoming susceptible to diseases. Larger areas might use several mixes with key species that link areas, but with a diverse overall range of species.
- **Simplify your timeline.**
  Choose plants in simple selections or mixes of three or four species that peak at any one time. Then change that palette of plants monthly, with further mixes of three or four additional species. The sequencing of plants then becomes simpler to achieve across a long period that is then extended with filler plants and geophytes (bulbs, corms, tubers, and rhizomes) and achieves the diversity mentioned above. The chapter on successional planting will help you understand this approach further.
- **Choose colour.**
  Conscious use of a colour palette with an underlying green structure typifies matrix planting. Therefore, use colour as a key element to engage people with your planting.
- **Complete cover.**
  Aim for complete coverage of the ground by using all the categories of layers set out above.
- **Consider other plant layers.**
  Increasingly, proponents of matrix planting are pushing the boundaries of what their landscapes require by considering shrub and tree layers in their designs. Whether this is for aesthetic reasons, such as their use as anchor plants on a large scale, or to improve biodiversity, utilising more than just perennials and grasses in matrix schemes is an important concept to consider. Habitat plays a big part in this, and returning to the idea of using planting that will thrive together in the same habitat and/or climate should guide you.

What you often lose with naturalistic planting is the concept of plant associations on a smaller scale, but you will continue to have association through habitat. Where you might lose control on one hand, you are more likely to achieve a more dynamic planting overall. Control is not totally lost, though. By selecting your plant mixes, including those waves of three or four species selections that perform at the same time, you retain considerable control over aesthetic decisions.

Using Several Mixes

For large areas, you might consider several mixes within your design. These may repeat key species in order to create some connection or rhythm between each distinct mix. This can be especially helpful if you want to create 'blooms' of individual species as outlined earlier, or if you want certain species to appear within set areas. Gradually, plants might self-seed and creep out of their originally assigned areas, but you can control this and plan to create a subtle change in appearance for visitors as they walk through large planted areas.

▲ Whilst the development of contemporary naturalistic planting is most often seen within the temperate climates of Europe, Australia, and North America, many other regions are experimenting with ideas around a natural aesthetic as well. It's not a new idea, and gardens such as this one on the island of Ischia, in Italy, have from their first planting used the principle of creating communities of plants that will naturally support each other to thrive in challenging conditions.

	LAYER	% SPACE
Design layers	structural/framework	10-15%
	seasonal theme	25-40%
Functional layers	ground cover	50%
	fillers	5-10%

NATURALISTIC COMPOSITION: VERTICAL LAYERS, THE ECOLOGICAL APPROACH

The development of naturalistic planting using a vertical layer approach is, to some extent, influenced by the canopy layer approach discussed earlier within the ornamental planting archetype. It also has similarities with, and is often described alongside, the matrix planting approach also detailed previously.

The approach discussed here was developed by Thomas Rainer and Claudia West as an accessible progression from earlier scientific studies, particularly those conducted in Germany. It focuses on designing communities of plants that are both resilient and naturalistic, with emphasis on choosing plants that are stress tolerant and, sometimes, competitors. It emphasises designed communities of plants that balance aesthetic and ecological functions, perhaps more so than matrix planting, which tends to prioritise people's experiences over ecological function.

Rainer and West have simplified the work of earlier proponents of designing plant communities based on scientific study, and have consequently made it more accessible to the professional planting designer. By using a sequential buildup of a small number of what they term 'design' and 'functional' planting layers, they allocate a percentage range of the total planted space to each layer to determine how much area is allocated and how many plants you will need for each layer. What follows, as in other descriptions of compositional archetypes above, is only a brief overview of this approach. It is recommended that, should you want to apply this approach, you read the work of these two leading experts.

Design Layers

The objective of the design layer is primarily to provide a pleasing aesthetic. These are the layers that will help create an overall planting atmosphere.

As Rainer and West explain, 'Design layers describe the tallest, most visually dominant species within a community. These are the plants which form your impression of the landscape. They draw your attention with their distinct architecture, tall height, and bold colours and textures.'

Design Layer: Structural/Framework Plants (10–15%)

The first design layer covers structural plants. These include trees, shrubs, and upright grasses and perennials with distinct forms. Just like with ornamental and matrix planting, they form anchors within the planting and might be used individually or in small groups.

Design Layer: Seasonal Theme Plants (25–40%)

These are the plants that bring seasonal colour or texture to the planting. They are not as tall or dominant as structural plants and will tend to be planted in masses or drifts. They support the structural plants when not in flower by functioning as a green backdrop.

Functional Layers

As Rainer and West put it, 'The functional layer describes the mix of low, ground-covering species. Unlike the more visible design layer, almost no one sees it. Its purpose is to hold the ground and fill any gaps to prevent weed invasion.'

Functional Layer: Groundcover Plants (approx. 50%)

The plants in this layer are low, shade-tolerant species used to cover open ground between other species. They meet our traditional understanding of groundcover, but in this approach, they also function as erosion control and a source of food. In the earlier matrix approach, this layer is where the low-growing, early spring bulbs that support pollinators would be planted.

Functional Layer: Filler Plants (5–10%)

Just like the filler plants in matrix planting schemes, these are the temporary plants that fill the gaps and add some seasonal interest.

Rainer and West take a very scientific approach to planting, but you will see process similarities with all the approaches described earlier. It shares an intention to engage people with nature as matrix planting also does, and for many planting designers it makes an ecological approach more accessible and straightforward to design. However, it still requires in-depth plant knowledge and creativity to allow you to design for a specific location, narrative, and client. You might still introduce seasonal themes and create dynamic changes in planting, although this vertical layer approach often results in a higher percentage of grasses—as much as 80% grass to 20% other plants. This might produce an atmosphere that feels more 'calming' than the naturalistic matrix planting approach described earlier, which to some degree emphasises visual excitement.

WHICH NATURALISTIC APPROACH SHOULD YOU TAKE?

The skill required in creating naturalistic planting relies primarily on your plant knowledge and a consideration of scale, mix, and control. Horizontal layers might support your choices through percentage allocations, but deciding on plant numbers is never a simple calculation. You will have to decide on the species and cultivar mix and understand the amount of control you'll have over plants. Whether one allows you to innovate more easily than another really comes down to your own creativity and imagination.

The major difference between the two approaches is that the vertical layer approach shares more concepts with the canopy layer approach used in ornamental planting and sets a distinct percentage of the space to use for each layer of plants. The balance of plant categories is quite defined, whereas the earlier matrix planting approach is perhaps more informal and flexible in its approach. This is why many planting designers might prefer matrix planting, especially if they are looking for a high reliance on flowering interest that changes dynamically over the growing year.

Some would argue that you can't rely on plants to do what science says they *should* do. However much you try to control planting through design, we know that plants take on a life of their own as soon as they're in the ground; no designer can hope to control every aspect of a planting design. But both approaches have their merits in creating naturalistic planting designs, and a planting designer might choose one approach over another for a specific project where a natural aesthetic outcome is wanted.

▲ Large infrastructure projects, such as this landscape built in 2008–2012 at the Queen Elizabeth Olympic Park in London, England, now regularly include areas of 'wild' planting that encompass not only recreational space but also meet sustainability goals of reintroducing permanent vegetation that can benefit wildlife as well as humans.

▶ The Institute for Nature Study in Tokyo, Japan, is an inspirational model of what can be achieved in an urban environment over the long term. This landscape is not only a great resource for city dwellers but helps the city breathe and supports the remediation of urban stormwater challenges.

▸ Within the landscape of an existing garden, a group of designers and gardeners in the United Kingdom are experimenting with planting based on sustainable goals to improve biodiversity by using existing aggregates found onsite and underlined by an aim to 'rewild' the landscape. They explore plant habitats and communities to find solutions that can adapt to a rapidly changing climate.

ARCHETYPE: WILD

Whilst often used as a way of achieving a conceptual idea of 'natural' planting, matrix approaches, even at their simplest, are a way for designers to deal with more complex ideas about what *is* natural. For some projects, a naturalistic approach may still feel too controlling and confining for stated requirements. Whereas matrix planting often strikes a balance between order and complexity, a wild planting archetype aims for a completely randomised design where the form of planting is spontaneous.

The invention of a completely new wild space or the return of a landscape to its original wild aesthetic is a relatively new concept in the Western world. In research terms, it's in its infancy. The definition of what constitutes a wild or rewilded landscape varies enormously, and with a changing climate the initial question should always be 'Do we want to return a site to its original wild landscape, or should we design a new wild version of the landscape'? Perhaps the most widely acknowledged definition focuses on the principle that humans are part of, rather than separate from, the natural world. It is a definition that supporters of naturalistic planting might also agree with, but this doesn't necessarily help us 'design' a new landscape. However, our planting design framework can also be used to wild a landscape, particularly as a strategic support to your design.

If we treat wilding as a strategy for planting, then the discovery and definition phases of the framework are immensely useful in determining the right objectives for the new wild landscape. Because definitions of wilding and rewilding vary so greatly, it is essential to define your intentions for your individual project through objectives and atmosphere, and even though the latter might be more about aesthetics, it will support your exploration of the site.

Your objectives could define how much you are prepared to engage and intervene with the existing landscape. A brown roof might require very little intervention other than its initial creation, whereas other planting intentions might still require an element of management to say, prefer native wildflowers over self-seeded ornamentals.

Mature projects are seldom available for us to study, whilst many recent attempts still in their infancy are open to scrutiny, but all will provide inspiration for the designer wishing to create a wild landscape. The Institute for Nature Study in Tokyo, Japan, is a great example of an inspirational long-term project where there has been minimal intervention for more than seventy years. It is an atmospheric landscape created in a relatively short period, following centuries-long human intervention. Equally, every gardener will understand how nature can take over a garden in just a few growing seasons. We can learn from that experience in moving towards creating a wild landscape.

Nature depletion and threats to biodiversity are being experienced globally, so wilding as a concept is an attempt to do something about those issues. Even small design moves, such as choosing plants over hard materials, increasing biodiversity in our gardens, and reclaiming urban landscapes through pocket parks, vertical green walls, and green roofs will have an impact. Indeed, from a human perspective urban greening efforts will perhaps have greater impact on a larger number of people than rewilding might do as part of countryside management, where the revival of wildflower meadows and positive agricultural practice as much as horticultural initiative is found.

There is also much discussion, and perhaps an unnecessary debate, about whether a 'rewilded' garden is really a garden at all. Gardening and gardens are part of the sustainability solution, and every client can build upon their experience of and support for nature by changing their gardening habits. Gardening organically, choosing plants for pollinators, allowing some wild patches to develop, leaving plants to die back naturally, and not 'tidying up' all add up as valuable contributions. Professional planting designers can encourage such activities alongside designing planting for their clients without having to engage in a rewilding debate.

CONTROL, COMPLEXITY, AND SCALE

For many modern planting designers, the naturalistic planting aesthetic provides a natural atmosphere that is desirable, but with an element of control that allows them to create waves of successional interest within the zonal constraints of a growing season. There is therefore a crossover between naturalistic and wild archetypes, much as there is between ornamental and naturalistic planting. The difference between archetypes and approaches is most easily viewed as the difference in the level of focus on control and complexity. A matrix planting will be delivered through plant lists which are predetermined, along with instructions on how the plants should be set out. It allows for a 'controlled spontaneity' in composition; no two planting layouts will ever be the same. A wild planting removes the control over the positioning of plants, typically by using seeded planting, but will still actually retain an element of control because the seed mixes are of course designed. Therefore, the designer retains a creative role in the planting's creation.

For many, control and complexity come down to the ability to work at different scales. This is why a professional planting designer will want to feel educated about different approaches and feel capable of applying them to different projects. A smaller space may require more order than a larger space, which might present opportunities for a wilder planted aesthetic. Indeed, it is arguable that matrix planting has been most successful in large-scale public spaces in urban centres while private residential spaces benefit from a more ordered and less complex matrix planting, one more akin to a crossover between the traditional ornamental mixed border and naturalistic planting.

Sometimes, the choice of a wilder landscape is accompanied by an attempt to achieve a sustainable, long-term landscape design with low-input aftercare. But it is possible that, like naturalistic planting, a wild planting might have a limited lifespan and require rethinking and replanting after the initial installation, to manage the landscape. The wilding movement is in some respects still in its infancy and so, as a planting archetype we should watch it, experiment, revisit it, and try to understand how it might be useful as a future approach to us as planting designers.

SUMMARY: STAY INQUISITIVE AND FIND YOUR PLANTING OPPORTUNITIES

The similarities between all the compositional approaches in this chapter indicate that it is entirely possible for you to develop your own unique planting design language. Further reading will also acquaint you with how you might take these approaches further if faced with landscape situations where, for example, you need to improve water management by designing a rain garden or are working in a particularly hostile environment, such as next to a roadside. You may even employ more than one approach within a larger landscape. Residential gardens and visitor attractions might include formal ornamental borders close to buildings and, as you move farther away on the site, the planting might become more informal by establishing matrix planting in woodlands and then, even farther out, seeded wildflower meadows.

Understanding modern planting design comes from being inquisitive about potential opportunities for planting and a willingness to have an open mind about what approaches and what plants you might use on any project. It starts with making time for the discovery and exploration stages of planting design. This informs our understanding of a project and will indicate what approaches will be relevant. Those early stages are undertaken by every successful designer, whether they are taking an ornamental, naturalistic, or wild approach. It will support the formation of a design narrative and will give you the confidence that you are taking the right structural or compositional approach to lead you to make judicious plant choices.

For all planting archetypes, a strong narrative will direct your thoughts and allow you to audit your plant decisions as you move on to the next stage in the framework.

Indeed, the development of a narrative to lead a design project—especially the planting design—might be most keenly needed for the development of a wild archetype, where the designer is removing a large amount of control in favour of spontaneity. If this is the narrative direction that many of our public landscapes are heading, our discovery and exploration phases will need to be watertight to ensure success and client satisfaction.

By choosing the right compositional archetype, you will continue to move forward with confidence in your planting structure. However, the archetypal approach you take won't choose your plants for you. You may have started a long list of plants as your ideas come together, but you will still have to make final plant decisions. This can be where some designers might stumble and fall back on their lists of favourites, their tried-and-tested plants. This misses an opportunity to find new, useful, and relevant species for your latest planting design. Try not to fall into the comfort trap and, again, keep an open mind.

The next chapters will consider the detailed selection of plants from the viewpoints of design qualities, successional planting, and the role that plants can play in creating sustainable landscapes. Following on from the composition of planting structure, you may start to feel there are many challenging factors to balance, but by showing patience, taking time, and getting your ideas down on paper at each stage, you will become confident and feel ready to move on.

◂ With the challenges of a changing climate and biodiversity playing a major part in the success of our planting designs, it is important that we be prepared to revisit our mature plantings to assess success against what we set out to do and to understand how to build upon that success in the future. We should always be asking whether we have met the attributes of planting design success.

CASE STUDY

TOM BANNISTER

Private Residence
Chester, United Kingdom

Climate: Temperate oceanic (Cfb)
Rainfall: 540mm (21.2") per annum
Temperature: Minimum +1 degree Celsius (34 degrees F)
Maximum +20 degrees Celsius (68 degrees F)
Soil: Poor, improved with imported topsoil

A planting design that addresses the practicalities of a new-build development with challenging soil conditions whilst giving a sense of purpose to a new, contemporary home.

PLANTING DEVELOPMENT

This was a typical new-development residential site where rubble and building materials had been compacted into a top layer of clay with no topsoil. This created a challenging environment for the planting scheme from the very start.

The designer wanted this garden to feel airy and romantic, whilst making the clients feel enveloped in the planting. The house has floor-to-ceiling windows, so it was also important to continue that sense of being embraced by the planting from inside. A second decree was to link the building to its rural environment.

PLANTING DETAIL

The designer used a similar approach to a vertical layer system. This started by studying the space and calculating numbers of plants required, then breaking down the border into several discrete areas and finally choosing mixes of plants for each area. With the space was measured and the percentage mix of grasses, perennials, and evergreens decided, it made it simple to choose species, breaking down numbers in categories further—such as the grasses, into five or six varieties. For this designer, following a development process helps him to create a cohesive, rhythmic scheme across sections of the site—dependent on sunlight levels and soil.

Repetition of plants throughout the different areas of the scheme is important; it gives cohesiveness and creates a balance in the overall garden. The designer wanted to offer something in every season rather than feature a 'star-a-month' plant, so he chose long-flowering species that would be self-sufficient even through periods of drought. Species that would not collapse in a sudden torrential rainfall were also desired, with preference given to those that had the ability to recover quickly.

CASE STUDY

KATE GOULD GARDENS

Private Residence
Buckinghamshire, United Kingdom

Climate:	Temperate oceanic (Cfb)
Rainfall:	817mm (32") per annum
Temperature:	Minimum +2 degrees Celsius (36F) Maximum +22 degrees Celsius (72F)
Soil:	Clay, with some areas of green sand

Negotiation with a family member and a profusion of year-round colour wins the day. Ultimately, this is a garden for gardening in, with an ornamental planting design that isn't precious—it's a place to plant and sit and dig, laugh and create memories.

PLANTING DEVELOPMENT

This designer works primarily in towns and cities, so gravitates to creating a backbone with evergreens. These plants create a strong emphasis on privacy and ensure the garden is 'dressed' all year round. A riot of summer colour is deployed in this garden, though. Gould says, 'I usually work on a less-is-more basis, but this garden, where my inner plant geek explodes, is very much based on more-is-more'.

This is Gould's mother's garden. It is the second garden they have created together, and the planting in part follows Gould's generally chaotic nature and her love of anything blue with a spire of flowers. There are often strong disagreements about colour choices or placements between Gould and her mother, and she often has to fight for an umbellifer. They generally compromise, though, and an umbellifer or agastache will be sneakily planted when one or other of them isn't watching the other.

In other clients' gardens, the designer works to create a picture that perhaps doesn't change wildly, so it will be easier to maintain (an important consideration in small urban spaces), but in this garden anything goes. From this approach (and in the garden she and her mother created together previously), exciting plant combinations have been forged. Sometimes these are combinations that work and sometimes they don't—but they all add up to a learning opportunity, and the designer says that the joy of waiting to see what and how things will develop over the seasons is still, after many years gardening, very exciting and rewarding.

PLANTING DETAIL

The original garden was poorly laid out, with over a third devoted to a car park. Now a diagonal path splits the garden, and this trompe l'oeil feature makes it feel so much larger. The site's original lawn was soon dug up and replaced with a parterre, to add additional winter structure.

There's ample colour, height, texture, and a feeling of being in the garden even when you are inside the cottage. The doors and windows are small in the cottage, but the planting continues right up against the outside walls to make the garden feel truly immersive. Many of the plants have lovely seed heads, so on a cold morning you can see *Rudbeckia* and grasses sugar-coated with frost just outside the windows. In the summer, the view through the cottage and out of the front door leads to a billow of *Hydrangea*, *Astrantia*, *Persicaria*, and *Salvia*.

The topiary and structure are important for creating the bones of the scheme; when the garden is quiet in the winter with really only texture to see, the evergreen background is vital, especially close to the house. Many gardens in this region peak in June, but this garden is just getting going. Its peak is from mid-July all the way to the frosts. From first hellebores to the last of the pale pink and deceptively delicate flowers on the *Schizostylis*, there is always something in flower being featured.

The only real challenge is curtailing a love of plants and keeping up with the weeding; many of the plants are prolific self-seeders. The garden is cold and wet in the winter. On clay, you would expect plants to suffer, but the ground is well worked and actually reasonably free-draining. It is mulched with manure and fed regularly, and consequently the roses thrive and other plants that you might expect to succumb to cold, wet winters (*Verbena*, *Salvia*, *Eremurus*, and even *Dahlia* tubers left in the ground) come back year after year.

The hard landscaping materials found in the original garden were reused for budgetary reasons, and planting is based on 'right plant, right place'. This means there is no plant waste and as plants grow and there is a need to divide, these are potted up and either sold for charity or distributed amongst the local gardening community.

CASE STUDY

ALEJANDRO O'NEILL GARDENS

Private Residence
Cap d'Antibes, France

Climate:	Hot summer Mediterranean (Csa)
Rainfall:	765mm (30") per annum
Temperature:	Minimum +4 degrees Celsius (39 degrees F) Maximum +24 degrees Celsius (75 degrees F)
Soil:	Rocky, thin soil layer with gravel mulch

A complex wild planting that connects people with nature and the larger landscape, requiring aftercare that nurtures and evolves the scheme.

PLANTING DEVELOPMENT

Connecting people with nature can be a significant challenge for clients who initially say they prefer a static landscape rather than one focussed on seasonal highlights. This designer aims to introduce his clients to a dynamic garden that he likens to an ever-changing orchestra. His goal is to help them appreciate the beauty of readable, well-balanced planting. He designs gardens like treasure maps, creating linked spots with paths that guide clients through varying atmospheres while maintaining overall harmony. Subtle transitions from one end of the garden to the other play a crucial role, allowing them to appreciate complexity and an order that at first glance might appear to be chaos.

This design creates an atmosphere that reconnects people with nature and the local landscape by relying on a complex and wild appearance. It carefully avoids the extremes of feeling either too wild or overly manicured, however. Achieving this balance involves thoughtful plant choices and meticulous garden management and maintenance, with a focus on refined pruning techniques. The biggest challenge is finding and hiring artist-gardeners who can nurture the landscape and help it develop over the long term to express vibrancy and complex dynamism.

PLANTING DETAIL

The designer has prioritised using materials that complement the landscape and shapes that harmonize with the existing architecture. The planting is inspired by the local flora, but with added colorful and complex elements. Creating spaces for both humans and wildlife is a key aspect of his design philosophy. In Mediterranean settings, he opts for small leaves, and wild-looking plants. Sustainability is crucial, so he chooses climate-adapted plants that require minimal resources and take into account unavoidable factors such as severe droughts.

Structural plants are crucial, especially in water-scarce regions during the summer dormancy period, as they provide consistency. A functional groundcover layer blends with a design layer, adapted to the Mediterranean context and focussing on emergent plants for what the designer refers to as the 'bubbly effect', or creating a magical atmosphere.

Successional planting is crucial here, and the designer blends different successional stages to achieve immediate impact. Maintaining naturalistic Mediterranean herbaceous borders requires adapting natural succession, as these areas would quickly become woodlands if left unattended. To preserve the ecosystem's integrity, and inspired by the Mediterranean *garrigue* ecosystem, pruning becomes essential. Many gardens have enriched soils, differing from natural conditions that surround them, so strategic pruning is key to ensuring a successional stage persists for as long as desired.

For plant selection, the designer has prioritised practical qualities like drought resilience, sturdiness during summer, and a tendency to self-seed. He focuses on creating cohesive communities, treating planting as a puzzle where each plant fits into the whole, and avoiding overly vibrant colours that may disrupt the Mediterranean look—he prefers those that blend well with the character of the region. Flowering isn't the primary focus, it's an outcome of well-crafted communities. In his work, O'Neill steers clear of temperamental plants and opts for species that have proven successful. He cherishes plants that establish themselves, adding dynamic elements and sustaining the garden's vibrancy over the years. Regular replacement of a few plants, ideally every two to ten years, ensures the garden remains fresh and evolves.

CASE STUDY

SURFACEDESIGN

Private Residence
Portola Valley, California, United States

Climate: Warm-summer Mediterranean (Csb) and exposed
Rainfall: 589mm (23") per annum
Temperature: Minimum -1 degree Celsius (30 degrees F)
Maximum +16 degrees Celsius (60 degrees F)
Soil: Existing soil amended with compost

A garden inspired by a botanical garden in Santa Cruz, California, with an amazing collection of plants; paths alternately direct footsteps and allow the visitor to get lost.

PLANTING DEVELOPMENT

The designers of this planting aimed to create an immersive experience for their adventurous client who is not afraid of exuberance. The client is a New Zealand citizen, and New Zealand and California have similarly temperate climates. Many New Zealand natives are considered exotic in California, but nevertheless recommend themselves as being climate-appropriate. The goal was therefore to merge California and New Zealand sensibilities. Employing plants from the Southern Hemisphere in a garden in California also extends the season of garden interest.

The entrance garden was designed to unfold as visitors make their way to the front door, creating layers of interest and framed views of specimen plants designed to be experienced as they move through the garden. Plant qualities that were important to the design emphasise vibrant, bold, and contrasting colours, sculptural form, low water requirements, and variations in height, texture, foliage, and flower.

PLANTING DETAIL

The specimen garden around the house highlights unique sculptural and ornamental plants featuring vibrant colour. These are set in pea gravel, which acts as a firebreak. The garden reveals a detailed and blousy beauty of its own as viewed against the architecture's striated, louvered façade. When a botanical garden is your inspiration, sourcing plants that feel truly unique can be challenging; there was a greater emphasis than usual on locating specimen plants here.

The Mediterranean temperate climate supports a mix of native and low-water-adapted planting. In the parts of the garden that connect to the adjacent hillside, the designers focused on a more native palette, while the more domestic entrance garden is allowed little more exotic expression.

The native meadow, placed far from the house, fades into the surrounding regional landscape. This surrounding chapparal shrubland is particularly susceptible to wildfires, so cleaning up the existing landscape and removing invasive species that would be the first to go up in flames gives mature trees on the site the conditions to thrive.

CHAPTER **8**

SELECTING YOUR PLANTS

◂ *Kniphofia* 'Tawny King', *Helenium* 'Sahin's Early Flowerer', *Foeniculum vulgare*, and *Ratibida pinnata* create a powerfully colorful combination at the Plant Specialist Nursery in Buckinghamshire, United Kingdom.

One of the advantages of following a framework process is that working through each of the phases will help to focus and steadily reduce the range of plants suitable and available for your project. Instead of being faced with thousands of choices, you will know with certainty what you are aiming for in terms of shape, form, seasonality, etc., based upon the demands of your project brief, the narrative and atmosphere that you have created, and your structural development work. You'll find that your early work has reduced the list of plants that are appropriate for your design. Now you need to reduce the list of potential plants even further by considering the qualities that your plant selection convey.

As well as creating your long-list of plants, it is useful to know what your suppliers can grow for you. A good relationship with plant growers is an essential collaboration for any planting designer, and by regularly supporting their business growers may well be willing to grow some specific species and cultivars that you use regularly, just for you.

DETAIL

Each time that you start a new planting design you are faced with a new set of possibilities. In the last chapter you saw that by exploring the spatial qualities of your landscape you can quickly develop a master plan. From there, following the framework will help you compose the structure of your planting. With experience and a sound knowledge of plants, the professional planting designer will naturally start to consider plants early in the process, but it is important that you don't make firm decisions until you've given yourself time to further research the plants that will best meet your requirements. At the start, the possibilities were endless and now they should start to become much more focused.

Your narrative, atmosphere, and project objectives—along with your structural development work—will guide you towards the important qualities that you want from your design and therefore the plants to select. Select plants based upon their qualities, not from a list of the plants that you know best. Even when a long list of possible plant ideas has been started, it doesn't commit you, but it does give you the space to research and consider what alternatives might be a better choice and to expand your plant knowledge.

Plants are incredibly varied in their characteristics and will both limit and create opportunities for your designs. Their practical and aesthetic qualities, both individually and in relation to other plants, will allow you to innovate in your work and create unique solutions for your clients. As with earlier phases of our framework, your final planting design will be a result of thorough exploration and research at each stage, but none so more as making your final selection of plants. And as you make your choices, you will expand your knowledge of plants and discover new plant associations and communities for use in your future designs.

The key qualities that will lead your plant choices are likely to be found in your narrative and especially your desired atmosphere. They can be obvious qualities, such as colour and form, privacy, and direction, but there are other qualities that might be less immediately obvious. A commercial client might ask you to provide impact at the entrance to a new development, or a private individual might ask you to provide winter fragrance in a small garden; you'll select other less-specific qualities yourself in creating your planting design.

FINDING YOUR PLANTING PALETTE

As you begin to select plants, you will find that returning to your project brief will be very helpful. Your narrative and desired atmosphere will be especially useful to remind you of the palette of plants that you are looking for and allow you to recognise plants that might be useful to your final design.

It's almost impossible for a planting designer to approach a new design without mulling over early ideas of what plants might fulfil the project brief and your overall planting palette. We all have our go-to plants and recently acquired knowledge of 'new' plants that we want to try out, but be very careful not to race to finalising plant selection. You should be aiming to give your client a unique design, not repeating what you've done before. Sure, you can use some plants that you know, even some combinations of plants that you've tried, tested, and love, but consider whether it's right for this project and its circumstances. This way, you are more likely to innovate with new ideas and inspire confidence in your design for yourself and client.

By now you are handling a lot of information from your project brief and development work and will appreciate why it is useful to get everything down on paper to free your mind up to explore your design and innovate further. Do the same thing with your plant ideas. If you get an idea for a plant that might fulfil your objectives and help create the planting atmosphere you desire, then continue with your planting long-list, drop yourself a quick note, and move on with the task at hand. You can return to your long-list later as you start to select plants, looking at the qualities those plant ideas have alongside researching others that might fulfil those same objectives and rules that you set yourself.

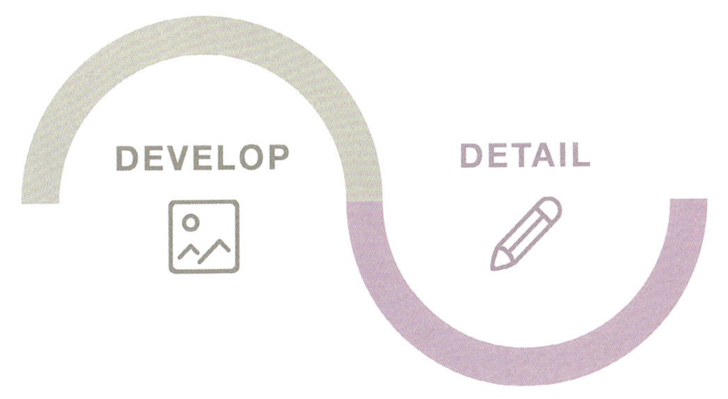

Design the masterplan
Design the structure
Start a longlist
Explore plant qualtities
Design succession
Select sustainably

◂ The development and detail phases are when you are making decisions about the plants that you will use. The advantage of following a process will be that you steadily narrow down the choices that are available to you, making selection easier and faster even when you need to explore the options that you do have.

USING PLANT QUALITIES TO SUPPORT YOUR DECISIONS

Choosing a compositional technique is, for some designers, how they are accustomed to creating a planting design. Listen to a designer describing their planting and they will often first talk about composition—we tend to understand plant qualities such as proportion and scale readily. Indeed, once we have decided on a master plan, the compositional archetypes discussed earlier aim to place planting in structural order, however complex the planting might be. These approaches help us to create and read a landscape as well as describe our design to our clients. They are practical tools that allow us to exert spatial control over a landscape

through plants, but we are also able to use more subjective design qualities and devices such as harmony, contrast, and pattern to realise our narrative. This is where the early creative design of the atmosphere in your proposed planting is most helpful. Accompanied by your narrative, your definition of planting atmosphere is a good way of understanding what design qualities you might employ to achieve your desired planting solution.

Visual hierarchy might make us determine priorities for plant qualities; that is, organising our planting according to the importance that we hold for them and often how our clients will see them. Sensory and functional qualities such as colour and screening may have greater importance because they have the most immediate impact. But don't forget that ecological and sustainable qualities may be of equal importance to you, and whilst they may not be so apparent, the client will come to appreciate them through their impact—for example, in welcoming birds into their garden. The successional nature of your design might also not be immediately evident to your client, but you will know that the overall quality of successional choices will add to an extended period of interest to fulfil a desire for year-round interest. Successional planting design and sustainability are discussed later, after we first look at plant qualities.

So what are the design qualities that will have such an impact on your eventual planting design? What follows is a description of some of the key qualities that are employed by designers—and not just by planting designers but also other design professions such as architects, interior designers, and graphic designers. You will find that some qualities overlap and many work in combination. Qualities such as colour, texture, and form are primary choices that can be easily understood and prioritised to make plant decisions. Then there are qualities that may be of secondary or of no importance at all—it is for you to decide. With experience you will find your planting design will become intuitive and, as you develop your own style they will, in varying degrees, become important to your work.

▲ Subjective plant qualities such as colour, harmony, and contrast play an important part in our choices. Here the overall mass of planting (left) displays these qualities. When you look closer (right) you can also appreciate the qualities in individual plants such as the fragile texture and pale purple colour of this *Echinacea pallida*.

▲ This design by Fisher Tomlin & Bowyer is a good example of how a naturalistic matrix of perennial planting in the foreground can connect with an ornamental planting behind it through a repetition of the same colour palette. The colour tones in the more ornamental plants are amplified for impact.

SENSORY PLANT QUALITIES

Aim to re-create your design atmosphere through the sensory and structural qualities of plants both in their use as individual species and especially in how they are used together. Of the many qualities of plants, those that are sensory are most likely to be emphasised by a client—they may be best able to articulate desires for qualities such as colour and fragrance over other more technical qualities.

COLOUR AND TONE

Colour and tone in planting are possibly the most contentious and subjective plant qualities within landscape design. Covering this very broad subject within a few pages is near impossible; many volumes are written every year on the use of colour in landscape design. Some designers will have developed house 'rules' for use of colour based upon scientific principles such as matching one primary colour with another, using a colour wheel, or another set of complex guidelines. Others will suggest it's best to be guided by other qualities first, such as balance; even the most flamboyant of planting designs might need a foil of a quiet colour to stop them becoming too chaotic for the viewer.

The way that colour is used in planting will also have an impact on the perception of the designed space. Cool colours will expand the feeling of space as clear tones seem to last longer than warm colours as sunlight fades and the evening takes over. Strong, bright colours will be useful where the sun is brightest; or, you might use a simple palette of colour to highlight a simple design layout. Colours will generally be used in contrast, in simple or complex palettes. What is important is that you develop a palette that will help guide your plant choices.

◂ Plant colours do not have to be subdued. In this ornamental border (top), a contrasting blue and white are used to dramatic effect whilst a more subtle blend of warm plant tones is used in another part of the border (bottom).

Choosing a colour palette requires experience and a willingness to experiment, but if you reference your earlier work on the planting atmosphere you should be able to make easy progress. Once you have designed your colour palette you can explore how to layer those colours through your design with the help of your compositional development work.

It can be very helpful to explain your colour palette in terms of the atmosphere you are aiming to convey; then words like 'bright', 'soft', 'vibrant', and 'muted' will direct you to the colours and tones that you should use. Tone is usually defined by the addition of grey to a given hue, which will make a colour less vibrant. On a scale, tone will recognise lightness or darkness. Science might dictate exactly how this is created, but only you as the designer can recognise how to use colour and tone to create a palette that you can then apply in the search for the plants you will use.

▲ Contrast can play an important part in emphasising colour. A simple Cor-Ten steel wall in this garden designed by Martyn Wilson on a reclaimed brownfield site gives emphasis to delicate *Deschampsia cespitosa* and *Knautia macedonica* 'Mars Midget' planted in front.

DETAIL

TEXTURE

Texture can be viewed in several ways in planting design, the most obvious being the characteristics of plant foliage. We might call something smooth or coarse, waxy, sticky, lined, or pitted to describe a texture, but texture is determined just as much by scale, size, and shape. Texture can also be found in bark and flowers. We recognise it subconsciously and often, but in planted spaces we especially judge and evaluate it in comparison to other nearby plants.

Texture can also apply to the look and feel of an overall planting design. A planting scheme focused solely on colour will be limited, but varying tone, shade, and particularly texture will add variety and interest. Repeating the same texture throughout a planting scheme can be monotonous. If you look at an image of a planting or a montage of your intended plants in black and white, the range of texture coming from those plants will appear in stark relief. It might all be too similar or too regular. Swap some of the plants being used to create more textural variety in your overall design if it seems that a lack of texture makes it feel bland.

▲ The planting at left displays a strong textural range in the autumn with a haze of flower and seed heads floating through grasses and strong foliage. Some individual plants, like the *Euphorbia characias* 'Portuguese Velvet', above, have a very strong textural quality of their own.

SCENT

Scent is often highly valued and appreciated by our clients. It will contribute to the immersive experience of large-scale planting schemes and add to the experience of your planting. Fragrant plants add a whole dimension to a garden. You can plan a seasonal progression of scent in much the same way that you might chose to provide succession of bloom time in your plant choices. Many plants are at their most fragrant in late winter, such as *Viburnum* spp. and *Chimonanthus praecox*. Fragrant spring bulbs also add early interest before the rest of your planting is flowering. Then there are *Rosa* spp., *Frangipani* vars., and *Melaleuca* spp. for summer.

Small, enclosed gardens will help contain fragrance, so for these, place plants where they can be appreciated easily, such as near the front of a border or by an entrance door—depending of course on the strength of the scent. Aromatic plants are often used for dual purposes; for example, the Mediterranean plants that are used in a hot gravel garden might provide aesthetic appeal but also be fragrant herbs for cooking. Scented foliage and flowers will also alert insects and animals either to their advantage as sources of food, or as a plant to avoid, so companion planting with fragrance in mind can be a key strategy for attracting pollinators as well as warning off undesirable pests.

In much the same way that too large a colour range might create visual tension in a planting, too many and varied scents can make a garden uncomfortable for visitors. This is critical when choosing to create a planting design with sensory elements, as too many different scents could confuse the visually impaired. Singular scents offered by a few dominant plants and placed carefully in key locations might however help this type of visitor locate, through scent, where they are in the garden.

◂ Roses are a classic choice for introducing scent into a planting design. This shrub, *Rosa* 'Mary Delany', is known for its long period of flowering and long-lasting fragrance.

SOUND AND MOVEMENT

The sound and movement of plants, particularly in conjunction with each other, will add to an immersive experience that can be used to great effect in gardens designed to enhance a sensory experience. Movement is seen as well as heard, and can have a mesmerising effect on the viewer, creating calm and meditative spaces. Consider the effect of grasses and restios in full bloom within a border and how the wind will move them. The sound of leaves rustling on trees and other plants such as bamboos are often also appreciated, especially in larger landscapes.

▲ The grass *Stipa tenuissima* in this design has foliage and seed heads that move with the wind and add to the immersive experience.

STRUCTURAL PLANT QUALITIES

To some extent, you will have already considered some of the structural qualities of plants in deciding on the development of a structural planting composition. Although there are similarities, we should also consider how the structure of a single plant in relation to other plants might impact your design.

▾ The simplicity of a single species of birch tree planted with just two species of groundcover creates a calming but still visually striking atmosphere.

SIMPLICITY VERSUS COMPLEXITY

Simple planting compositions can still be very effective in engaging people with a landscape. Modern landscape design might call for a minimalist approach of pared-back, limited planting palettes, for example, to pair with modernist architecture. Naturalistic 'prairie' or 'meadow' styles of planting can be structurally simple and may contain a high proportion of grasses. But whilst they might look loose and unstructured, the naturalistic meadow is often created with a very complex range of plants to create a community. The intensity of a design is often accompanied by a complexity in the range of planting employed both at any single time and in succession over a growing season, to ensure something is always peaking.

Complexity will become more important as we consider future climate change and efforts to improve biodiversity. We might need to learn to use resilience techniques such as waterwise planting to change our approach as designers, for example, to improve the longevity of plant choices we make and how plants become mutually supportive within a design. Developing complex planting patterns can be one way of engaging with biodiversity.

▲ The complexity of bright colours in this ornamental border adds a lightness to the planting while dark jewel-like seed heads pop through swathes of perennial flowers to add focal points.

◄ A complex mix of grasses and perennials creates a beguiling mix of colour, structure, and movement.

MASS AND VOLUME

In a three-dimensional planting world, we define mass and volume in relation to hard landscaping or architecture as much as to other plants. The solid and semi-solid spaces are the mass of plants and architecture; the voids are the empty spaces between them. Mass is the solid body or grouping of visual elements, whereas volume is its three-dimensional form. Designers might describe a 'massing' of plants where several individual plants of a single species are grouped to provide seasonal drama within a planting scheme.

▲ This design by Piet Oudolf in Bottrop, Germany, masses areas of single species and low hedging to create drama within the larger mixed perennial planting.

SHAPE AND FORM

Plant shape and placement create a visual dynamic within a space and its overall form. Too many different shapes may be visually unreadable, whereas a single shape might be too dull. This is, for example, why a naturalistic design that focuses on a matrix of plants growing to between 06.m/2' and 1.2m/4' in height might also include specimen trees, shrubs, and individual perennials within the matrix to create strong anchors within the planting, enhancing the overall form of the planting to create a more varied aesthetic.

▲ The vertical form of the fan palms *Chamaerops humilis* projecting from amongst a much lower layer of mixed shrub and perennial planting gives dramatic shape to the landscape; Italian cypress *Cupressus sempervirens* repeats that vertical shape and form to added rhythmic effect.

Consider the overall scale of your site when choosing plants. Here, a grand vista leading to a prominent glasshouse benefits from an avenue of flowering cherry trees that have been set back so as not to disturb the main view. Tulips and other spring bulbs are planted within the grass, at ground level, to allow for a more intimate experience of plants at a human scale.

PROPORTION AND SCALE

Proportion is the size of an object in relation to surrounding objects within a landscape; scale is the relationship between an object and a fixed object, usually a human. Plants should be chosen to be in proportion with the landscape, including buildings and other architecture, and more often in scale with the people using the landscape and viewing the planting. With experience, a planting designer might learn to use out-of-scale specimen plants such as trees and large succulents to create heightened drama within a landscape.

An ornamental planting that is structured in an incremental way will include a wide range of plant sizes, graduating from specimen trees down to groundcover. In contrast, layered planting approaches including matrix planting will often use a much narrower range of plants by season so that plants can be appreciated as a mass. For example, a spring layer of planting may be low, formed from spring bulbs and groundcover, and transition into an early summer layer of low perennials and finally a layer of tall perennials and grasses in late summer.

LINE

Line creates a sense of direction and movement. A straight path likely encourages fast movement through a space; a curving path is likely to slow visitors down. The use of line in planting often appears as the placement of a tree or a group of plants, such as a formal avenue, as much as it does in the two-dimensional layout of a space.

Vertical lines within an individual plant's structure, such as the tall stems of subfamily *Bambusoideae*, might lead your eye skywards; the horizontal branching of a tree such as a *Cornus controversa* or *Ginkgo biloba* may even draw the eye out to the surrounding landscape.

The path here displays a strong sense of direction emphasised by the vertical and horizontal lines of the pergola through which climbers grow.

BALANCE AND CONTRAST

Visual balance is formed by the structural use of plants. An avenue of single-species trees will appear balanced, but so could a group of different trees and shrubs within a border if there's a perceptible repetition to their appearance, or from larger groups of massed plants as we walk through a planted space. Other visual tools, such as colour, can be used to create balance. The converse of balance is contrast; using groups of plants with very different characteristics to highlight difference can also create balance if, say, soft petals are contrasted in proportion with sharp foliage.

▸ Here the button flowers of *Helenium* 'Waltraut' balance the form of the globe heads of *Echinops bannaticus* 'Blue Globe', but uses contrasts in colour to great effect.

▸ Two very different cherry tree species create balance by throwing the contrast of their vertical and horizontal form to frame the view and path to the bench beyond while maintaining a similar bloom colour.

▲ An arch made from trained *Laburnum* x *watereri* 'Vossii' trees has its own moment of flowering drama, but for the remainder of the year the arch will focus the view on the statue beyond, itself framed by solid evergreen hedges.

EMPHASIS

Much as we might use a specimen plant to anchor or focus our eye within a landscape, plants can be used to emphasise a particular view or architectural feature. We might highlight the entrance into a new area of garden or planting, or we might use plants to lead us to the end of a walkway. Compositional approaches, however relaxed and informal, all include an element of framing focal points and anchoring plants. A repeated use of single specimens, particularly hedges, is a popular and effective way of achieving this.

▲ The similarity of habit in the plants along this double-planted border bring harmony to the design by tumbling towards the path at a fairly uniform height although their colours vary widely.

HARMONY, UNITY OR VARIETY

Without unity and harmony, a planting design might feel chaotic and unreadable. Harmony brings different design elements in a landscape together; unity is the use of similarity in these elements to create a visual and conceptual connection. It can be achieved through the repetition of similar elements within a planting design: for example, the repeated use of a single genus of plants, such as *Iris* spp., but appearing in different varieties within a garden. Or repeating a single species, such as *Anigozanthos manglesii* within a larger design. The use of multistem trees is a popular modern device to create harmony with different species.

Variety is the complement to harmony and unity, and stops a planting design from becoming uninteresting and too repetitive. There is therefore a balance to be struck between these qualities through different seasons. For example, a mixed-species woodland might start with a simple blanket of a single species in spring such as *Eranthis cilicica* or *Viola banksii*, which transforms into a varied mix of late-spring flowering plants, and then a more complex layer of summer perennials before dying back to a harmonious groundcover of green foliage.

▲ Plants evolved different growth habits as coping strategies in their unique environments. For example, certain evergreens might grow densely to resist wind; humans might capitalize on that habit to prune or form them into a desired shape or function, such we often do with hedges.

HABIT

The habit of a plant is the general form of a plant in terms of its growth. A tree might be upright, erect, or ascending, but can also be spreading and weeping. Habit often relates to the horizontal and vertical form of a plant, and plants are often selected according to the designer's need for a particular form. For example, the upright *Thalictrum delavayi* will create a haze above a perennial border, while a spreading, clumping alpine such as *Rhodohypoxis* spp. might work well to seem to pop spontaneously out of a gravel garden.

PATTERN QUALITIES

Pattern qualities refer to the way in which we can weave and layer plants together, repeating them in a way that feels harmoniously predictable. We know plants will have a life of their own, seeding, spreading, and growing, so aftercare is often specified to maintain desired pattern qualities in a planting design.

PATTERN, REPETITION, RHYTHM

Patterns in planting design relate to how colonies of plants work together. It might determine how you mass individual species, or how you mix a range of plants to make a layout that appears to create a larger shape or visual tapestry. More formal compositions often rely on an element of strong pattern precisely to convey formality, but informal compositions can also employ subtle or natural-seeming patterns based on structure to anchor the overall scheme.

In a similar way to complexity and simplicity in planting design, too much contrast can create tension in a scheme. Pattern and repetition can reduce visual confusion and bring rhythm and movement to a design. Rhythm in planting can act like pattern, and results from the repetition of elements in the landscape. This may come from built structures in a design, such as the use of climber supports, but plants can also be used as repeated elements to unify a design and create a sense of movement. Repetition and rhythm may also be created with other plant qualities, such as form or colour—or even an individual species repeated as an anchor through a landscape. The ribbon method of laying out planting (see Chapter 7) will help you create a feeling of movement that leads your eye through a planting scheme, bringing a sense of order and purpose.

‣ Topiary pyramids give a strong visual rhythm to the border overall, especially in autumn when the planting is starting to die back (left) but also as a dramatic contrast to other planting layers through the year (right). Their repetition along the border draws visitors down its length.

▸ A Mediterranean planting of mainly aromatic plants displays a repetition of form that brings the overall design together.

▸ Whilst matrix planting might seem spontaneous and informal, it actually relies on an element of pattern and rhythm created by the planned repetition of species through a planting.

ACCENT

Accents can be used to add striking drama to a planting. This is often achieved through unexpected variation on a theme, such as how 'architectural' plants are employed amid otherwise low-growing species to give strong moments of punctuation. Or groups of accent plants, such as spiky *Agave* spp. within a border planting, may create that one needed, dominant, bold form to act as a visual foil to softer plantings around them, but might also be used as a single specimen to create a sculptural accent within a softly planted border.

▲ The African plant *Aloe spectabilis* (above) accents the open, flat, rocky landscape it grows in and instantly creates a dramatic atmosphere. Similarly, *Yucca rostrata* accent their landscape (left), while the blue *Agave americana* adds a sculptural and contrasting shape to the group.

▲ Plants within a large-scale ornamental border can be planned to transition colour slightly to create a changing dynamic as visitors immerse themselves in a garden, or just to meet a horticultural requirement, such as shifting cultivars from those that prefer bright sun to those that need part shade.

SEQUENCE

Sequence refers to how transitions in plant qualities might change such as a gradual change in texture, shape or colour. Sequence in a single colour might include a gradual change from a darker shade through to a lighter shade and might be accompanied by a change in the numbers of each plant used depending on which shade will be dominant or subordinate. Sequence on a larger scale may see a gradual change from one form of planting to another.

How to Research Plants

Every region and climate zone will have different resources available to help you find the plants that fit the criteria for your design. Wherever you are in the world, there are good places to get information and advice about plants. The Resources section in this book is a useful place to start; it includes digital resources as well as more traditional sources. Here are some more general recommendations:

DEFINITIVE PLANT BOOKS

Many countries have issued definitive plant books that will help you identify plants to use in your designs. They are tried-and-tested resources for everyone and often contain a large database of plants that are sorted by colour and tone as well as seasons of interest, which can make your research easier. Some are issued with botanical gardens and organisations such as the International Plant Names Index (IPNI.org), a useful resource from three world-renowned contributors: the Royal Botanic Gardens, Kew; the Harvard University Herbaria; and the Australian National Herbarium. These publications will be up to date with their naming of plants and can provide you with alternatives to plants you know or cannot source.

SPECIALIST BOOKS

A large range of specialist planting design books are also available. Some are classics—they tend towards promoting certain design archetypes and will supplement this book well. However, you should always be mindful of a book's publication date, as older editions may well ignore the impact of a changing climate and contain plant recommendations that are no longer appropriate due to invasiveness, etc., or have out-of-date scientific names.

SPECIALIST NURSERIES

Specialist nurseries are a great resource, especially if you are researching native plants, a particular style of planting, or a community of plants. Develop a relationship with these nurseries in your area for the support and information they can provide.

ONLINE RESOURCES

Similar to definitive plant books, you might find there are some definitive online plant databases for the region that you work in. These websites can be great, but be aware that if they are also selling plants, you might find they are only highlighting the plants that they want you to buy from their stock; use judgement. They might suggest alternatives if they haven't got a plant you are looking for, which can be helpful, but again, watch for bias.

Online digital resources are available both with a regional focus and as global databases. Online resources such as World Flora Online (worldflora-online.org) are essential tools for viewing plant species diversity and can inform your work. Botanic gardens often provide scientifically accurate information, such as the Royal Botanic Gardens, Kew's Plants of the World Online (https://powo.science.kew.org).

ASK YOUR COMMUNITY

Planting designers comprise a large, diverse, and generous industry with many years of collective experience. Network within your profession and you will find people who are happy to make suggestions. Social media apps like Instagram can be very helpful if you hit a wall and want suggestions for plants you could consider. They are also great for discovering the plant passions of others. Start up a conversation and see what comes back to you.

FUNCTIONAL QUALITIES

Functional plant qualities refer to the usefulness of plants to resolve landscape challenges, as opposed to their use for purely aesthetic value.

VISUAL PRIVACY AND SCREENING

The request to add plants that will increase or create privacy is possibly one of the most frequent from clients, especially in urban and suburban areas, where they are aware of overlooking neighbours. Even in the countryside, clients may have a desire to partly shut themselves away from neighbouring properties, a poor view, or even to divide acreage up into smaller, more intimate spaces. Where fences and other boundaries cannot achieve the height required to provide privacy, plants will often be a good solution.

Strategically placed trees can quickly provide privacy by screening out direct lines of sight into our homes and landscapes. Pleached trees and avenues create formality, while mixed plantings keep things feeling informal. Planted as mature specimens or in close plantings and with good aftercare, plants can quickly create a dense screen. At a lower elevation, hedges can also be established quickly, and many nurseries are even able to provide large plants and 'instant hedging' that will provide immediate height.

DETAIL

Plants will also screen an undesirable view of a built structure, such as a shed or neighbour's house. In tight spaces, a planted green wall is an effective screen, whether you use the traditional method of training upright or climbing plants against a structure or install the modern pocketed growing systems, often fabric, that are affixed to a wall and enable you to install a permanent vertical wall of plants. For larger spaces, you may be able to plant a wider screening boundary of plants to distract from the view beyond.

▸ Traditional *Taxus baccata* hedging, a popular evergreen screening, can often be sourced in large sizes to create immediate impact for a client.

▼ Noise pollution in our cities can be a public health issue. Anything planting designers can do to reduce the impact through planting will be welcomed. In this city, public cycleways are set back from roads whilst layers of planting reduce noise on one side and act as a windbreak for winds coming off the lake on the other, making a much more pleasant environment for cyclists.

▲ Widely seen in rural settings, windbreaks can be used to reduce the impact of strong air flow on planted landscapes. These will be in leaf when the vines beyond are also in leaf; protection is less important in winter.

AUDITORY PRIVACY

Noise pollution is a cause of health issues in humans, and it also impacts wildlife. It is not unusual for a client to want to try and reduce the impact of noise generated beyond the boundaries of their property. Trees especially have an ability to deflect and absorb more high-frequency than low-frequency noise, making them ideal for sound barriers.

The closer trees are to the noise, the better, but the depth of planting will also have an impact. Deeper barrier planting is better. Height is a consideration, too, and generally trees up to 10–12 meters (30–36 feet) are most effective; any taller and their lower branches can be lost so their ability to absorb noise declines. Shrubs and hedges will also absorb noise closer to ground level.

Always test the impact of deciduous species on sound reduction from busy highways, even if at a very large distance, as in winter the leaves will not be present to alleviate intrusive noise. Generally, broad-leafed evergreens and conifers will be most effective at absorbing noise, although broad-leaf species of deciduous trees are also effective deflectors of sound. Thriving local or regional native species are likely to give you the best long-term resilience.

WIND ATTENUATION

Gardens and landscapes in exposed locations are often open to winds that can damage property and other plants. Windbreaks and shelterbelts are designed as semipermeable barriers that reduce wind velocity and provide shelter for other plants. The semipermeability is an important feature; we want these to slow down and filter wind, not block it entirely as solid boundaries create swirling eddies of wind on either side that can be forceful enough to damage plants.

Windbreaks are defined as relatively narrow structures for wind defence, such as hedges and single rows of trees, and therefore are possible in small gardens where space is limited. Shelterbelts are created from a mix of taller trees and shrubs planted in at least three staggered rows; these require a deeper space. Again, resilient local or regional native and near-native species are likely to give you the best result. They will also provide shelter and habitat for wildlife, reduce moisture loss in soil and plant foliage, and can protect plants from salt-laden winds in coastal settings.

CREATING SHADE

Whilst many clients, especially in urban settings, may feel that they have enough shade cast from surrounding buildings, you will also find clients who deliberately want to create shade. People often appreciate shaded seating areas and, for everyone, eating areas will be more comfortable with overhead shade that will also help reduce glare. Strong, direct sunlight can be a health issue in many countries, and with a changing climate this is becoming increasingly prevalent. Shade gardens are to be encouraged. Many plants thrive in shady conditions, and woodland gardens full of shade and ephemerals can feel quite magical. Trees can be positioned to cast part shade or occasional shade at certain times of the day, and climbers can be used over structures like pergolas and arches to create tunnels of green.

▲ The shade created by plants, especially trees, will be appreciated in hotter climates and can be used to reduce the temperatures inside nearby buildings.

DIRECTING MOVEMENT

When planted alongside paths, plants can direct movement effectively. They naturally restrict where pedestrians and vehicles might go and lead them in a particular direction. For paths with high pedestrian traffic, planting resilient shrubs at intersections can stop people from cutting corners through planting beds or adjacent lawns.

▲ A simple grass path can be used to direct visitors between planted borders, slowing them down with a curved circulation pattern, and engaging them with a variety of plants to stop and consider. Grass paths should be lined with reasonably compact plants at the edges that can avoid being mowed along with the lawn; always be aware of the need for aftercare.

ENVIRONMENTAL AND ECOLOGICAL QUALITIES

People will be affected by and will affect their environment, especially within their own landscapes, yet it often falls to the planting designer on a project to engage and inform those clients of the opportunities and challenges that their own landscape presents. These are often based on the ecology of the site; therefore, the future of our approach to planting design is very much linked to an understanding of local ecology.

Whilst many of the functional qualities of plants might also provide environmental benefits, there are useful ecological opportunities that come from using plants in the landscape. The role of plants in providing environmental and ecological benefit is discussed throughout this book, especially in the chapter on sustainability, but the following are some of the main qualities that are also of design value.

STORMWATER MANAGEMENT

The directing and regulating of surface water has become increasingly important for planning authorities because of our changing climate. More severe bursts of sudden rainfall are being experienced around the world. Engineered water management strategies are seen not just at roadsides but also in new housing developments, especially those developed on floodplains. Rain gardens are a popular and attractive form of remediation. They utilise natural soils and plants to enhance landscape, support habitat and biodiversity, and improve the aesthetic value of urban areas. In public spaces, the use of native and near-native plants is commonly, but not universally, seen.

▾ In this street in New Jersey, United States, extensive use is made of linear bioswales, a design feature increasingly implemented in urban centres. They are designed to slow down the dispersal of rainwater rather than capture, store, and infiltrate rainwater, which is a function of rain gardens.

HABITAT CONSERVATION AND RESTORATION

Understanding habitats and their role in ecology will become increasingly important. Planting designers are often tasked with *conserving* ecosystems as a regulatory requirement worldwide, whereas when we set out to *restore* habitats, we aim to increase biodiversity and gradually reverse habitat loss caused by urbanisation, intensive agriculture, and pollution. Plants will play a major part in achieving this and the later chapter on sustainable planting solutions explores practicalities further.

▲ Planting designers are increasingly concerned with the opportunities that exist to improve ecology and the environment through their work, including via habitat restoration and creation. Natural habitats such as this one in the Lesser Caucasus can also serve as inspiration to us for designing resilient plant communities.

CLIMATE CONTROL

Plants, especially trees, can have a significant cooling and shading effect on a building, especially in hot climates. On a larger scale, an avenue of trees along both sides of a road will reduce the outside temperature beneath those trees and create a more comfortable environment to move through.

POLLUTION

The process of phytoremediation involves using plants to clean up contaminated environments by taking advantage of their ability to concentrate elements and compounds in their environment and detoxify contaminants. Whilst planting designers might not generally have cause to use this process, it is possible that planting will need to contribute to absorbing common toxins frequently in the near future, especially in urban areas. Through photosynthesis, plants can also reduce the level of carbon dioxide in the atmosphere.

▲ Inspiration for many relatively new approaches to planting design has come from our natural landscapes, including prairies, meadows, and places like this, the Goegap Nature Reserve in South Africa. Such designs do not necessarily aim to be accurate re-creations of natural landscapes, but borrow principles that established the original, such as using communities of plants that will thrive in the same conditions, to guide the design process and discover plants that can be included in a new way.

PROMOTING COMPLEXITY AND BIODIVERSITY

Successful planting design will increasingly be measured by its ability to support and improve biodiversity. The level of control that we exert through our planting designs can deliver a level of complexity, but we should be careful not to just mimic nature for aesthetic reasons. We must consider how we can support and improve the nature around us within our designs.

Biodiversity in planting design is emphasised throughout this book (and covered in more detail later). Whilst it is listed last in this chapter, it is not without reason that consciously designing for biodiversity—whether at a client's request or by stealth—is a major contribution to a more sustainable landscape that the planting designer can make.

◂ If we are fortunate enough to be asked to create new woodland or areas of forest, we may bring in specialists, but our objective should be to ensure that what we are designing supports future biodiversity.

A garden where the diversity of ornamental plants is relatively simple requires more attention to auditing choices and their performance. This garden in Odawara City, Japan, is based on *Hydrangea* spp. and *Iris* cultivars; these will require good management to ensure that the clarity of design is preserved from year to year.

SUMMARY: MAKING AND AUDITING YOUR PLANT CHOICES

The work that you have done on preparing a project brief, developing your ideas, and composing your planting structure and a planting palette has led to this moment. You are now ready to make your final selection of plants. Focus on making definitive choices based on a thorough understanding of the objectives for your planting design and the qualities that individual plants and communities of plants will contribute to it.

Whilst this chapter demonstrates that there are diverse plant qualities, it is likely that the atmosphere that you first developed as part of your project brief will quite quickly lead you to make relatively easy choices based on aesthetics—but always consider functional qualities when deciding how to use plants, such as resiliency, one of the attributes of future planting design success.

Sometimes you will encounter trends for a particular style of planting or a fashion for individual plants. For example, over the past twenty years there has been a strong trend to use grasses to varying degrees within planting schemes, sometimes as a main feature, other times to support other planting. We've seen that grasses might play a vital part in a vertical layer approach, but also that ornamental borders can contain a proportion of grass species. Trends can be good; they might lead us to make choices that are good for biodiversity or resilience. Fashions are perhaps not so useful and remind us of the importance of making choices based on a sound understanding of what our objectives are rather than implementing short-lived aesthetic preferences.

There is a lot to be said for the idea that one generation prefers the fashionable aesthetic plant qualities of their grandparents' generation and not of their parents, but in a rapidly changing climate, we need to think beyond just aesthetics and consider our environmental impact in our work. The following chapters discuss two important areas of a planting designer's work in detailing designs. They also build upon plant qualities to promote longevity, permanence, biodiversity, and resilience. Successional planting will extend the value of a planting design through a growing year, and choosing sustainable plants and planting techniques will support resilience and 'futureproof' your designs.

As you make detailed planting choices, draw your final planting plans and write your schedules of plants and instructions, revisit your project brief and atmospheric mood boards to determine if you have truly met your objectives. Auditing your choices against your initial ideas is good practice and will give you confidence when presenting your final design to your clients. It's a great way of ensuring that you have taken into account the four attributes of planting design success—connection, innovation, complexity, and resilience—in proportion important to your design.

CASE STUDY

FISHER TOMLIN & BOWYER

Blind Veterans UK
Sussex, United Kingdom

Climate:	Temperate marine, microclimate formed from surrounding wall
Rainfall:	790mm (31") per annum
Temperature:	Minimum 4 degrees Celsius (39 degrees F) Maximum 21 degrees Celsius (70 degrees F)
Soil:	Sandy loam

Planting design provides an inspirational place for people who live with disability. Here, design innovation requires an in-depth understanding of the particular needs of the client.

PLANTING DEVELOPMENT

Blind Veterans UK help vision-impaired ex-servicemen and women rebuild their lives after sight loss as they work to regain independence and to live the life they now choose. The designers had previously worked with the charity, designing a woodland garden in North Wales before being commissioned to create this garden as a focal point and enhancement of an existing centre on the south coast of England. Previous experience of working with the members, staff, and charity volunteers greatly informed how this landscape should be developed, especially the planting design.

Vision impairment can affect our enjoyment of the outdoors in different ways. The brief was to create a community garden that everyone could enjoy, particularly in the warmer months, and for servicemembers to be able to guide themselves around the garden. Colour and scent were of obvious importance for passive enjoyment of the planting, but there was also a mandate to impart a sense of community. This is achieved through the structural landscape via sculpture, paths, seating, and practical, active therapy areas.

PLANTING DETAIL

Whilst the senses are important when designing for vision impairment, the common conceptions of features that 'should' appear in a sensory garden were too simplistic for the needs of this demographic. The enhanced sense of smell many vision-impaired people develop can be overwhelmed by too many different scents; this design therefore focused on distinct fragrances to differentiate zones. A rose walk where the fragrance of traditional hybrid roses predominates, for example, helps the visitor navigate the garden.

Colour is still important for the vision impaired. The designers spent time with servicemembers to understand what colour contrasts especially stood out. Interviews revealed that strong contrasts, such as yellow against blue, are easier to learn and follow. The first objective of the planting was that the vision-impaired visitors should be able to appreciate the design, but the staff and volunteers also made it clear that it was equally important for the planting to project a positive mood; they often referenced the desired colour saturation as 'joyful and encouraging'. Interestingly, the first iteration of this project (the design has since been used as inspiration for other sites) prompted landscape architect professionals working in public gardens to reveal that they appreciated and remarked on the impact that colour had on those using the spaces. They had also experienced similar visitor reactions, whereas designers who predominantly design for private spaces showed more reluctance to using the more contrasting, stronger colour palette of this design.

The planting is ornamental, with a fifty-fifty balance of shrubs and perennials across a third of the area. This requires relatively low maintenance, a benefit when the planting is maintained by volunteers with no guaranteed schedule of work. Trees were sourced at a larger size to provide immediate shade. The remaining space is divided equally between a kitchen garden—also a space with a distinct scent—and a colourful pictorial meadow with changing waves of interest through the summer and then extended with spring bulbs for earlier warm-weather enjoyment. Autumn and winter see fewer visitors, although maintenance allows for a natural dieback to support wildlife.

CASE STUDY

SUSAN COHEN

Montclair Residence
New Jersey, United States

Climate:	Warm continental climate/humid continental climate (Dfa)
Rainfall:	1198mm (47") per annum
Temperature:	Minimum -3 degrees Celsius (27 degrees F) Maximum +31 degrees Celsius (88 degrees F)
Soil:	Loam with imported compost, neutral pH

Designed to overcome the practical challenges of an existing space and microclimate, this planting manages to create a Californian vibe in New Jersey.

PLANTING DEVELOPMENT

The designer was asked to create a 'California in the seventies' vibe to complement a new pool house addition on this property. The planting beds had already been built, so the challenge was to make them work with the overall story the renovation was trying to tell. Additionally, California has a Mediterranean climate and Northeastern America is very different, much more harsh and with much wider temperature swings across the seasons. These designers use the same methodical planting design approach consistently on each project they design—but the process varies with the individual constraints of each project.

PLANTING DETAIL

A limited colour palette simulates the feel of what might be found during the springtime bloom seasons in the rolling hills of Southern California. Grasses harken to the tans of the chaparral. Greens, then blues and yellows, follow as accents. The space receives full sun and there is a big dog to consider, so plants had to be tough to make the edit. Additionally, the client has a second home elsewhere and would not generally use this property in high summer, so the scheme had to include plants that show particularly well in spring and fall. Factors like these make each planting plan unique to site and owner.

The biggest challenge was the limited size of the existing planting beds. One in particular is only two feet wide. Space to be allocated to plants is often added as an afterthought when the planting design isn't considered until very late in the construction process.

The designers followed a framework planting design process to arrive at three main elements that came to define this space: repetition, triangular placement of plants to make it feel that they zigzag through the scheme, and ruthless editing. A huge list of possibilities was whittled down to just a few, with final plant lists that are remarkably brief but not in any way less effective in the final planted space. Within that scheme, successional blooms are very important. A specific sequence that allows some colours to fade fully before others dominate makes the garden seem completely fresh with new hues every spring and every fall.

CHAPTER **9**

SUCCESSION AND SEASONAL IMPACT

One of the most sought-after outcomes for most every planting design is achieving year-round interest. Along with low aftercare, it ranks as one of the most requested planting objectives by clients. The concept of all-year, all-round interest with high flowering or foliage impact across every season will, for many designers, feel insurmountable. You will certainly not achieve this from relying on a single plant, nor be able to achieve it completely across a whole landscape. A design approach known as successional planting is the best approach to achieving continuous interest throughout the year within a garden or landscape.

◂ As autumn arrives, the plants in this ornamental design retain structure and colour, extending planting interest. Allowing the plants to gradually fade, to reveal seed heads, and leaving spent plants in place rather than clearing provides valuable shelter and food for wildlife.

The primary objective of successional planting design is to retain visual interest across at least a major part of the year. It is based on the principle of creating waves of flowering periods that will peak at different times. Each wave is formed from a group of plants that create interest when they reach a flowering peak and then give way to another group. Often, before or after they flower, a group of plants or individual plants will provide some other form of additional interest, such as interestingly shaped seed heads, thus adding value to their position within the overall planting.

Successional planting is most likely to be focussed on supplying interest from early spring to early autumn, but the mandate may be extended further—into winter. Midsummer is usually thought of as the period of absolute peak interest (and in some ways the easiest to achieve), then other plants are used to bring forward and extend interest on the months to either side. Outside this period, individual plants might provide further interest to fulfil some smaller seasonal peaks, perhaps with autumn foliage colour or by offering winter flowers.

▲ Whilst they might be considered monotonous on their own, grasses often supply a foliage backdrop in dormant seasons, supporting flowering perennials and then providing drama and movement in the autumn and winter. This planting design by Piet Oudolf at Pensthorpe in Norfolk, England, uses *Astilbe chinensis* var. *taquetii* 'Purpurlanze' and *Molinia caerulea* subsp. *arundinacea* 'Transparent' to grab the visitor's attention outside of peak flowering season.

Winter / spring	Late spring / early summer	Summer peak	Late summer	Autumn flush
Early bulbs, flowering shrubs and trees	Later bulbs, early summer flowers including perennials and shrubs	The main attraction including perennials and non-hardy annuals	Long and late flowering perennials, grasses and foliage	Autumn foliage colour and the last of the flowers if mild

FIND YOUR STARTING POINT

Aim for a rhythm of seasonal interest with peaks across a long period of time with few, if any, blank spaces. As a starting point, consider at what point the main planting climax should be. Your client might have a view on this if they are away for a significant part of the growing season. For example, it's not unusual for a client to be away on vacation for a month during midsummer, so your starting focus might be early summer. It doesn't mean that there will be a complete blank when they are away, but it will help you to plan your main planting peak for when your client is at home and can most appreciate the garden.

If there is no preference, your own experience will help you understand where the main peak of interest might naturally arrive. A changing climate has made our work that much more unpredictable, but over time you will find that your own experience in the region where you work will show you where to start your successional design. Aim to find the main peak of planting interest for your regional climate and then extend your planting out from there, usually in both directions, before and after, to an earlier and later growing season.

It is very unlikely in a traditional landscape setting that the whole garden or landscape will peak at the same time—you should be able to maintain and enhance a rhythm to the planting that avoids large blank spaces and will always give you some interest.

Whilst compositional techniques primarily focus on an approach to planting *structure*, some of the archetypes discussed earlier usefully also inherently include a way of extending planting to engage the audience with several flowering peaks through the growing season.

Using Seasonal Charts

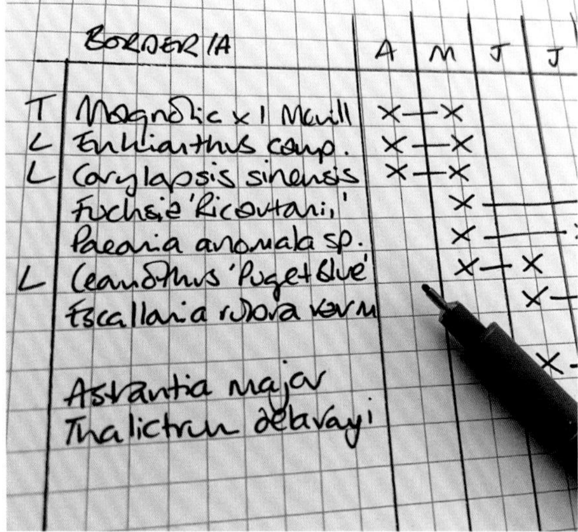

Start with simple hand-drawn charts to explore the plants you are considering to see how they work together. To start, abbreviate plant names and use monthly columns to understand what you are designing with, then transfer your solution to a computer spreadsheet with full scientific names and colour once you have made your decisions.

One of the most useful ways of exploring successional planting is to create seasonal charts, sometimes known as spreadsheet schedules. Whilst seasonal charts are useful for exploring how plants will perform in combination with others—when they will peak and what they might bring by way of colour to an overall planting design—they are especially useful in helping select plants for a long multiple-season succession of plants.

The chapter on delivering your work contains more examples of actual seasonal plant charts, but for now here are some ideas for communicating seasonal changes in your work:

- **Start with your primary plant choices**
  The simplest way to start exploring how your plants will work together is to start by entering the primary plants that will predominate in your design. If you have an objective for an early summer peak or a succession of peaks, how do your chosen plants interact with that?
- **Build upon your primary choices**
  You will quickly see in graphic form how your primary plant choices are working together. Do they create the peak of interest you want? Do you need something else to support these plants? Do you have too many different species? Could you swap some for plants that will peak earlier or later?
- **Consider interest from attributes beyond flowers**
  Interest doesn't have to come from flowers alone. Sometimes we choose plants for their foliage, which might support other plants when those are flowering. For example, a plant with purple foliage might be a perfect foil for colourful flowers before it flowers itself. That foliage might continue to support other plants once those flowers are finished. Evergreens are a great example of shrubs that will provide year-round structure and interest from foliage with just a relatively brief period of flowering interest. Grasses and restios can be especially useful as supporting actors before flowering in the late summer to early autumn. Other features, such as interesting bark or fruit, can also add to the usefulness of a plant; flag those in your seasonal chart as well.
- **Introduce colour to your chart**
  Use colour in your chart to indicate the actual colour of each plant at different times of the year. Flower colours are easy enough, whereas periods of foliage interest can be represented by their shade of green or another colour. A detailed colour chart will help you understand how your colour palette is working alongside a plant mood board.
- **Use your schedules to explain more**
  The great thing about using a spreadsheet programme for your seasonal plant charts and schedules is that you can then add extra information, such as key plant data (spread and height, numbers required for orders, costs and aftercare requirements) as you develop your final design.

SUCCESSIONAL PLANTING FOR AN ORNAMENTAL ARCHETYPE

The concept of successional planting is based on attempting to achieve all-year, all-round interest through plants that peak at different times. It's not an especially new idea, indeed it goes back hundreds of years to the traditional mixed border that uses an ornamental incremental planting design approach. Christopher Lloyd, a master of successional planting, created his designs using an ornamental archetype that makes available a wide range of plants that we might assess as horticulturally compatible, while allowing us to select according to the principle of creating successional planting interest.

This ornamental approach can, however, create a relatively static planting design where different plants simply provide different periods of interest through the seasons. You might experience one group of plants predominating before another takes over. For example, the periods of planting interest will be spring bulbs, then flowering shrubs and early perennials before a peak summer perennial flowering which is then further extended by long-flowering perennials and grasses. Occasionally annuals and more tender plants might be brought in to temporarily to fill gaps. Shrubs that provide a foliage structure through peak seasons might be selected to flower out of the peak season for added value to the overall design.

◂ Fig. 1. Spring.

◂ Fig. 2. Summer.

◂ Fig. 3. Autumn.

◂ Fig. 4. Winter.

▸ Explore successional planting through design elevations to help you assess structure through the seasons. Adding colour will help you understand and highlight the changing blossom and foliage of the plants you are using. You might also use seasonal mood boards to explore how plant colour and other qualities might change.

A good technique to improve upon this approach is to use plants that have multiple uses or features across the growing season. These are the plants that are more than just flowering stars—they contribute seasonal foliage, bark, and fruiting interest but also structural support for other plants and out-of-season interest through features such as seed heads (which also support objectives for biodiversity).

Some plants might be doubly useful in providing physical support for others as well as acting as a foliage backdrop; grasses are a great example for large-scale plantings where they can anchor a design physically as well as visually. Then, when other plants die back, they start flowering late in the summer and into autumn. So with successional planting, consider what a plant can give to a border not just through its flowering peak but how it might contribute different types of interest at different times.

SUCCESSIONAL PLANTING FOR A NATURALISTIC ARCHETYPE

The ornamental approach will be familiar to many designers and is a highly controlled way of organising successional waves of interest. However, succession can be more challenging for naturalistic planting, which relies on distinct *communities* of plants. This is an opportunity, however—by using a community of plants that work together horticulturally (in terms of aspect, soil, moisture, and climate) you have already narrowed down your plant choices and made your eventual planting palette easier to decide upon. The challenge then is to understand how these plants can be divided and organised into groups that peak at different times and provide waves of interest across a long period. It therefore does require a thorough familiarity with the plants that are to be used.

Naturalistic planting design approaches often aim to simplify planting methods. As a starting point, the use of communities of plants that work together in the same conditions will simplify the plants that are available to use. Simplifying structure at a higher level with a repetition of trees, large shrubs, and grass species is a common approach. Simplifying the timeline for plants is a natural progression where the designer will choose plants in focused mixes of just three or four species that peak simultaneously. Sequencing plants across a long period then becomes easier to achieve from month to month, with further extension of the period of interest through filler plants and geophytes.

GRASS RIPPLES AND MEADOW			
TYPE	QTY	SUPPLIER	NAME
Grasses			Calamagrostis x acutiflora 'Karl Foerster'
Biennial			Daucus carota
Grasses			Ammophila arenaria
Annual			Eschscholzia californica 'Alba'
MIX 01 - SEA			
TYPE	QTY	SUPPLIER	NAME
Perennial			Cynara cardunculus
Perennial			Artemisia 'Powis Castle'
Perennial			Eryngium maritimum
Grasses			Helictotrichon sempervirens
Perennial			Perovskia atriplicifolia 'Blue Jean Baby'
Grasses			Poa labillardierei
Perennial			Crambe maritima
Perennial			Eryngium x zabelii
Perennial			Origanum laevigatum 'Herrenhausen'
Bulb			Iris 'Black Swan'
MIX 02 - DUNES			
TYPE	QTY	SUPPLIER	NAME
Grasses			Chionochloa rubra
Perennial			Carex buchananii
Perennial			Eyngium yuccifolium
Perennial			Gladiolus tristis
Perennial			Kniphofia thomsonii
Grasses			Pennisetum macrourum
Shrub			Phlomis chrysophylla
Shrub			Phlomis fruticosa
Perennial			Scabiosa ochroleuca
Perennial			Silene uniflora (sea campion)
Perennial			Sisyrinchium striatum
Perennial			Stachys byzantina
Shrub			Teucrium flavum
Grasses			Nasella tenuissima
MIX 03 - SUNSET			
TYPE	QTY	SUPPLIER	NAME
Perennial			Dierama pulcherrimum
Perennial			Erigeron karvinskianus
Perennial			Cirsium rivulare 'Atropurpureum'
Perennial			Foeniculum vulgare 'Giant Bronze'
Perennial			Kniphofia thomsonii
Bulb			Gladiolus communis subsp. byzantinus
Perennial			Armeria maritima 'Splendens'
Grasses			Chionochloa rubra
Grasses			Panicum virgatum 'Shenandoah'
Perennial			Origanum laevigatum 'Herrenhausen'
Succulent			Aloe striatula
MIX 04 - CALM/LINKING MIX			
TYPE	QTY	SUPPLIER	NAME
Succulent			Agave-Havardiana
Grasses			Sesleria nitida
Perennial			Crambe maritima
Kintsugi Walk and Beds			
TYPE	QTY	SUPPLIER	NAME
Conifer			Juniperus squamata 'Blue Carpet'
Perennial			Cynara cardunculus
Grasses			Helictotrichon sempervirens
Perennial			Crambe maritima
Bulb			Iris 'Black Swan'
Grasses			Chionochloa rubra
Perennial			Gladiolus tristis
Perennial			Erigeron karvinskianus
Grasses			Sesleria nitida
Grasses			Calamagrostis x acutiflora 'Karl Foerster'

HEIGHT	SPREAD	COLOUR	J	F	M	A	M	J	J	A	S	O	N	D	NOTES
1.8	0.5 - 1	Wheat													
0.9	0.3	Airy umbels of off white													
1	0.6	Wiry grey green foliage and buff flowers													
0.4	0.3	Blue feathery foliage, white flowers													

HEIGHT	SPREAD	COLOUR	J	F	M	A	M	J	J	A	S	O	N	D	NOTES
1.5 - 2.5	1 - 1.5	Silver evergreen foliage, purple flower													bring structure through year
0.6	0.9	Silver - semi evergreen													
0.5-1	0.1-0.5	Semi evergreen foliage, blue globular flowers													
1.4	0.6	Evergreen grey blue foliage													
0.75	0.5	Permanent grey structure, light purple flowers													
1	0.7	Semi evergreen blue foliage, transparent cream flowerheads													
0.75	0.6	Blue green leaves, dense white flowers													
0.5-1	0.5	Silver green foliage, blue thimble flowerheads													
0.6	0.45	Mauve pink flower clusters													
0.9	0.3	Deep purple flower, narrow grey green leaves													

HEIGHT	SPREAD	COLOUR	J	F	M	A	M	J	J	A	S	O	N	D	NOTES
1-1.5	0.5-1	Dense tussock of red tinted leaves													
0.75	0.75	Brown orange arching leaves													
1.2	1	Evergeen bluish green foliage, grey/blue/cream flowers													
0.75	0.2	Dark green leaves, pale lemon trumpet flowers													
1	1	Sparse foliage, pale orange flowers													
1.5	.0.75	Buff white flowerheads													
1	1.2	Evergreen, golden flowers													
1	1.5	Evergreen grey green shrub, deep yellow flowers													
0.8	0.6	lemon flowers													
0.15	0.15	Semi evergreen, white flowers, blue green foliage													
0.8	0.5	Semi evergreen, pale yellow flowers													
0.45	0.55	Evergreen mat forming, silver													
0.5	0.75	Evergreen, grey green leaves, pale yellow flowers													
0.6	0.3	Semi evergreen, pale blonde buff panicles													

HEIGHT	SPREAD	COLOUR	J	F	M	A	M	J	J	A	S	O	N	D	NOTES
1 - 1.5	0.1 - 0.5	Long narrow evergreen leaves, nodding pink flowers													
0.3	0.5	White and Pink													
1.2	0.6	Dark crimson flower													
1.8	0.45	Bronze/yellow flowers													Short lived
1	1	Sparse foliage, pale orange flowers													
0.9	0.1	Deep red flowers													
0.2	0.3	Evergreen tuft of foliage, clusters deep pink flowers													
1-1.5	0.5-1	Dense tussock of red tinted leaves													
0.9	0.9	Deep burgundy panicles													
0.6	0.45	Mauve pink flower clusters													
1.5	1.5	Evergreen with yellow racemes of flowers													

HEIGHT	SPREAD	COLOUR	J	F	M	A	M	J	J	A	S	O	N	D	NOTES
1.3	1.3	Evergreen grey blue leaves													
0.6	0.45	Blue grey foliage, white flowers													
0.75	0.6	Blue green leaves, dense white flowers													

HEIGHT	SPREAD	COLOUR	J	F	M	A	M	J	J	A	S	O	N	D	NOTES
0.3	1.5	Evergreen bright blue grey													
1.5 - 2.5	1 - 1.5	Silver evergreen foliage, purple flower													bring structure through year
1.4	0.6	Evergreen grey blue foliage													
0.75	0.6	Blue green leaves, dense white flowers													
0.9	0.3	Deep purple flower, narrow grey green leaves													
1-1.5	0.5-1	Dense tussock of red tinted leaves													
0.75	0.2	Dark green leaves, pale lemon trumpet flowers													
0.3	0.5	White and Pink													
0.5	0.5	Semi evergreen blue green, white flowers													
1.8	0.5 - 1	Wheat													

DETAIL

SELECTING PLANT BLOOMS FOR NATURALISTIC DESIGNS

One useful technique for approaching succession in large-scale naturalistic planting is to compare your selection to that in nature. We often experience single-species 'blooms' within larger plant communities. This is especially the case in meadows, where there may be a predominant native species such as *Leucanthemum vulgare* (ox-eye daisy) and *Ranunculus acris* (meadow buttercup) in Europe, *Eschscholzia californica* (California poppy) on the West Coast of the U.S. or *Xerochrysum bracteatum* (strawflower) and *Rhodanthe* spp. in Australia. Your project brief may call for a light touch, in which case a simple planting with seasonal impact and that relies on a series of single or double species blooms can be a useful approach to take.

SUMMARY: SUCCESSION WITHIN THE PLANTING DESIGN FRAMEWORK

DETAIL

Successional planting requires a very clear understanding of your planting design objectives such as colour, structure, and scent. If you develop an extensive project brief and a strong planting narrative to lead your design, this should not be a challenge.

This method of stretching the season of interest sits very much within the wider framework for planting design. It encourages the designer to consider a broad range of plant types, species, and variety that are suitable for the horticultural qualities of the space being designed. It should also support the attribute of improving complexity and biodiversity within planting but, most important of all, it requires the planting designer to observe and learn, in order to develop a wide knowledge of plant performance.

▸ Blooms like this *Drosanthemum hispidum* in West Coast National Park, South Africa, are a natural phenomenon that might inspire single-species waves of planting and moments of superbloom spectacle within a naturalistic planting design. They are especially useful in designs using predominantly native species.

CASE STUDY

RICHARD WILFORD

The Great Broad Walk Borders, Royal Botanic Gardens, Kew
Richmond-upon-Thames, United Kingdom

Climate: Temperate marine, influenced by proximity to London
Rainfall: 625mm (24.6") per annum
Temperature: Minimum +4 degrees Celsius (39 degrees F)
Maximum +22 degrees Celsius (72 degrees F)
Soil: Varies along length; overall cultivated sandy loam

A planting feature created on a grand scale to attract visitors whilst linking back to the history of the site and telling the story of a modern botanic garden.

PLANTING DEVELOPMENT

The planting designs at this World Heritage Site are heavily influenced by the location and purpose of each garden within the Royal Botanic Gardens overall. Some designs, like the Great Broad Walk Borders, are mostly designed for aesthetics, but must still include some link to botany or the science being performed at Kew.

The brief was to create a summer display for when visitor numbers peak, and also to transform a dull, uninspiring path into one that could showcase a range of flowers that would draw even more visitors. The Broad Walk was originally intended as a promenade to the Palm House, which opened in 1848. The original planting design by William Nesfield consisted of an intricate pattern of beds, with trees, shrubs, and perennials. The current designer wanted to re-create the impression of the long promenade but in a more contemporary style, using bulbs for spring colour but relying heavily on summer-flowering perennials. He also sought to make a link to the RBG's research—for example, highlighting plants in the daisy family in one section, the mint family in another, both areas of study at Kew.

PLANTING DETAIL

Visitors to Kew are mostly likely to reach the Great Broad Walk Borders from one end or the other, or at the middle point, where it crosses other paths. The design immediately emphasises the Walk's substantial length, and encourages exploration of the whole path. Topiary yews at the front of the borders provide rhythm and give a sense of the scale of planting straight away, from wherever you join the Walk. Then, as you walk down the central path, the planting design changes. The borders are a based on a geometry of a series of circles bisected by the path, with each circle joined to the next by short, narrow connecting segments.

Each circle has been planted in a different style and with a different choice of plants. In this way, they encourage visitors to move along and explore the next section, sure to hold something new. Interpretation plaques appear at regular intervals. Places to sit and enjoy the planting and to have a break are provided to encourage lingering, but they are set in, so the view down the borders is uninterrupted and visitors sitting down do not feel 'in the way' of other people.

Establishing scale that feels appropriate was very important here; the length and 8-metre (26-foot) width of the existing path meant the borders needed to be wide in order to fit the landscape proportionately. An existing avenue of cedars that lined the path was another challenge; although set a few metres back from the path, the large trees that cast shade and leach moisture. The borders are designed so the widest sections (the semicircles) fall between the trees and therefore receive maximum sunlight. Interviewing the horticultural staff about how the soil profile changes along the Broad Walk also informed the planting.

Repetition is an important tactic for linking the various sections of the border together; repeating a plant from one section to the next is often enough to provide a visual link. In this case, topiary yews punctuate the whole border at regular intervals and enhance the perception of perspective from either end. They provide a constant visual element that helps to orient visitors before they process the distinct plantings of each semicircle and also provide year-round structure as evergreens.

Summer is a long season in the garden, lasting from May to early October in London, so the planting necessarily changes over that period to provide a series of peaks rather than just one. The borders look very different in September to what they look like in May. The continuation of colour and interest throughout the summer has to be maintained, however, and this directive influenced the choice of plants and where they were planted. As one group fades, another takes over. Herbaceous perennials are perfect for this type of display, with such a range of colour and flowering time to choose from. To extend the season of interest, bulbs are planted for spring colour, and start flowering in early March. Grasses are used to provide some extended interest in autumn, with their autumn colour enhancing the borders, along with the seed heads of other perennials.

The main consideration to support sustainability is the use of hardy perennials that do not need regular replacement. Cuttings are also taken of some plants and grown on at Kew, for replanting. The aim is to let the borders evolve while keeping more vigorous or spreading species under control, but without having to keep to a rigid design strictly contained and without having to replace everything that doesn't survive.

CASE STUDY

GREEN OVER GREY

The Vancouver Centre
Vancouver, Canada

Climate: Indoor 'tropical' environment
Rainfall: Artificial irrigation as required
Temperature: Minimum +18 degrees Celsius (64 degrees F)
Maximum +22 degrees Celsius (72 degrees F)
Soil: Aggregate substrate that uses a hydroponic method

A strong design narrative inspired by nature aims to engage visitors whilst demanding specialist expertise to achieve a thriving living wall.

PLANTING DEVELOPMENT

Designing a hydroponic living wall involves a meticulous balance of art, science, and horticultural experience. The designer often looks to nature for inspiration for these vertical installations. It is his hope that having a connection to nature in the midst of a city will motivate people to want to protect the natural spaces that we have left in the rural world.

For the Vancouver Centre, the lushness and aesthetic appeal of these living walls was paramount. Careful attention is paid to colour palettes, textural contrasts, and spatial arrangements to create visually stunning and harmonious compositions. The overall design is based on leaf patterns, which become abstract lines that travel across all six atrium canvases and tie them together. The other two walls (which are in different areas of the building and not visually connected to these six) have distinctly different designs.

PLANTING DETAIL

The objective was to create an atmosphere where people could enjoy the walls from the seating in front, as well as from below. As these walls are over 9 metres high (30 feet), they have a lot of impact when seen from below. The leaves of the larger specimens in particular are breathtaking when viewed from this angle.

The designer also wanted to create a sense of botanical awe when selecting the plant species. The walls have upwards of eighty unique plant species, with some very rare additions coming from the designer's personal collection. Using a large diversity of plant species is something that he is keen on—it not only makes the living wall more botanically interesting, but also helps to figure out which plant species work best on any given section. Each wall has its own microclimate, temperature fluctuations, natural lighting schedule (exposure), shadows, air flow, etc. There are even areas on a living wall that are more or less moist depending on the distance from an irrigation line, etc. It requires a fair amount of science to get things just right and ensure the wall's long-term health.

Humans now live inside 'tropical' environments where the temperature is between 18 and 22 degrees Celsius, every day, all year. This is why what are considered houseplant species in Canada had to be used here; Green Over Grey does use native plants outside, but native plants require cold seasons to thrive—and here in Vancouver, a rainy winter. If they do not have a winter period, then they will start to get stressed and will eventually die.

The living wall system is hydroponic and uses many tropical plants that can be classified as epiphytes—a key rule for the brief as well as a helpful one for growing vertically. Challenges included gaining access to these very tall walls, which is overcome best using scissor or boom lifts. Calibrating the water pressure for the irrigation system across all the areas of different needs and sizes was also challenging. A sustainable solution is always aimed for, and this includes the system using 100 percent recycled materials, such as the wall's waterproof backing panel, made from post-consumer waste. All plants were also sourced locally.

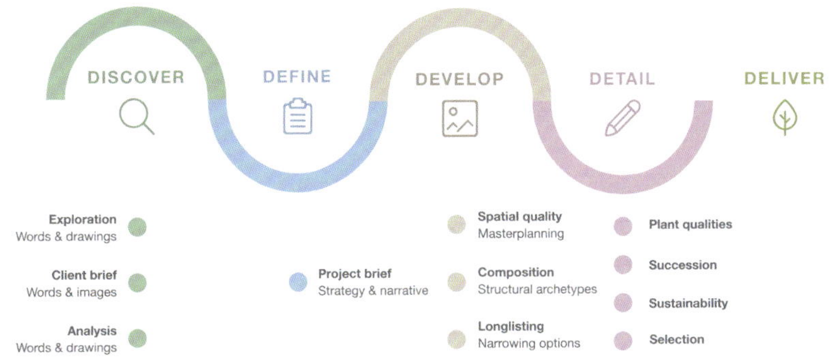

CHAPTER **10**

TOWARDS A SUSTAINABLE PLANTING APPROACH

◂ Small, undeveloped corners in urban areas are increasingly being seen as potential sites for pocket parks. A movement to introduce green infrastructure that started in the late twentieth century has taken on a more serious aspect due to the changing climate; more radical use of urban space is now often supported by planning regulations.

Planting designers are in a unique position to change opinions and attitudes about what is possible in support of the environment we live in. Much has been written about an apparent disconnect between humans and nature and the importance we give to plants. This disconnect differs between cultures and how closely we are connected to nature, land, and the benefits that plants bring to our lives, but although there is a disregard for nature, we also often find a perception that nature, and particularly plants, are a solution to the challenges of a changing climate.

It is perhaps too convenient to say that people don't see plants, that they are somehow placed lower on the scale of importance to humans and animals. Yet whilst there is a sense of perceived lower status for plants, the tide is turning in recognition that they are part of the solution to the predicament we find ourselves in.

In framing your planting designs, you will very likely consider sustainable practices as you progress through the framework steps. For example, you might consider ecology early on as part of the survey stage and define your project brief in terms of environmental objectives. The development stage will help you consider compositional approaches which, whilst being primarily about planting structure, will often encourage sustainable approaches and resilient plant choices. This chapter focuses on helping you consider factors that can support your design choices *and* help you reflect upon the sustainability of your design.

DETAIL

The drivers of sustainable development are recognised as economic well-being, social equity, cultural preservation, and environmental protection. In terms of landscape and plants this translates into a consideration of factors such as soil fertility, use of resources including raw and recycled materials, drinkable water, breathable air, food security, availability of green space, embodied energy, and embodied carbon.

A changing climate has prompted a change in attitudes towards plants—this gives planting designers an opportunity to improve our environment. Our role within a design team can be important in contributing to sustainable solutions. We can amplify the awareness and appreciation of plants within the environment, local ecosystems, and cultures where we find ourselves working. Where once clients questioned the need for perceived 'high-maintenance' planting, they have now started to understand the role that plants can play in their lives, whether that's for their own well-being or for nature's. There is also more understanding that aesthetic movements align with low-aftercare gardens. For example, a naturalistic planting allowed to die down naturally over a winter season can provide wildlife benefits of shelter and food as well as being relatively easy to maintain, since debris is left to mulch down where it once grew.

▲ A roof garden that blooms with sedum in the summer can completely transform the outlook of surrounding buildings, help reduce internal building temperatures and support wildlife. It may seem like a very simple solution to the planting designer, but it often fulfils a role within large designs that include meeting sustainability metrics for planning approval.

SUSTAINABLE PLANTING DESIGN IDEAS AND PRACTICES

Whilst the outlook across a whole range of indicators for sustainability seems challenging, planting designers are in a fortunate position to call upon many tested tools and approaches that will enable us to design planting in a sustainable way. As professionals, people are also often willing to listen to us and trust our expertise. Following are some key ideas and practices to embrace so that they become second nature within your work as you design while incorporating sustainability as an end goal.

▲ Understanding climate trends is important to the work of the planting designer. We cannot predict the future, but there is a substantial body of information indicative of the direction we can expect our current climate to move. Tropical atmospheres might be challenging to create in temperate zones, should weather and seasonal patterns change.

▶ Gardeners understand the importance of healthy soil. Our planting designs should be accompanied by an understanding of how we can use the soil that we have and how to improve it through the production of organic compost. We can even encourage our clients towards zero-waste gardening, where all debris is used onsite, whether as compost or mulch.

UNDERSTANDING WHAT YOU ARE WORKING WITH

Scientific evidence shows that we are increasingly capable of predicting future weather patterns. However, whilst we might like to think that we are technologically advanced enough to predict patterns at a macro level, we are generally not so good at predicting the impact of a changing climate on our individual gardens, landscapes, and projects unless we garden there regularly and develop an understanding at the micro level. We understand that the weather is less dependable, with less demarcation between seasons. Spring and autumn might be fleeting, or we might experience milder winters with plants flowering earlier and for longer. Plants might be less able to cope with temperature extremes, leading to loss. Regularly working within a locality will help us understand what we are up against, but how will weather patterns affect each individual project we work on?

You should not take a broad-brush approach based on macro predictions, but spend time to discover and define how local patterns impact each project. Nature is incredibly complex—even within a single landscape you might see a flowering plant species growing well in one area but failing in another. Consider factors such as local microclimate and the type and presence of existing vegetation, and use clues from existing biodiversity. Taking the time to find out what you have in front of you and to familiarise yourself with the nuances of each individual site is more important than ever.

THE QUALITY OF YOUR PLANTS STARTS WITH HEALTHY SOIL

Soils are a complex and complete self-contained ecosystem made of minerals, water, organic matter, air, and living organisms. A healthy soil provides the means for plants to grow and supports habitat, the air we breathe, the food we grow, and the water we drink. We know that different soils have different properties based on their composition, so for each project we should test the soils we have to make plant choices appropriate to the prevailing conditions.

We also need to nurture the soil that we already have before rushing to bring in new soil. The experienced gardener understands the importance of soil stewardship: regularly adding organic matter, improving drainage, eliminating compaction, mulching, and choosing plants that are suitable for the soil at hand. Growing nutrient-hungry edibles might require a greater input of organic matter and the use of techniques such as no-dig and crop rotation, but the principles of working to maintain health are the same.

Encourage composting, maximise plant cover in your projects, and avoid as much disturbance as possible. On your working sites where other hard landscaping elements such as paving and boundaries are being built, it can be easy for a landscaper to forget about protecting the soil

from compaction whilst work is underway, or to underestimate the protection that existing vegetation, especially trees, require. It's your role as planting designer to remind your landscaper of these important factors to protect your eventual planting medium, and to specify at the outset of a project how existing vegetation should be protected and to indicate which areas for planting must be protected throughout the construction period and when newly planted.

Using Other Substrates

We are not always blessed with a perfect soil that allows us freedom to choose a wide and diverse group of plants. Soil, climate, and moisture availability determine what we can grow more than any other factors. The challenges that we face with soils and also the waste that is prevalent on redevelopment sites has led to a great deal of research on the use of different substrates as growing media. This is particularly true for brownfield sites, where previous industrial land is being transformed to create new landscapes meant to fulfil objectives such as water management or leisure space.

The use of substrates and soil alternatives is growing, and the planting designer is well placed to follow these developments and look for opportunities to use what was previously thought of as waste materials for planting. You could experiment if given the opportunity, but there is already a body of research and evidence available for planting in settings such as previous freight train yards, and using road building and building waste materials. It is challenging, but it can be very rewarding to create planting designs with materials onsite rather than importing new soils.

▲ This design by Amanda Grimes highlights the potential to reuse building waste as a substrate for planting as well as to recycle materials to create a garden. It might not be to everyone's aesthetic taste to have a garden like this, but it does question the need for high-cost materials if we can create sustainable gardens in this way.

MANAGING WATER CONSUMPTION

The amount of water consumed by gardens and landscapes varies widely, but there is consensus that water for residential gardens accounts for 3 to 5 percent of total water use in Northern Europe. This will of course vary with weather patterns and climates in different regions. Water management systems, such as rainwater harvesting into simple storage for garden use, and more sophisticated 'grey' water harvesting are often used to benefit planting, usually when natural rainfall is seasonally unavailable.

Surface water runoff from the widespread use of impermeable paving is a challenge for all urban areas, but the development of sustainable drainage systems has also become more widespread in recent decades. These include rain gardens, increasing the amount of green space available by including green roofs and replacing impermeable surfaces with permeable paving systems, swales, infiltration trenches or basins, and soakaways. In some countries, these have become regulated requirements for development.

Ultimately, these systems and approaches will cost money to install and manage. Developing a successful budget therefore often means combining these with a sustainable approach to designing planting for the conditions that you are presented with. A focus on right plant choice, where you plant for the conditions that you have (i.e., the rainfall and drought you experience), will in theory reduce the need for artificial irrigation beyond plant establishment. Think of it as allowing the water management systems to continue to do their work without rendering plants dependent on them and thereby adding stress to the system.

▸ Benchakitti Forest Park in Bangkok, Thailand, is an example of a new type of sustainable urban park appearing more frequently worldwide in recent years. In the former Tobacco Factory area, this public site covers 178 acres. The design narrative aims to improve public understanding and knowledge about ecology, forests, hydrology, and the environment of the urban community. The park aims to preserve the ecological environment of the city, retaining water in the rainy season and producing clean water using wetland plants including rare indigenous trees of the central river basin. All existing trees onsite were preserved and integrated into the park design.

BIODIVERSITY IS ABOUT JOINED-UP THINKING

Biodiversity is defined as all the different kinds of life that you will discover in a single area, and the variety of that life. It includes animals, plants, fungi, and microorganisms such as bacteria that make up the natural world. Each species will work together in an ecosystem, maintaining balance and supporting each other and everything in nature that we need to survive. The loss of habitat is a very real threat to biodiversity. For example, a 2023 report revealed that 34 percent of plants and 40 percent of animals are at risk of extinction, with 41 percent of ecosystems in the U.S. at risk of range-wide collapse. It is a similar picture around the world, with biodiversity hotspots such as Japan recording a continuing trend of biodiversity loss.

Retaining existing vegetation is a particularly worthwhile approach to help restore and develop further habitat. To work with the principle that the most sustainable landscape is the one where you retain as much of what already exists as possible renders an early exploration of your site critical. An assessment of existing vegetation will reveal what can be incorporated into your new planting design. Whilst it might be tempting to start completely afresh, retaining existing trees and other plants will give immediate biodiversity value and help maintain at least some of the habitat already present onsite, while saving valuable resources and money.

Not all projects will come with substantive areas of vegetation and wildlife; new residential or commercial development on brownfield sites might be limited in their biodiversity or have contaminated land that has to be cleaned for new building development. Increasingly, these developments will include planned communal areas of green space where imported, manufactured soils and water management systems are designed; here you could be faced with creating a new ecosystem almost from scratch, especially as pertains to plant life. Nature will find a way of arriving, but you can support it by looking at the potential beyond your site and how you might link habitat through green urban corridors, choosing plants that support and increase diversity within the neighbourhood you are working within.

You can also encourage biodiversity at a residential scale, for whilst you might be confined to design for garden spaces, wildlife doesn't experience those constraints. Insects and small mammals will move between gardens within a neighbourhood, pollinators like bees and butterflies are known to travel many miles for food, and of course birds and larger mammals will travel long distances in search of food and safety. Larger landscapes might have more potential for wildlife habitat, but you can still treat small landscapes like pocket wildlife reserves with small yards and gardens forming part of a larger ecosystem that might include nearby gardens, parks, common grounds, and woodlands. Indeed, in some heavily urbanised areas our private gardens, all joined together, function as a large wildlife park.

◂ Whilst planting designers often work in fairly controlled settings and focus on creating spaces for people, there will be times when you are able to improve biodiversity through your work. In larger landscapes, the influence of existing life, especially plants and animals, will allow you to focus on supporting an even more biodiverse future landscape, and to support the needs of wildlife as much as people. It might require a light touch or a larger intervention, but you have the power to influence the direction taken.

◂ The sustainable planting designer will try to retain as much existing vegetation as is possible; an early assessment of the site in the discovery stage of your design will enable you to identify where you can retain and enhance existing planting. Existing bluebells *Hyacinthoides non-scripta* provide valuable habitat in this woodland near Sheffield, England, and will provide a dramatic bloom in spring before other plants introduced by design might make an appearance.

In support of biodiversity, expect to design insect and wildlife habitat, remove the need for toxic chemicals such as spraying off existing weed cover prior to planting, include natural water features, and consider lawn alternatives such as wildflower and perennial lawns. Every element of our biodiversity is codependent: plants, insects, animals, humans. The sustainable planting designer can design planting with this in mind to enhance ecological value for wildlife, especially the essentials of water, shelter, food, and places to raise young while still improving client well-being.

The traditional *avenidas* of orange trees in Seville, in southern Spain, have proved resilient and adapted to increasing temperatures that have resulted from a changing climate. They are a major cultural feature of the city's landscape and also meet environmental requirements, such as reducing pollution and urban temperatures, thus earning their place as a sustainable choice on many levels.

LONGEVITY, RESILIENCE, AND ADAPTATION

The practice of stewarding a biodiverse landscape can help build resilience. Designing and gardening with the characteristics of soil, climate, current conditions, and resources that come included with your site will set you on a positive road to design success. But planting designers are also increasingly being asked to design for and anticipate an unpredictable future. A key factor in the success of a sustainable landscape is to create some measure of longevity for your designs in order to achieve permanence in your planting. Planting techniques and aftercare have a role to play and are discussed further below, but you should consider the adaptability of plants in coping with a changing climate and changing biodiversity early on in your design process.

This is not an easy task. However, you will discover that there are many people working on determining what plants will adapt well to a future climate within every region, from academics at land-grant universities in the U.S. to local nursery owners to professional gardeners. You too can build that knowledge base and share your experience with others. Often, the conditions you might now be experiencing in your area will have been experienced somewhere else, either today or in the past. The wide body of existing evidence and information can help you make adaptable plant choices now. Read widely and educate yourself either through formal or informal channels about what others have learned, particularly through horticultural science, about resilient, adaptive species. Some of the approaches in this book, such as using communities of plants that thrive in the same conditions, will be helpful in creating resilience in your own designs.

Always evaluate the accuracy of information that you do find; some designers might advertise their plantings as sustainable, but this can be a matter of interpretation. A new planting scheme might be lauded for its wildlife credentials and score well on creating habitat, but what if existing habitat was eradicated in its creation through use of herbicides? What impact does the planting have if it has only been designed to last for ten years and needs substantial aftercare? For example, permanent and diverse vegetation that offers year-round form and structure with planned successional value is better than, say, a large-scale perennial planting with no trees nor shrubs that peaks for just a few summer months and requires substantial aftercare.

Actively work to learn from other planting designs that you can see have successfully incorporated sustainable elements, and replicate inspiring ideas—but only where they will work sustainably for your designs. The most useful tool for the planting designer is assessing the success of your own experiments and initiatives, then applying those lessons to future designs. Individual species' success might be useful to understand but there is much more useful knowledge to be had by objectively evaluating the overall success of your own designs, scrutinising how your plant choices have worked together (or not), and measuring the benefits they have added. Likewise, if you are fortunate enough to be invited to work in an unfamiliar climate or region, your challenge will first be to define what success will look like in that new locality and to develop a sustainable planting design that is tailored to that new ecosystem.

SIMPLICITY VERSUS COMPLEXITY

Approaches to design will vary, but there is now a strong argument for complexity in planting design. Why? Although biodiversity doesn't care much about a formal v. informal planting aesthetic, we are learning that complex plantings often better support resilience in a planting scheme.

Whilst naturalistic planting archetypes often display complexity as part of their aesthetic, ornamental planting can also be complex in its design, and should not be dismissed as inherently being any less sustainable. A formal ornamental design might need high-energy inputs to maintain an aesthetic and long-lasting successional planting, but it can still be complex and relatively sustainable if managed well. Building resilience and longevity into your designs and planning for appropriate aftercare that is not reliant on chemical interventions will contribute sustainability.

▼ This garden features both ornamental and naturalistic plantings. Plants are partially used as boundaries instead of hard materials, which are generally kept to a minimum overall, and surfaces are free-draining. It has complex planting and supports wildlife by including aquatic areas as well as hedgerows.

In many regions it is possible to design diverse, engaging planting with native plants exclusively. This planting in Australia provides a richness of colour and experience that appeals to human senses and thereby forms an emotional connection. In other regions of the world planting that is 100 percent native might not provide the desired richness of experience or aesthetic.

USING NATIVE AND NONNATIVE PLANTS

The sustainable planting designer will often choose to use a high proportion of native and near-native plants to support biodiversity. Some designers adhere to a philosophy of only using native plants, whilst others are unconcerned where a plant originated. Often a blended approach is required to work most effectively on any given project, so it is useful to have a grasp of the benefits of native v. nonnative plants so you may work nimbly and form your own approach.

From a planting design perspective, its first important to understand that the definitions of some terms vary according to location. For example, in Britain and Ireland, a native plant is defined as either a plant that arrived naturally since the end of the last glaciation (i.e., without the assistance of humans) or one that was already present (i.e., it persisted during the last ice age). In Australia, a native plant is any plant included in the Australian Plant Census, except those identified therein as naturalised, and the definition also includes any hybrid or cultivar for which all parents are Australian native plants. In Canada, a native plant is defined as one that 'occurs naturally in a particular region, ecosystem, or habitat prior to European contact'.

Generally, a plant is considered native if it has occurred naturally in a particular region, ecosystem, or habitat without human intervention. Therefore, a nonnative is defined as being in some way introduced or manipulated by humans, and this definition may be further divided. For example, in the U.K. nonnatives are divided into two categories. The first, 'archaeophytes', are long-established plants that behave like natives. These might be familiar plants that people now think of as native or wild due to their widespread presence, but which were actually ancient introductions by humans; these are often edibles, such as *Salvia rosmarinus*, introduced by the Romans. Global exploration around the year 1500CE brought radical changes in trade, agriculture, and industry as well as human demography. Plants introduced in this era are deemed 'neophytes'. Global plant migration was radically altered at this point, as species acquired a transactional value. In Australia, a nonnative species is defined differently, as 'a species that has been introduced into the country by human intervention (either deliberately or accidentally) since the end of the last ice age'.

Many plants grown for ornament are neophytes. In some regions of the world, especially those that established

colonial empires, familiarity with commonly found plants might mean it is easy to assume they are native when they have actually only been present for a few hundred years. Many nonnative introductions have also become invasive, sometimes dangerous weeds. Therefore understand the ramifications of using natives and nonnatives wherever you are working.

Native plants do offer many benefits when designing for sustainability. They likely require us to use less fertiliser and pesticide; they tend to require less water; they help keep the air clean; and they support local wildlife. Some nonnatives also offer these benefits, of course, but native plants, as a whole, more readily promote biodiversity and stewardship of our natural world.

Your approach to using natives is very much about your own belief in their importance. Whether you use only natives will often be a choice made according to your location. For example, in the U.K., using only native species might be considered limiting. There simply isn't as much breadth and variety of plant life in the region as there is compared to South Africa, for example. Including colour interest might require looking to nonnative ornamental plants; but you can still work to include nonnatives that contribute a wildlife benefit and or a benefit for human well-being as part of your sustainability goals. Indeed, some U.K. native species are losing their resilience due to climate change, and so nonnatives may become more important to bolster the health of schemes in the future.

By contrast, native plant palettes in regions such as Australia naturally present designers with a rich and broad variety of flowering plant species—there, native species number around 20,000, whereas introduced species are still relatively few, at about 3,000. In contrast to a designer in the U.K., the Australian planting designer can comfortably create rich, engaging designs with exclusively native plants. Because of the wide range of climates experienced in that country, they may further choose to select species that are native to one distinct region of the continent.

How we use natives and nonnatives in the future will likely be based upon how we balance our predictions of resilience. A changing climate simply influences our ability to choose which plants will meet our design objectives. Strong and differing opinions exist on this topic, but your challenge is to define and act according to your own views.

▲ It is useful to investigate why some native plant species are traditionally used for common landscape features, such as hedgerows. This native hawthorn (*Crataegus monogyna*) is widely used in England because of its resilience and availability. Mixed native hedgerows are also found, but hawthorn is often the predominant plant, simply because it supports other plants and species so well.

▲ Sustainable objectives might influence the choice of hard materials as much as plant selection. Be mindful that aesthetics might push you towards a material, such as gravel, that is not always associated with sustainable sources. Consider locally available materials and carbon impact before making your final choices.

▲ In Norway, turf roofs are a traditional element that still prove effective in modern schemes. They provide insulation for buildings as well as bring nature into proximity with people.

HARD MATERIALS AS ELEMENTS OF PLANTING DESIGN

Whilst this book is focussed on planting design, hard materials do make an appearance in nearly every landscape we design, so best practices for including them must be considered along with plant choices. Some materials go hand in hand with building resilience into a landscape or making choices suitable for a future climate. For example, permeable paving surfaces such as small-unit bricks might be used minimally in conjunction with a ribbon driveway where plants form as much of the surface as the hard materials, reducing impact on the overall sustainability of that design. In contrast, a naturalistic dry-climate wildflower planting might use gravel over a weed membrane, as a mulch. If the membrane is plastic and the gravel harvested from a river hundreds of miles away, these materials effectively reverse all the positive benefits provided by a naturalistic planting. We say local is better, but how do we define the boundaries of what is considered local? What is the impact of removing material from a natural waterway on wildlife habitat? There is no simple answer to these complex questions, but bearing the impact of hard materials in mind when the time comes to select them means being prepared to make decisions that will best meet your sustainability objectives.

INCORPORATING PLANTS AND ARCHITECTURE

The twenty-first century has seen an interest in greening our urban centres in whatever ways we can. Sometimes that means that, with limited space, we are making our buildings work harder by installing green walls and roofs. Of course, planting green walls is nothing new—we have planted against walls for centuries, training plants up. The traditional 'wall shrub' or climber is an easy-to-create feature within your planting designs and, if chosen well, the shrub or climber can give pleasure over more than one season.

Modern green wall systems use technology to create planting in places that call for some drama, drawing attention say for a new hotel or HQ office. These systems can often demand a lot of water, so they don't necessarily entirely fulfil a sustainability objective even though they do introduce plants in unexpected places.

Green roofs are perhaps more advanced in meeting sustainability objectives. They are widely used as a means of

◂ This roof garden above a four-storey townhouse in Brooklyn, U.S., designed by Todd Haiman, is unusual in that it creates a relaxed, almost wild atmosphere in the middle of the city, where formal plantings are often popular. The naturalistic planting immediately removes you from the urban setting and into the countryside. The growing medium depth ranges from just 100mm (4") to 200mm (8"), requiring an experienced understanding of what plants will thrive in such a harsh environment.

retaining some of the green space that might have been lost to development, or indeed to reintroduce plants to the built environment. Northern Europe, for example, is noted for having used green roofs for insulation for centuries. Trends in green roofing are moving towards suggesting a diverse planting approach. Systems range from very simple planting of a low range of plants, such as sedum, to much more complex systems that might employ a biodiverse range of plants; these will likely be high (up to 85 percent) in grass species and rely on native species and wildflowers to fill in the rest. Retrofitting a green roof is not a simple task, however, so you will most often find that green roofs are built in as requirements for new developments.

USING SUSTAINABLE TECHNIQUES AS PROJECT OBJECTIVES

Many planting techniques can be combined with the framework's design approaches to benefit the sustainable landscape. The designer can specify and develop these with their clients and landscapers to best serve the objectives of each project. Some of these techniques are suggested below, and there are also resources available in the appendix to help you investigate these further.

◂ Planting across a broad, paved space will introduce multiple benefits: reducing the impact of raised temperatures created by large expanses of concrete, creating shade for pedestrians and cyclists, and filtering pollutants.

POLLUTION FILTERS

Many of the approaches described here focus on our choice of plants, how they are planted, and their aftercare, but the planting designer can compose plants to provide other benefits, notably to block noise and filter air pollution. Trees and shrubs are used to combat the effects of airborne pollution as well as ambient noise, especially next to highways.

Air pollution has caused a global health crisis, but plants are effective at filtering particulate matter and air pollutants such as nitrogen oxides. Evergreen rather than deciduous plants will provide better year-round reductions in pollution, but avoid plants that produce allergy-inducing pollen, such as *Betula* spp., and work towards creating a biodiverse selection rather than relying on a single species over one area.

PEAT-FREE MATERIALS

The preservation of rare peatland habitats for their unique biodiversity and environmental benefits has now been regulated by many countries home to peat bogs, and laws are aimed at banning peat in both private and professional use. Peatlands are important carbon stores and so contribute to climate change alleviation. They can also play a role in helping prevent localised flooding. In recent years, research into peat-free composts has developed suitable quality replacements for peat-growing mediums, such as coco coir, and it is relatively easy to source plants that are grown entirely peat free or beyond its use for small plug plants.

PERMACULTURE

Permaculture is an approach that focuses on living and growing in harmony with nature. It is about treading lightly on the earth, and is used worldwide. Concepts such as forest gardening and no-dig methods would fit within this movement. Elements of permaculture can be used both in small-scale gardens and larger-scale agricultural systems. Although often focused on edible landscapes, the principles of permaculture can be applied to ornamental plantings.

WATERWISE PLANTING

Waterwise planting practice advocates using plants with low water demands and designing plants in communities that have similar needs to encourage more efficient water use. This method emphasises stewardship of the soil, delivering water directly and efficiently to a root zone created by planting densely and with good groundcover, organic mulching where possible, and reducing areas of lawn.

This approach is commonly paired with other design directives and terms such as 'drought-resistant', 'drought-adaptive', 'drought-tolerant', where plants are used in similar ways. 'Xeriscaping' can also fall into this category, if the main aim is to eliminate the need for artificial irrigation.

DETAIL

LAWN ALTERNATIVES

A desire for a traditional, expansive lawn often tops a client's wish list. Families will want a soft area for children to play on, but traditional lawn care practices can rely heavily on water, fertilisers, and pesticides that have a negative environmental impact. Even worse is the suggestion of using artificial plastic grass. What alternatives and techniques could you be using and suggesting?

- If grass is a must, choose grass varieties that are native to your region and will have adapted to your climate. They will tend to be less demanding of water and more resistant to pest and diseases.
- Propose sustainable aftercare, such as adjusting mow heights to leave blades of grass longer, which stresses the plant less. Start to mow later and finish mowing earlier in the growing season.
- Encourage a move away from the 'perfect lawn' as an opportunity to create lower-maintenance gardens with lawns that look after themselves.
- Suggest design alternatives such as wildflower meadows or perennial plantings that include native grasses and plants, to deliver benefits to wildlife. Point out how the complexity of this visual scheme can add interest to a home landscape. These can also be planted with seed rather than turf, for significant savings.

▲ A natural wildflower meadow, such as this one at Diamond Valley Lake in California, U.S., can inspire alternative uses for spaces currently dedicated to lawns. Moments of colour simply provide joy that a traditional lawn cannot. Research indigenous wildflowers in your region and you might even be able to help improve the biodiversity of plants in a small way.

DETAIL

EDIBLES

Creating opportunities for growing edibles will encourage us to consider more than the ornamental value of a garden and promotes understanding of the environmental impact of large-scale farming, still largely reliant on chemical applications to crops and soil structure. It can be introduced to our planting designs in just a small area of raised beds, or we can choose to plant orchards and even substitute some ornamental plants with edibles in borders. The needs and desires will vary with each client, but discuss edibles and the appeal and health benefits of a garden-to-table lifestyle with clients as an aim to increasing sustainability.

▲ A large kitchen garden sited next to a house will provide easily accessible opportunities to grow seasonal vegetables and fruit. In small or balcony gardens, even a few pots can provide a bountiful and continuous source of fresh herbs.

EMBRACING SUSTAINABLE AFTERCARE

Part of your work will be to specify the aftercare that is required for the planting you have designed. The following is just a brief list of aftercare objectives you might consider for the development of your sustainable planting schemes.

- Commit to 100 percent organic methods and always avoid harmful chemicals.
- Always consider any necessary replacement planting in line with the original objectives (e.g., choosing new species and cultivars that will thrive in with the existing community of plants without becoming invasive).
- Develop creative use of resources—recycle and reuse things like supports and labels.
- Commit to creating a zero-waste site where any debris is composted and used back on the planted areas.
- Make an effort to preserve existing native plants.

- Grow from seed or propagate on or near the site to minimise transportation miles.
- Remove invasive species when they become obvious.
- Use alternative fuel for your tools (e.g., battery over petrol power) and retain traditional methods (e.g., scything meadows over mechanical mowing).
- Replace fences as they gradually fall into disrepair with a hedge layer instead of a new fence.
- Create monolith trees when they die to generate habitat and allow them to decompose onsite.
- Support generating nourishing decomposition layers through natural plant dieback rather than clearing.
- Continue to emphasise building up a healthy soil.

Making an informed plant selection that reduces the need for maintenance inputs is challenging at first, but a skill that you will build over time. Landscapes that feature a high proportion of amenity lawn will likely require more higher-energy inputs than a mixed herbaceous planting; similarly, onsite composting of green waste can reduce the need for energy input. It takes planning and convincing a client (and possibly their gardener), but you will reap the benefits of reduced costs and increased wildlife presence.

▼ A dead hedge in the Wuhle River area in Berlin, Germany, constructed from cut branches, saplings, and foliage performs a barrier function whilst creating a decomposition layer rich in food, nesting material, and shelter for insects and birds.

▲ Our gardens, yards and communal spaces are one of our greatest assets for wildlife. Whilst we can measure the impact of our planting designs on a project-by-project basis, we shouldn't lose sight of the impact we can have by joining up these habitats with other planting beyond our project boundaries.

SUMMARY: ASSESSING YOUR WORK

Measuring impact is increasingly a goal for many designers. There is already a useful body of research and evidence around the beneficial effects of engaging sustainable design objectives in development work—and not just in landscape but in other professions such as forestry. The behaviour of nature and wildlife can inform your work in precise ways; keep an open mind to these. Many governments have introduced laws and permitting requirements to improve biodiversity, especially for new or large-scale building sites, and these require systems for measuring compliance, if not success on a more esoteric or emotional level. Measurement systems that assess concepts such as embodied carbon are in their infancy but increasingly available, both commercially and free-to-use. Institutions such as the U.K.'s Royal Horticultural Society support and develop sustainable design indicators. They are not always perfect, but they do allow us to assess our work, and at a basic level we can assess the success of indicators such as wildlife improvements with the engagement of citizen scientists and local or national science-based organisations.

We all have a role to play in designing landscapes that minimise the risk of disruption, pollution, or interference of other natural systems. A forward-looking goal should be for plantings to provide positive long-term sustainable benefits. As clients start to demand more climate-resilient and nature-based solutions, the adoption of the sustainability concepts outlined above is becoming an important element of the planting designer's work. Their application will hold variable importance from project to project, but we should approach *all* our design work with a consciousness of what we can contribute to making a more sustainable planet. You might not always succeed in your sustainable objectives, but that doesn't mean you shouldn't aim high. These are ideas and tools we can employ that will make a real difference, to planetary health and with all the complex challenges an ever-changing climate presents, we should be voices for sustainability—we are in a unique position to do so.

CASE STUDY

BETHANY WILLIAMSON

The Cliff House
Bellarine Peninsula, Victoria, Australia

Climate: Temperate oceanic (Cfb)
Rainfall: 540mm (21.2") per annum
Temperature: Minimum +6 degrees Celsius (42 degrees F)
Maximum +24 degrees Celsius (75 degrees F)
Soil: Varies, including sand

Planting that merges modernist architecture with a windswept site on a dune and settles the house into its coastal environment. The key design intent is for the garden to look like a continuation of the surrounding natural ecosystem, as though the sand dunes are wrapping around the house.

PLANTING DEVELOPMENT

This house is designed around a central courtyard, with a pool and roof garden atop the garage. The roof garden design is critical in enhancing the feeling of being in nature, as it is visible from most rooms. Additionally, the planting creates a visual barrier from beyond the concrete walls to afford privacy while the clients use and entertain in the outdoor spaces, and also provides a buffer from the wind.

The planting designer's approach to this design relies on a naturalistic appearance. To that end, she uses long sweeps of plants, usually punctuated by one or two other scattered species as emergents; this also ensures a variety of plant textures to provide visual interest. Colour is an important part of the approach as well, though at times throughout the year, it is featured as various shades of green if flowers are not part of the seasonal scheme.

The designer says, 'Repetition and balance are two key techniques we employ often in our gardens, and were two important techniques in this garden. We are trying to design the garden so if feels like a continuation of the surrounding sand dunes. The use of repetition helped to make this garden feel more natural'. Successional planting wasn't an important aspect of this design, which relies on mostly native or indigenous coastal plants, and most of these don't display a lot of change through the seasons.

PLANTING DETAIL

Plants are selected first for their ability to survive in the harsh, salty, ocean-facing conditions, and next for their aesthetic. The plants work with each other in tone, and with the colours of the weathering house.

The main focus had to be on creating a palette of plants that could handle the seaside conditions. Once a shortlist of suitable plants was created, visual characteristics and colouring were considered. The designers aimed for a variety of greens, blue/silvers, and brown/rust colours; but within these colours, they looked for a variety of textures. For example, the *Correa alba* features soft, grey-green round leaves and wheat-brown stems—this works well next to wispy grass *Poa labillardierei*, which has a wheat-coloured seed head. Next to this sits a short *Dianella* 'Little Jess', whose thick leaf and bright-green hue works beautifully next to the *Ficinia nodosa,* with its thin green blade and a brown flower spike. In turn, that ties back to the *Correa alba* stems and *Poa labillardieri* seed head.

Sustainability was a theme for this planting narrative from the outset. A variety of planting types were considered to provide shelter to various local birds, insects, and small animals living and moving through the surrounding sand dunes. The designers arrived at a mix of grasses, various-sized shrubs, and dense groundcovers to create ample opportunities for a variety of creatures to take shelter.

Irrigation was also an important consideration, as the aim was to rely on rainfall alone if possible. In the end, they installed drip irrigation, to be used sparingly; it was a must to combat the constant wind that constantly dries out the soil. The roof garden is essentially a large planter box with a lack of soil profile, so the soil level was mounded slightly to create extra soil depth. Even with minimal irrigation on the roof, the plant selection has created a thriving, interesting, and beautiful garden space.

CASE STUDY

DUNCAN CARGILL

Private Residence
Norfolk, United Kingdom

Climate:	Humid temperate oceanic (Cfb)
Rainfall:	660mm (26.0") per annum
Temperature:	Minimum +1 degrees Celsius (34F) Maximum +22 degrees Celsius (72F)
Soil:	Well-drained loam

A planting design that embraces existing horticultural conditions and a surrounding wilderness landscape to create a sustainable planting that anticipates climate change and brings together mown and self-seeded lawn, schemed beds, and the meadows beyond.

PLANTING DEVELOPMENT

This designer's approach is usually led by balancing existing environmental elements, such as the climate, built and natural surroundings, in-situ plantings, and the practical brief. The studio's own style is one of relaxed formality. Here, the client asked for an existing space to be reconsidered. The landscape dictates the planting style, and the building suggests the structural approach.

This large garden is set on loamy, sandy soil—wet, but well-draining. The planting area immediately in front of the house is planned as a dry garden to accommodate the current substrate of gravel over sand, building rubble, aggregate, and flint. The design relies solely on the weather conditions for irrigation, which also helps to control the most vigorous self-seeding plants from the adjoining meadow and anticipates increasingly dry summers.

The nearby water meadow itself was the inspiration for this design. Undisturbed for hundreds of years, except during seasonal grazing, it had a tangible sense of calm timelessness. The building has a hard-line modernist silhouette, so its position in an ancient landscape brought about an opportunity to create a scheme that could contrast and complement it. Its materials—concrete, wood, and glass—serve as a backdrop that provides texture, shade, reflection, structure, scale, and presence against a free-flowing, naturalistic-style planting.

PLANTING DETAIL

The garden is seen from indoors out and can be enjoyed from several points and levels. The first view of the planting is from the first floor of the house, through huge square framed windows with balconies. The designers were conscious not to put any obstacles in the way of these, to retain a view of the long background belt of trees in the distance. Visitors notice this expanse immediately, then turn attention to the landscaped, detailed part of the view in the foreground.

The view out and down presents a circular mown-grass area that balances the unapologetically rectilinear nature of the architecture. Early sketches experimented with different sizes of open lawn, but all parties settled on a diameter of 18 meters (60 feet); this leaves plenty of room for amorphous planted beds to splay out from its edges, on all sides.

Fairly formal planted beds provide interest from early spring to July, after which time the scheme melds with the wildflowers and the meadows beyond. Plantings in the existing beds are organised by grouping them into heights, then colours, and then into flowering seasons. The grasses are put to one side. These are then mixed with a new palette of silvers, rusts, and blues, which turn to whites and golds in new beds encircling the new grass area. The planting peaks twice, first in May and June with rich greens and spots of colour, and then at the point at which the grasses are drying in July and August and appear in form and texture closest to the grasses in the surrounding meadow. This blurs the boundary between garden and landscape beyond. In autumn the whole garden is left to die back naturally, including the dry planting area, which creates a ghost of summer structure all through the winter.

CASE STUDY

RIOS

Mariposa Gardens
California, United States

Climate: Oak woodland on a gentle slope
Rainfall: 240mm (13.4") per annum
Temperature: Minimum +2 degrees Celsius (36 degrees F)
Maximum +35 degrees Celsius (95 degrees F)
Soil: Well-draining loam

A garden equal parts legacy and fresh inspiration, designed to delight the visitor walking the gardens through a procession of plants, with an emphasis on seasonal changes.

PLANTING DEVELOPMENT

Sprawling across four acres, this property presents pockets of surprises and preserves the legacy of the site's George Washington Smith home and Lockwood de Forest III heritage gardens. Inspired by the Spanish Colonial Revival style, the curated landscape returns the site to its full historical glory while adding modern sensibilities. This garden celebrates the act of working with nature through sensible cultivation and knowing what thrives in this place to bring out the true spectacle of nature's beauty.

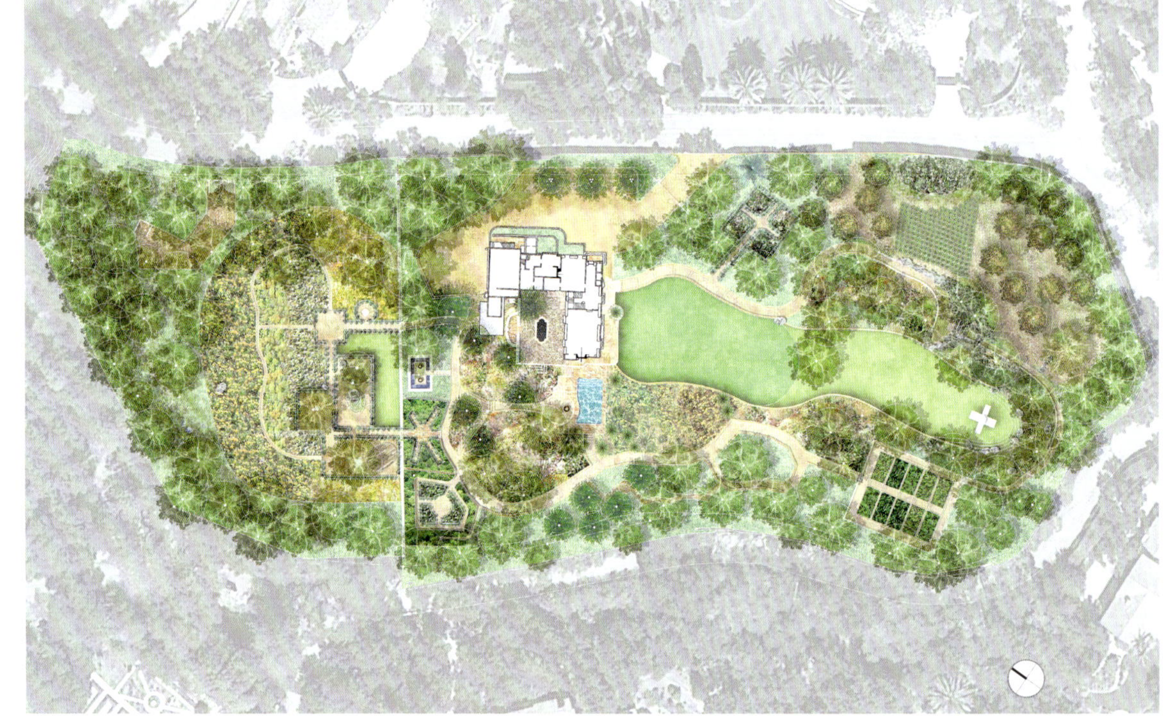

The project was started in the drought of 2014, with a directive to reduce water usage. Working carefully within the Mediterranean climate, the horticultural intervention spanned over six years. The original lawn areas were significantly reduced from 21,000 sq. ft. to 6,000 sq. ft. and replaced with a wide variety of California native and climate-appropriate plants to increase habitat.

Rain gardens dotting the site absorb any dry season runoff and have capacity to capture rainfall from high-intensity storms.

The Santa Barbara sandstone boulders found throughout the site were reclaimed from the 2018 floods and repurposed. An integrated pest management plan eliminated the use of pesticides and increased soil biology.

PLANTING DETAIL

The various gardens, curated with a high level of horticultural intervention, feature many unique or rare climate-appropriate plants that enhance the original California chaparral habitat. California coast live oak trees (*Quercus agrifolia)* encircle the estate and frame walkways and garden rooms. Coastal rosemary (*Westringia fruticosa*) and dwarf olives (*Olea europaea* 'Montra') reinterpret the earlier formal boxwood borders. A yellow garden recalls the faraway mountain backdrop, and its native palette invites pollinators with a splash of sunshine. A lushly planted yoga and meditation deck encourages the whole family to share moments of peace and reflection.

CHAPTER **11**

COMMUNICATING YOUR DESIGN IDEAS

◂ A simple pen-and-ink sketch can help communicate your overall planting concept to a client without forcing you to commit to individual plants or even plant qualities early in the project development stage. It's an easy way for non-visual clients to come to understand your ideas.

To achieve your design objectives, you will rely on different tools and methods and work methodically through the planting design framework. The preceding chapters have shown you ideas for how your planting design can be delivered to your client and colleagues. You may recognise which will be of most use for any given design style or direction, and some communication tools and presentation strategies also appear within the case studies.

USING SKILLS YOU'VE MASTERED

Your work as a planting designer is not all about planting plans—those big sheets of paper that contain endless circles, labels, and numbers. Indeed, often in contemporary planting design we find we might not need detailed plans at all, if and when they can be replaced with plant schedules and instructions to enable a more naturalised and spontaneous layout of plants. Planting plans do still have a place, even when presenting a naturalistic archetype, but you should also recognise that you have many other tools in your kit to communicate your ideas to clients and collaborators.

This chapter concentrates on how all these tools might be used together, and so, here is a reminder of what skills you have already worked to develop.

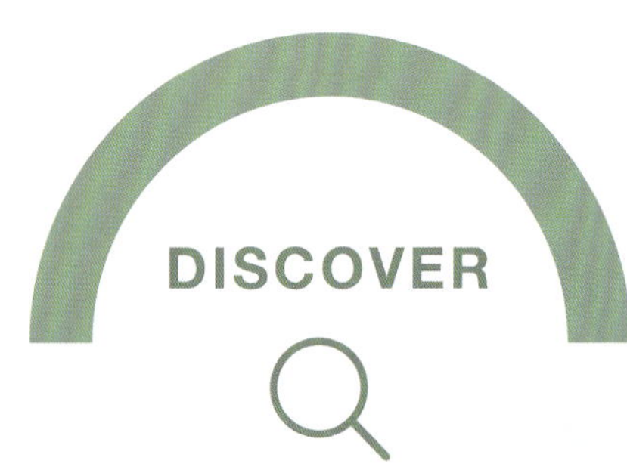

Key skills

- Survey maps and overlay sketches
- Digital apps for collecting environmental data

Advanced skills

- Information maps to present your analysis
- Mood boards to prompt client discussion
- Public consultations to prompt response

Key skills

- A project brief that highlights primary discovery material
- Overall objectives to create a strategy for your design and rules for specific areas and requirements
- Constraint review to determine your design limitations
- Verbal narrative creation
- Visual narrative creation of atmosphere using mood boards
- Using headline, strapline, and outline copy to pitch your idea verbally

Key skills

- Master-planning in 2D with elevation sketches and plans to explore character
- Selecting a compositional archetype to determine planting structure
- Evaluating best processes to build ornamental and naturalistic designs
- Transferring elevations and perspectives into 2D plans

Advanced skills

- Long-listing plants using lists and plan overlays
- Master-planning in 3D with perspective sketches and plans
- Delivery of ornamental planting through a ribbon layout technique
- Delivery of matrix planting through spreadsheet and instructions
- Model-making

Key skills

- Creating a plant palette
- Selecting plants by qualities to meet your project objectives and desired atmosphere
- Extending interest through successional planting
- Introducing sustainable solutions into your designs
- Finding resources to research plants
- Creating seasonal charts

Key skills

- Matching your message to your audience
- Hand drawing v. CAD
- Creating usable planting plans
- Photographic plant library
- Mood boards
- Specifying suppliers and sources
- Aftercare and management plans

You may want to study some of these techniques and methods further using the resources presented at the end of this book. This would be especially useful when developing skills in the composition of planting archetypes, as the resources list some of the leading proponents of those styles. You should also develop confidence in some of the drawing methods described, including sketching (for yourself or clients) and mastering CAD skills (for working with other professionals).

MATCHING YOUR MESSAGE TO YOUR AUDIENCE

We all process ideas and concepts in different ways. Some people might respond best to words, whilst others will find photographic images and illustrations more engaging. Your customers might not read everything you give them; it's up to you to assess what to prioritise to prompt a useful and productive response. This approach to presentation is often referred to as 'visual hierarchy', and designers need to develop efficient strategies for communicating their ideas—in other words, to match their message to their audience. Quite often you will get a clue about whether a particular client better responds to words or images from the outset, but sometimes you need to use both to ensure they understand your intent, especially when 'the client' is a team of people or when you are undertaking an exercise to gain feedback and input from the public.

Colour and contrast will be key to your presentations. We all react to and engage with colour presentation techniques. Just as in our choice of plant colours, presentation colours can suggest calm, urgency, or other emotions. A planting design that emphasises textures and a range of foliage might be best presented as a natural palette of greens to highlight structure and leaf shape; a bright and colourful design might be presented with dramatic contrasts. When you are close to your design, it may become evident the colours to use, and you will develop a house style that you can adapt for each project. Even if you are not using computer-aided design (CAD) programmes (more on this to follow), you can use commonly found software such as Microsoft PowerPoint and Apple Keynote to easily create effective presentations.

Scale, 'white space', and typography will all matter in your presentation layout, as does the practicality that clients need to be able to read what you have written or typed up at a glance. For example, many clients will struggle to read long lines of copy across a presentation in a landscape format; present text in narrow columns or as bullet points across several pages. This also gives you the opportunity to add white space to help legibility and to drop in images that illustrate your written ideas.

There is always the likelihood that your presentation will be reviewed by people you don't actually get the chance to meet, making clarity of vision paramount. This is especially true of commercial projects, where clients, planning regulators, and other stakeholders might receive a copy of your presentation without having the benefit of hearing you explain your ideas in person. Very private clients might also review your presentation without meeting you—as a side note, these types of clients often share plans with friends and family, which can be an opportunity to increase your clientele base among a specific demographic.

In short, there are a surprising number of times you may have to leave drawings for someone to interpret without you. Public engagement and feedback sessions are very common for publicly accessed projects, but even if planning authorities and community committees ask you to present a scheme, you can still leave behind a report afterward to remind them of what you have said. Professional teams may have different agendas to private clients, but will hopefully respect your expertise as you would theirs.

Essentially, always try to have decision-makers present and leave something with them—a hard copy of your presentation is ideal. Consider your audience, their level of experience with planting design, their comfort level with your expert advice; all these factors lead to proposal approval. Use your presentation again later to help brief contractors and suppliers as well, to increase buy-in.

▸ The ability to present convincing images of your proposed planting is crucial. Whether you do this through hand drawing or using CAD, as in this design by Caroline Briones for a Chilean landscape where drawings are overlaid on photographic images of the actual site, a combination of reality and inspiration are important.

Elevation.
Sea Garden
Scale 1:50

Perspective.
Paula's Garden

CREATING GREAT PLANTING PLANS

HAND DRAWING VERSUS CAD

There is no rule that defines whether hand-drawn plans are better or worse than computer-aided design (CAD) for presenting your work. Planting designers need to use a range of tools to present plans. These can include photographic images, graphic illustrations, and planting schedules as well as traditional 2D plans. However, if you are going to work as part of a professional team, you will be expected to produce workable CAD drawings as part of the overall project design drawings for architects and landscapers. If your intention is to work for yourself, then you may be happy and adequately prepared if you continue with your own hand drawings, supplemented by spreadsheets and written instructions where appropriate.

If you decide to learn new CAD skills, look beyond the big software titles and decide what you need from them. For example, there are entry-level software programmes available that provide reasonably simple CAD aimed just at producing planting plans. Their simplicity also comes with a more affordable price tag. Just remember that when working with others, whatever you produce should be exportable into another professional software programme.

GUIDELINES FOR WORKING DRAWINGS

The primary function of working drawings is to instruct others. These are not the place to give a visual impression of the eventual mature planting or establish mood. The best drawings should be understandable and clear. For a contractor to implement your design, or even for you to set out plants for someone else who will plant them, you should produce working drawings with all physical setting-out details and the applicable necessary information. A few guidelines follow to help you keep plans clear and will help you gain the respect of your colleagues.

▸ Working drawings should contain clear annotations and details, such as scale and print size, to support whoever is setting out the plants. Colour is optional, although on a larger scheme it may help delineate between different areas or species.

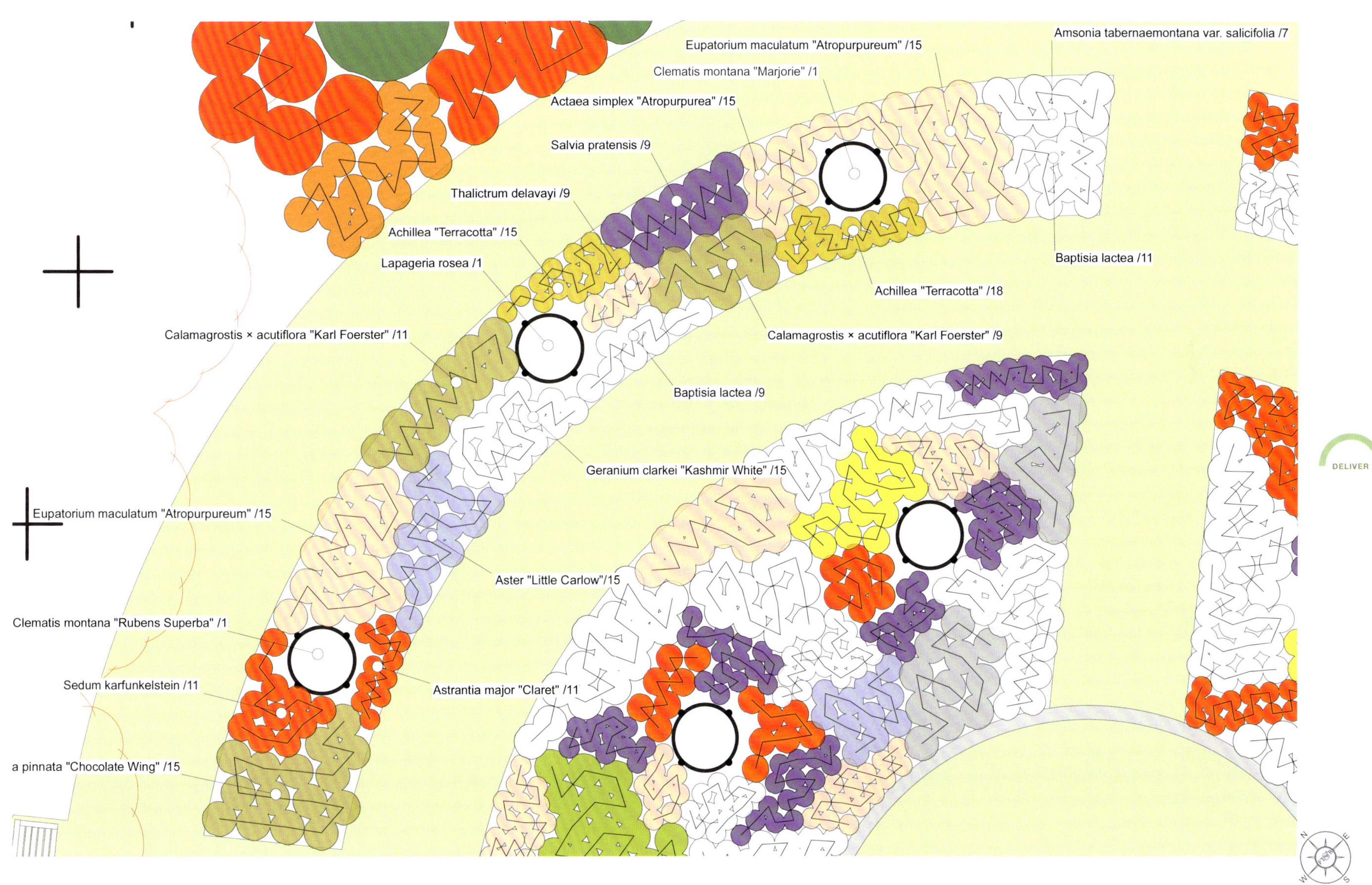

Amsonia tabernaemontana var. salicifolia /7
Eupatorium maculatum "Atropurpureum" /15
Clematis montana "Marjorie" /1
Actaea simplex "Atropurpurea" /15
Salvia pratensis /9
Thalictrum delavayi /9
Achillea "Terracotta" /15
Lapageria rosea /1
Baptisia lactea /11
Achillea "Terracotta" /18
Calamagrostis × acutiflora "Karl Foerster" /11
Calamagrostis × acutiflora "Karl Foerster" /9
Baptisia lactea /9
Geranium clarkei "Kashmir White" /15
DELIVER
Eupatorium maculatum "Atropurpureum" /15
Aster "Little Carlow"/15
Clematis montana "Rubens Superba" /1
Sedum karfunkelstein /11
Astrantia major "Claret" /11
a pinnata "Chocolate Wing" /15
N
E
S
W

Choice of Scale

Detailed planting plans should be at a comfortable scale for you to work with in creating the design, and also in communicating your intentions to anyone who uses your information—especially landscapers. Generally, strategic master plans that show, for example, a woodland area with no detail will be produced at a larger scale of 1:250 to 1:500. General amenity plantings, including matrix plantings, should be at 1:100 and for detailed ornamental planting a scale of 1:50 is preferable.

Plant Location

It is useful to include an outline of buildings if present on the site, or hard and soft landscape areas sufficient to locate planting areas. Critical dimensions for the setting out of planting beds themselves should be included—which will often be within the overall setting-out drawings, but irregular beds may need specific drawings. Dimensions for locating trees, especially where close to services, can be useful especially on large commercial sites where heights and positions are vital; once planted, trees cannot really be moved. Satellite-guided positioning software is sometimes used for accuracy down to 100mm (4") on commercial and large-scale schemes.

Annotation

In hand-drawn images, try and keep annotations clear and neat. Where you have several plans, you should also include a simple location key, so the user knows where the area at hand is situated.

Never use abbreviations or keys, because they are simply difficult to follow and can be easily misinterpreted. It takes long enough for the person onsite to identify plants and their positions, but more importantly it is difficult for someone who must approve your plans, such as a planning officer, to continually have to reference abbreviations, and you don't want to antagonise *them*!

Remember always to show the scale and the sheet size needed for printing so that drawings will be printed at the right scale and size.

Scientific Names

Plants' scientific names enable horticultural professionals to communicate across all specialties, wherever we are in the world, so we'll always know which plant we are discussing. Common names vary widely from region to region, so they do not provide consistency and are open to misunderstanding. There are conventions for binomial nomenclature, and accuracy is important; when writing botanical names for plants on your plans and schedules in a regular planting plan, use the genera, species, subspecies (if it exists), variety and/or cultivar (again if they exist). Only the cultivar will have a vernacular name. Taxonomists change plant names occasionally as new science emerges about plant families, but don't worry—if you are working within the planting world, you will find changes clearly tracked in the resources available to you and from colleagues, such as nurserymen.

Further rules for botanical nomenclature include the naming of hybrids, interspecific hybrids, and forms. It is useful to understand these; for example, a hybrid rose might have a trademarked name, but for most purposes an accurate scientific name is all that is required to help someone to locate and source plants. A good botany book will help you do this (see the Resources section in the appendix).

Specify Sizes, Specify Types

In researching plants for your palettes, you will discover data about their habits, seasonal performance, and other factors. Eventual or mature size will be important to how you lay out the plants and calculate the numbers of plants that you will need. But plants will not usually be delivered at mature size, so you will need to decide upon what size and in what form your plants should be supplied. For example, a tree can be sourced as bare root, root balled, or containerised. You will specify which is best for your project depending on budget, time of year, availability, etc.

Annotate size or age of nursery stock either on a separate schedule or on your drawing plan, especially if you are intending to use different sizes of the same species at once—for example, if you need to delineate between which stock size is used where for hedging, perhaps one area is being planted for immediate screening with mature plants while another area that uses the same plant may be allowed to grow in to save money.

Plant Spacing

Many experts will tell you that the simplest way to determine how far apart to space individual plants is to use the average of the mature spread of two plants to be planted next to each other. Therefore, two shrubs that will spread to 1.2m (4') and 1.8m (6') should be planted 1.5m (5') apart. This method can be useful for trees and shrubs, but the calculation can also be an over-simplification. Clients might not want to wait for plants to mature or, for example, we might be adding rapidly growing groundcover to provide a form of sustainable waterwise planting.

Most plant resources will supply measurements of a species's mature spread and height. Check the maximum spread—then plan to plant a little densely. Two-thirds mature size is a good indicator of size if you want plants to knit together over, say, two growing seasons in a fairly tight distribution, if a goal is to have little visible soil. Be aware that plants will generally perform poorly if there is competition for water and light, however, so this 'two-thirds' method works best for smaller plants, especially perennials, not larger shrubs and trees. Good aftercare guidance will also direct lifting and dividing plants as they mature.

Where you are planting shrubs and trees that will take some time to mature, consider drawing a view like that used in matrix planting. Use shorter-lived infill plants in the spaces around those shrubs and trees to provide interest in the short term, knowing they will eventually die out as the main specimen matures.

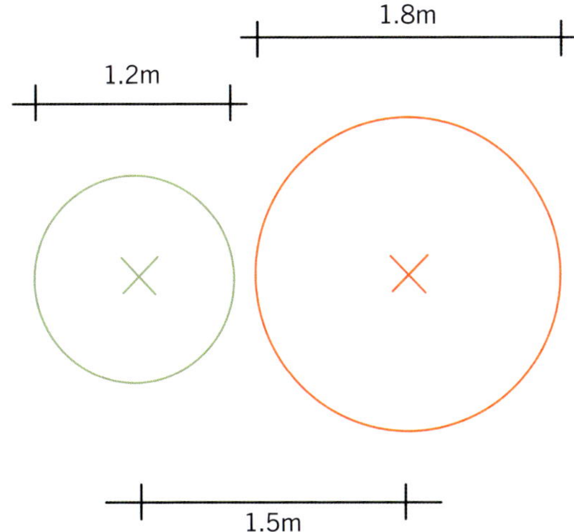

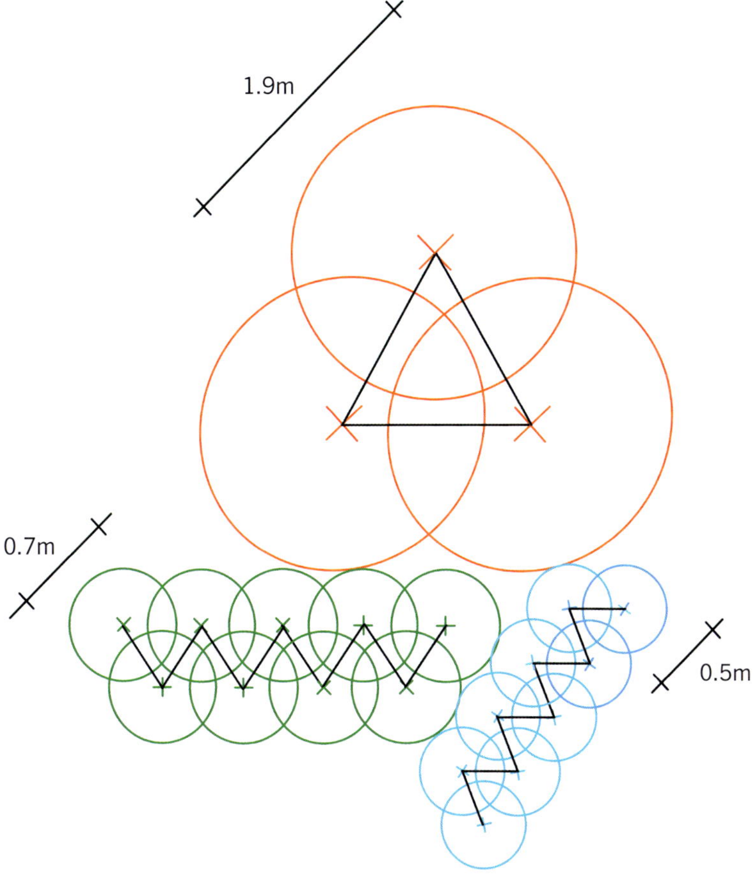

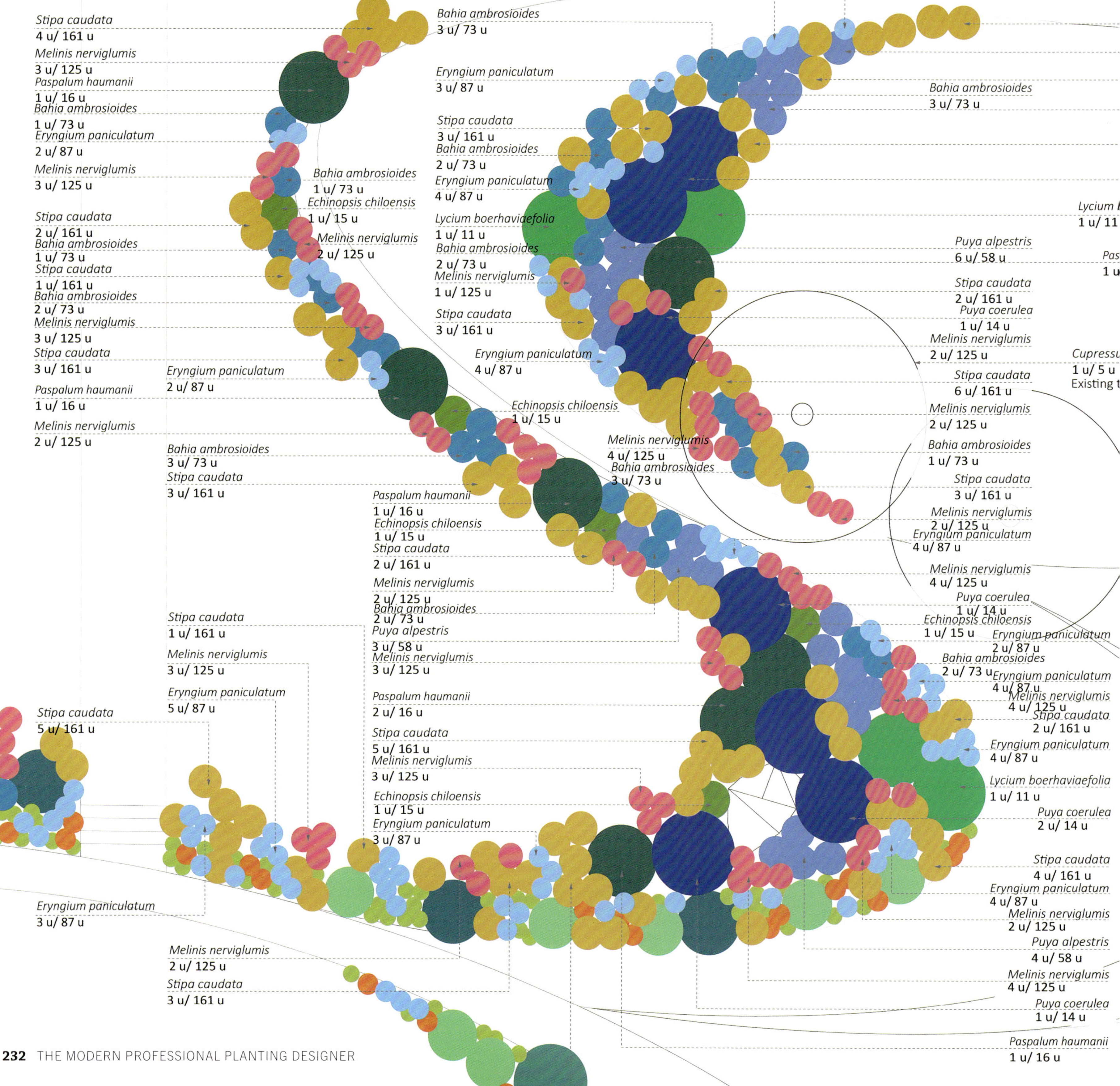
Stipa caudata
4 u/ 161 u
Melinis nerviglumis
3 u/ 125 u
Paspalum haumanii
1 u/ 16 u
Bahia ambrosioides
1 u/ 73 u
Eryngium paniculatum
2 u/ 87 u
Melinis nerviglumis
3 u/ 125 u
Stipa caudata
2 u/ 161 u
Bahia ambrosioides
1 u/ 73 u
Stipa caudata
1 u/ 161 u
Bahia ambrosioides
2 u/ 73 u
Melinis nerviglumis
3 u/ 125 u
Stipa caudata
3 u/ 161 u
Paspalum haumanii
1 u/ 16 u
Melinis nerviglumis
2 u/ 125 u
Bahia ambrosioides
1 u/ 73 u
Echinopsis chiloensis
1 u/ 15 u
Melinis nerviglumis
2 u/ 125 u
Eryngium paniculatum
2 u/ 87 u
Bahia ambrosioides
3 u/ 73 u
Stipa caudata
3 u/ 161 u
Stipa caudata
1 u/ 161 u
Melinis nerviglumis
3 u/ 125 u
Eryngium paniculatum
5 u/ 87 u
Stipa caudata
5 u/ 161 u
Eryngium paniculatum
3 u/ 87 u
Melinis nerviglumis
2 u/ 125 u
Stipa caudata
3 u/ 161 u
Bahia ambrosioides
3 u/ 73 u
Eryngium paniculatum
3 u/ 87 u
Stipa caudata
3 u/ 161 u
Bahia ambrosioides
2 u/ 73 u
Eryngium paniculatum
4 u/ 87 u
Lycium boerhaviaefolia
1 u/ 11 u
Bahia ambrosioides
2 u/ 73 u
Melinis nerviglumis
1 u/ 125 u
Stipa caudata
3 u/ 161 u
Eryngium paniculatum
4 u/ 87 u
Echinopsis chiloensis
1 u/ 15 u
Melinis nerviglumis
4 u/ 125 u
Bahia ambrosioides
3 u/ 73 u
Paspalum haumanii
1 u/ 16 u
Echinopsis chiloensis
1 u/ 15 u
Stipa caudata
2 u/ 161 u
Melinis nerviglumis
2 u/ 125 u
Bahia ambrosioides
2 u/ 73 u
Puya alpestris
3 u/ 58 u
Melinis nerviglumis
3 u/ 125 u
Paspalum haumanii
2 u/ 16 u
Stipa caudata
5 u/ 161 u
Melinis nerviglumis
3 u/ 125 u
Echinopsis chiloensis
1 u/ 15 u
Eryngium paniculatum
3 u/ 87 u
Bahia ambrosioides
3 u/ 73 u
Puya alpestris
6 u/ 58 u
Stipa caudata
2 u/ 161 u
Puya coerulea
1 u/ 14 u
Melinis nerviglumis
2 u/ 125 u
Stipa caudata
6 u/ 161 u
Melinis nerviglumis
2 u/ 125 u
Bahia ambrosioides
1 u/ 73 u
Stipa caudata
3 u/ 161 u
Melinis nerviglumis
2 u/ 125 u
Eryngium paniculatum
4 u/ 87 u
Melinis nerviglumis
4 u/ 125 u
Puya coerulea
1 u/ 14 u
Echinopsis chiloensis
1 u/ 15 u
Eryngium paniculatum
2 u/ 87 u
Bahia ambrosioides
2 u/ 73 u
Eryngium paniculatum
4 u/ 87 u
Melinis nerviglumis
4 u/ 125 u
Stipa caudata
2 u/ 161 u
Eryngium paniculatum
4 u/ 87 u
Lycium boerhaviaefolia
1 u/ 11 u
Puya coerulea
2 u/ 14 u
Stipa caudata
4 u/ 161 u
Eryngium paniculatum
4 u/ 87 u
Melinis nerviglumis
2 u/ 125 u
Puya alpestris
4 u/ 58 u
Melinis nerviglumis
4 u/ 125 u
Puya coerulea
1 u/ 14 u
Paspalum haumanii
1 u/ 16 u

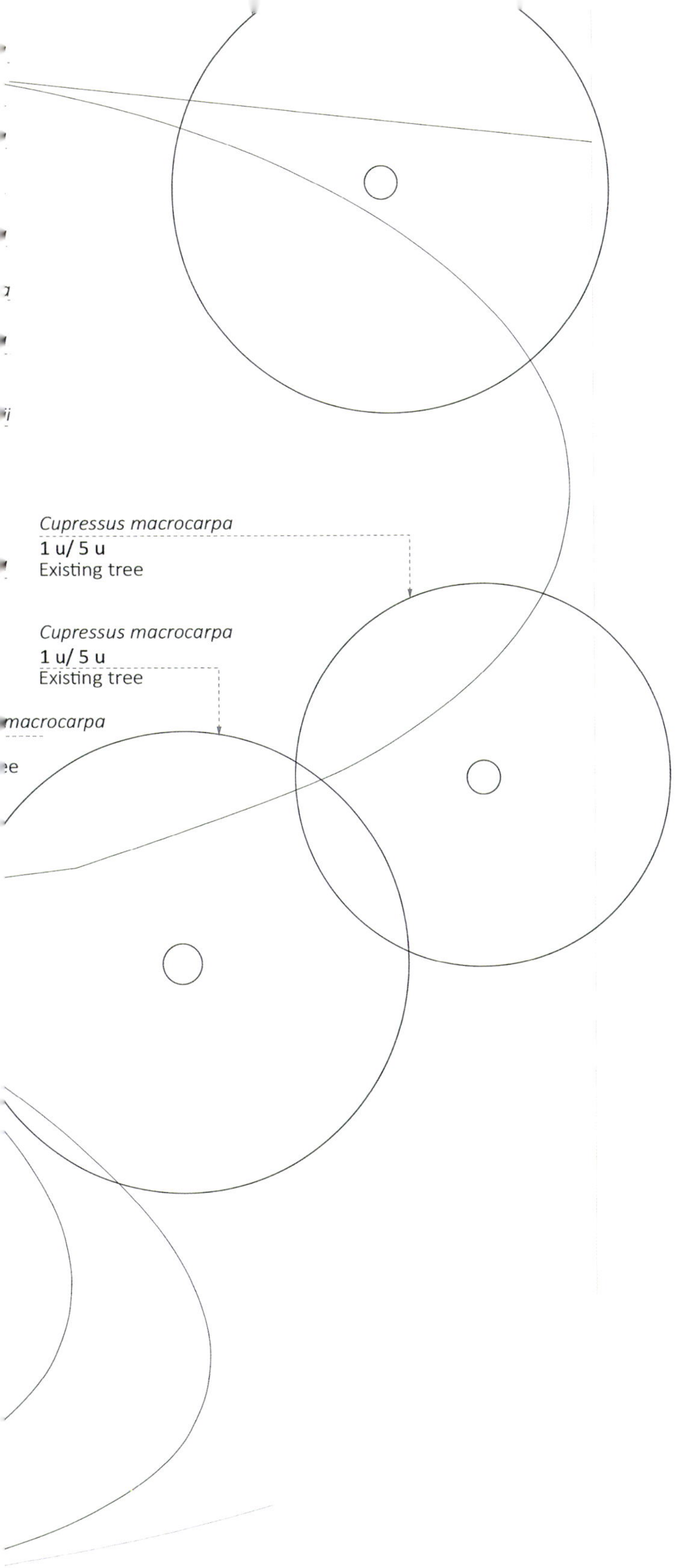

Cupressus macrocarpa
1 u/ 5 u
Existing tree

Cupressus macrocarpa
1 u/ 5 u
Existing tree

macrocarpa

ee

Use of Colour

Generally, simple black-and-white drawings with tidy annotations and circles to indicate placement and spread are appreciated by those who will use your drawings for setting out. In some cases, though, it is useful to use colour; this is especially true for complicated schemes, to help delineate groups of plants. Colour-coding symbols can lead clients to assume that this is an accurate representation of the final plant's colour, though, so take care to explain when presenting to them.

◂ Be prepared to break down your planting plans into manageable segments that will be usable onsite when laying out plants. This plan by Carolina Briones is complex but easily understandable because of the colour that has been added to indicate individual plant species.

MOOD BOARDS AND SKETCHING

By now you've gathered that mood boards or vision boards are a great way to communicate your ideas to your clients. They can take a wide range of forms, but are especially useful to the planting designer for conveying an underlying narrative and atmosphere. These inspirational boards can include images other than individual plants—consider including any images that represent the atmosphere you are trying to achieve through planting. Images of fine art, textiles, or even everyday objects can inspire an understanding of plant qualities, such as colour and texture.

You can also use mood boards to explain individual character areas and themes linked to specific spaces within your overall planting design. Make them engaging and descriptive so that your clients understand the overall feel of the planting. A useful tool for relating your plant choices back to your narrative is to include an image from your atmosphere mood board alongside your plants. For example, if you are using a piece of fabric for your colour inspiration, you could include a fragment of that fabric as an image alongside your plant drawings or images. This immediately links your plant choices back to your original narrative. If you've created a great elevation for a location, include that as well with a few descriptive words that reflect your planting design objectives for the area featured.

Finally, you can create boards that show palettes of the actual plants to be used. They don't have to include every plant you are using but they will give a feel for your plant palette. It is useful to your client if you collect them together by location rather than by type for example, a mood board that explains a single area of a garden.

Elevation.
Paula's Garden
Scale 1:50

Sea Garden.
Scale 1:50

Detail: Seasonal Charts

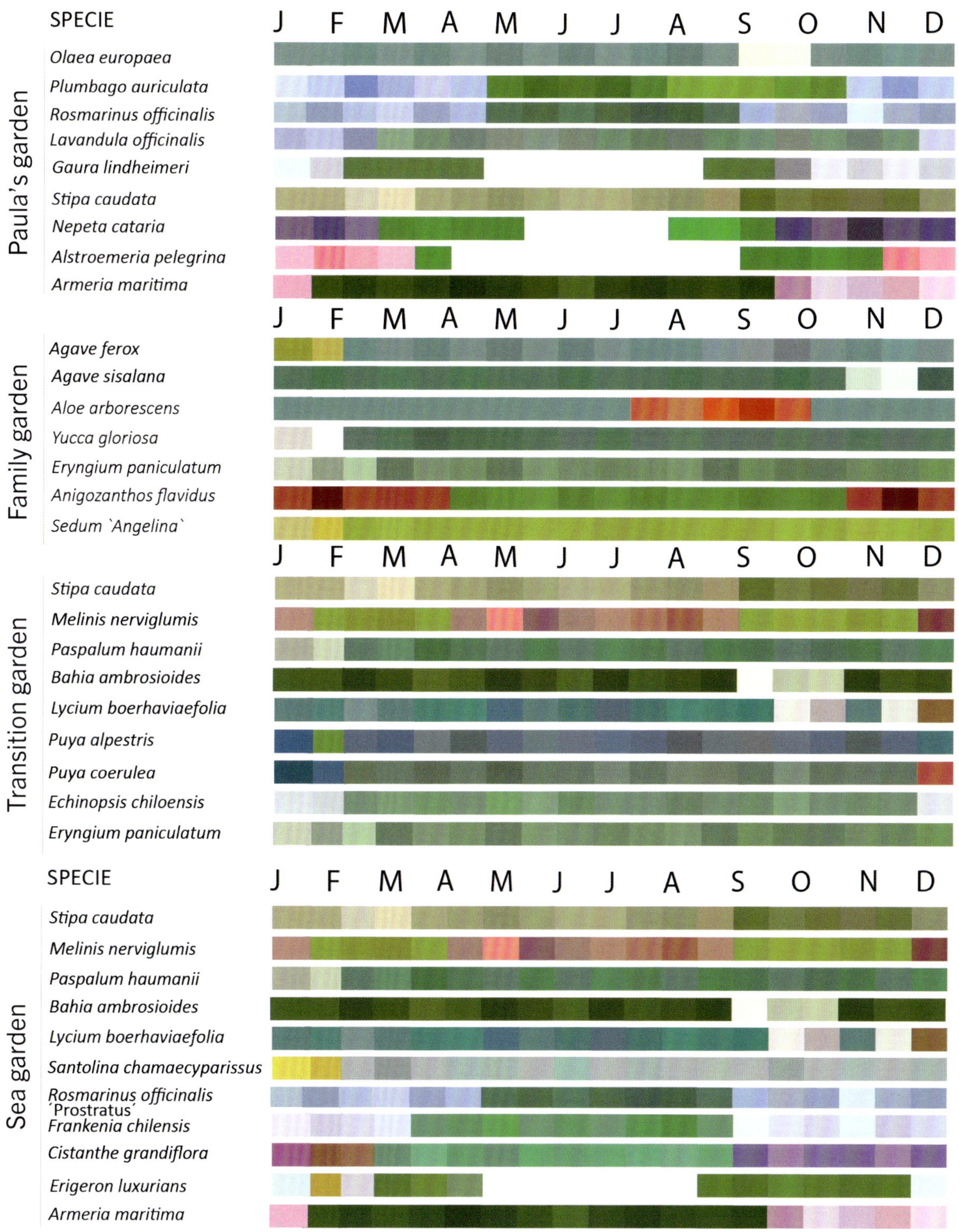

SPECIE J F M A M J J A S O N D

Paula's garden

- *Olaea europaea*
- *Plumbago auriculata*
- *Rosmarinus officinalis*
- *Lavandula officinalis*
- *Gaura lindheimeri*
- *Stipa caudata*
- *Nepeta cataria*
- *Alstroemeria pelegrina*
- *Armeria maritima*

J F M A M J J A S O N D

Family garden

- *Agave ferox*
- *Agave sisalana*
- *Aloe arborescens*
- *Yucca gloriosa*
- *Eryngium paniculatum*
- *Anigozanthos flavidus*
- *Sedum `Angelina`*

J F M A M J J A S O N D

Transition garden

- *Stipa caudata*
- *Melinis nerviglumis*
- *Paspalum haumanii*
- *Bahia ambrosioides*
- *Lycium boerhaviaefolia*
- *Puya alpestris*
- *Puya coerulea*
- *Echinopsis chiloensis*
- *Eryngium paniculatum*

SPECIE J F M A M J J A S O N D

Sea garden

- *Stipa caudata*
- *Melinis nerviglumis*
- *Paspalum haumanii*
- *Bahia ambrosioides*
- *Lycium boerhaviaefolia*
- *Santolina chamaecyparissus*
- *Rosmarinus officinalis ´Prostratus´*
- *Frankenia chilensis*
- *Cistanthe grandiflora*
- *Erigeron luxurians*
- *Armeria maritima*

◂ Seasonal information presented as a very visual chart can be useful in developing a design, and also to illustrate your intentions to a client. A combination of attractive elevations and a richly coloured seasonal chart for this design by Carolina Briones brings the concept alive.

◂ Consider nurseries a real resource. You may not want to select specimen plants at a nursery unless they are over a certain size, or you may be looking for something different or with a character other than standard sizes and shapes. At this tree nursery, for example, you would probably be happy to accept the nursery's suggestion of a plant that fulfils your planting design's needs.

SPECIFYING SUPPLIES AND SOURCES

Different regions have different requirements for specifications. For example, there are conventions and specifications in Europe that define standards for trees and plants grown in different ways, such as containerised or field grown. Australia has a national plant specification and construction code. In the U.S., different states will have different requirements for working documents. It is up to you to research how plants are specified according to where your site is, and to create plant specifications that are understandable and useful to your suppliers.

Some sources are noted in the Resources section of this book, to help you get started.

Your suppliers will usually support you by explaining how they like designers to specify their needs at the outset of a job, but here are a few useful tips:

- Deliver plant lists in the form of digital spreadsheets to your nurseries. Don't expect them to respond to a plan, which can be misunderstood and presents plants in a way where they could be accidentally missed. Nurseries can transfer your spreadsheet list directly into their software.
- If you are using specimen plants, visit the nursery and pick them out yourself, or at the very least ask for photographs of the plants that are being offered to you. Tag them as being reserved for your order. This will avoid disappointment when the plants arrive and ensure that the nursery has the stock you want, when you want it.
- Your nursery will not want to store plants that you have ordered for very long because they have limited space; take delivery as soon as you can after ordering. That said, there is nothing worse for your landscaper than when plants arrive onsite too early, so try to balance site needs and nursery delivery schedules.
- Visit plant nurseries regularly, and definitely let your key suppliers know you appreciate them and feel loyal, but be prepared to review different sources each year. Trade shows are a great way of finding potential new suppliers. It's a good idea to arrange a visit before placing an order. Over time you will undoubtedly form close relationships with a few suppliers; if you communicate well and clearly and pay invoices on time, they will look after you.

Building a Personal Photographic Library

Whilst it might be easy to search for royalty-free images of plants off the internet, creating your own photographic library of plants and plantings will give you a rich resource for future projects without having to spend time hunting for that perfect image. It doesn't have to take a lot of your time to create. The site visits when you return to assess your work are ideal opportunities to take good images of plants. File them by scientific name on your computer, and/or group them by use, style, or condition—for example trees for drought or winter-flowering shrubs.

Taking photographs of planting designs regularly will also help you build a library of plant atmospheres that may be useful in the future. You may never use them, but a resource like this can even be useful for inspiration when you're creating a new narrative or atmosphere. You can credit the designer and location for formal use, but you will put your interpretation on the scheme that you create.

GOOD HORTICULTURAL PRACTICE

Your design efforts will amount to nothing without support from good horticultural practices including soil preparation, planting methods, soil and moisture management, plant protection, and great aftercare. Just as there are different specifications for plant sourcing, there are also different accepted methods of horticulture, such as for bed preparation. It's for you to find out what is the accepted method where you are working and for your design.

However, you cannot beat having a good grounding in horticulture yourself. Whilst this book is about design and not horticulture, there are many references to horticultural principles and practice throughout the book because it's critical to planting success. Ask around about others' experiences with different in-person and online introductions to the general subject. Whether or not you earn a certification at the end, any amount of added education will stand you in good stead. If one area piques your interest, investigate courses in more detailed areas.

Many horticultural books also cover preparing for planting. Some will cover soil amendments, others more esoteric areas, such as planting in waste aggregates. The more you understand how your plants will be handled, planted, and cared for, the better. Learn the basics of staking, protection, mulching, and irrigation.

To build your knowledge base so you can be fully conversant with other professionals about what your plantings will need to thrive, look for courses and books that cover:

- Plant classification, structure, and function
- Plant nutrition and maintaining plant health
- Plant cultivation, including ecology
- Identifying plants
- Soils and their use
- Care and plant protection
- How to identify pests and diseases
- Sustainable practices

AFTERCARE AND MANAGEMENT PLANS

Just as your design success will rely on good horticultural practice, your plantings are only as good as the aftercare that comes with your design. There are two ways of assuring great aftercare: the first is to bring in specialist aftercare services, and the second is to provide clear, understandable instructions in the form of a management plan.

It can be a challenge to find good aftercare companies, but they are out there. As you would to find any service provider, ask your colleagues for recommendations and testimonials. Develop a good relationship with your industry colleagues by explaining what your design intentions are and sharing your management plan. Consider any suggestions the aftercare provider may have, but remember that ultimately you are the designer, and you make the design decisions. Plan for seasonal or annual reviews—a good moment to review the success of aftercare plans in place.

Your clients and colleagues may refer to aftercare as 'maintenance', but this can, in their minds, reduce what is actually required to a bit of tidying up and cleaning; well-designed plantings will account for detailed aftercare requirements to keep the overall scheme looking as intended and healthy. Even the simplest planting design can require different interventions through a growing year, such as checking supports, clearing the previous year's debris, pruning, and checking for and treating pests and diseases. Seasonal changes and a changing climate will have an impact on growth rates and times. Subtle changes might have different impacts from year to year, for example, colder-than-usual spring nights can lead to grasses not growing as tall as they might do later in the growing season.

Your management plan might not be able to cover every eventuality, but you can present how the planting should be managed in a simple report format that includes:

- Design intentions
- Overall seasonal tasks (use seasons, not months, as the start of a season can vary from year to year), including when to start, slow down, and finish cutting grass or when you want perennials to be cut back
- Annual tasks, such as checking tree stakes and ties
- Specific tasks for individual plants, such as dead-heading and pruning, if you have a preference

Regular site visits to review your planted designs can be especially useful to ensure long-term success. If you include just two seasonal visits in the first growing year, you will have the opportunity to review how your plants have grown, how your design is working, make changes if needed, reconnect with your client—and ask them if they know of anyone else who could benefit from your services. You can take photographs for your plant library and marketing. If you extend visits to the first two growing seasons, you will discover even more. You might not have the time to carry out repeat visits to every client, but if they take an interest in your visit, they'll likely ask you to help them develop their landscape further in the future.

◂ When hiring the modern professional gardener, their knowledge of horticultural techniques should be matched with their attention to health and safety and use of sustainable methods.

CASE STUDY

CW STUDIO

Moneypenny Headquarters
Wrexham, United Kingdom

Climate:	Temperate oceanic (Cfb)
Rainfall:	831mm (33") per annum
Temperature:	Minimum +2 degrees Celsius Maximum +20 degrees Celsius
Soil:	Amended heavy clay

Connecting a working building with nature and making a direct improvement in the lives of its clients, employees, and visitors.

PLANTING DEVELOPMENT

This new landscape for a corporate headquarters building is regularly opened to visitors and for employee family days. It is a large landscape that originally comprised agricultural fields, rough grassland bisected by existing hedgerows, and a ditch.

The intention is to give the impression that the planting is moving in gradually from the surrounding meadows towards the building. Employees and visitors are encouraged to experience the tall planting as they approach the building; it's a moment of transition where they can experience nature and the seasons close-up, and learn to anticipate the next season's unique attributes. Farther away, the meadows, woodland edge, and wetland allow staff to get away from the office, either to wind down or to be inspired as they go in to work.

PLANTING DETAIL

Nearest to the building, the designers wanted to create a loose mix of ornamental grasses and perennials within a semi-evergreen structure. They rely primarily on hornbeam (*Carpinus betulus*) hedges, as texture at these points is more important than colour. Landscape lines and edges give a formality to the entrance progression, lead the eye, and create viewpoints; they also create contrast to the meadows and wetlands farther from the main building. The designers explain that the paths feel carved out of the planting, and the hedges have been extruded directly from the ground.

Soil compaction of the existing heavy clay, along with poor storage of excavated soil, led to challenges in its reuse. The soil required substantial consideration and amendment to be brought back into use. Existing yew hedges (*Taxus baccata*) were swapped for native hawthorn (*Crataegus monogyna*) to adjust the planting design to this challenging soil.

Successional planting is important here, and the designers shared seasonal images with the client so that they could understand the dynamic shifts the planting would create between seasons, from spring bulbs to winter seed heads. A mandate for simple aftercare kept the planting choices relatively simple as well; all the plants work hard to give more than a single season of interest, and the designers relied on robust, tried-and-tested plants, but used them in innovative ways to provide an inspiring, immersive experience.

To make the most of a ditch that fills with water seasonally, the designers transformed it into a wetland and oriented watery surfaces to reflect the building in the distance. New boardwalks add formality, and tall grasses replace the expected reeds, allowing immersion in the planting for visitors traversing it. Micro-pools and islands within the wetlands enhance biodiversity by providing habitat for nesting birds, and the area aids in water filtration and purification.

The meadow achieves sustainable objectives as well, namely by using five different types of rich native seed mixes to create grassland across a large area. Existing woodlands at the boundaries were extended into the site with new trees, and an orchard was planted as a tasty resource for staff.

Following the opening of the new building, staff attrition and sickness has dropped, productivity has increased, and applications to work at Moneypenny have doubled.

CASE STUDY

ANDREW SMITH-WILLIAMS

Ceramics Studio
Rye, United Kingdom

Climate: Humid temperate oceanic (Cfb)
Rainfall: 770mm (30.3") per annum
Temperature: Minimum 3 degrees Celsius (37 degrees F)
Maximum 21 degrees Celsius (70 degrees F)
Soil: Sand and sandy loam

A presentation for a planting project to accompany an imagined new building nestled within a coastal sand dune setting.

PLANTING DEVELOPMENT

The imagined client here is a ceramic studio collective; the organisation plans on opening a purpose-built studio and workshop space to serve the nearby creative hub in the town of Rye, which is located behind the dunes of Camber Sands. The existing site is currently used as a car park. The garden would enhance the new building and provide a resource for the surrounding community, inspiring creativity. Dealing with planting in sandy coastal conditions is a key objective.

The narrative is ‘Turning Earth’. ‘Turning’ representing the shape and movement of the dunes, the shape of the potter’s wheel, and the fluidity of ceramic glazes. ‘Earth’ refers to the visual attributes of the raw materials used in ceramics and, tones to be used in glazing, and the requirement for the garden to be grounded within the ecology of its extended surrounding landscape.

Thinking about the mixes will be viewed from different vantage points and where height, simplicity and energy is most required within the space.
How can the mix themes influence how the plants are laid out? - dunes defined with waves of grasses.

Bottom right: Exploring adding more structure.

PLANTING - DEVELOPMENT

THE GLAZED BEDS MIX LAYOUT:

Before I move into the planting plan I wanted to define the layout of the mixes in the glazed beds - using the initial sketches as the basis for this.

The beds have been extended to now encompass the south side of the Kintsugi walk so you can walk between the mixes to give more consistency and a more obvious rhythm to the planting.

MIX 01: SEA
MIX 02: DUNES
MIX 03: SUNSET
MIX 04: CALM
KINTSUGI WALK PLANTING
INNER BED

Mixes defined using 1mx1m squares to allow easy transition to the planting plan.

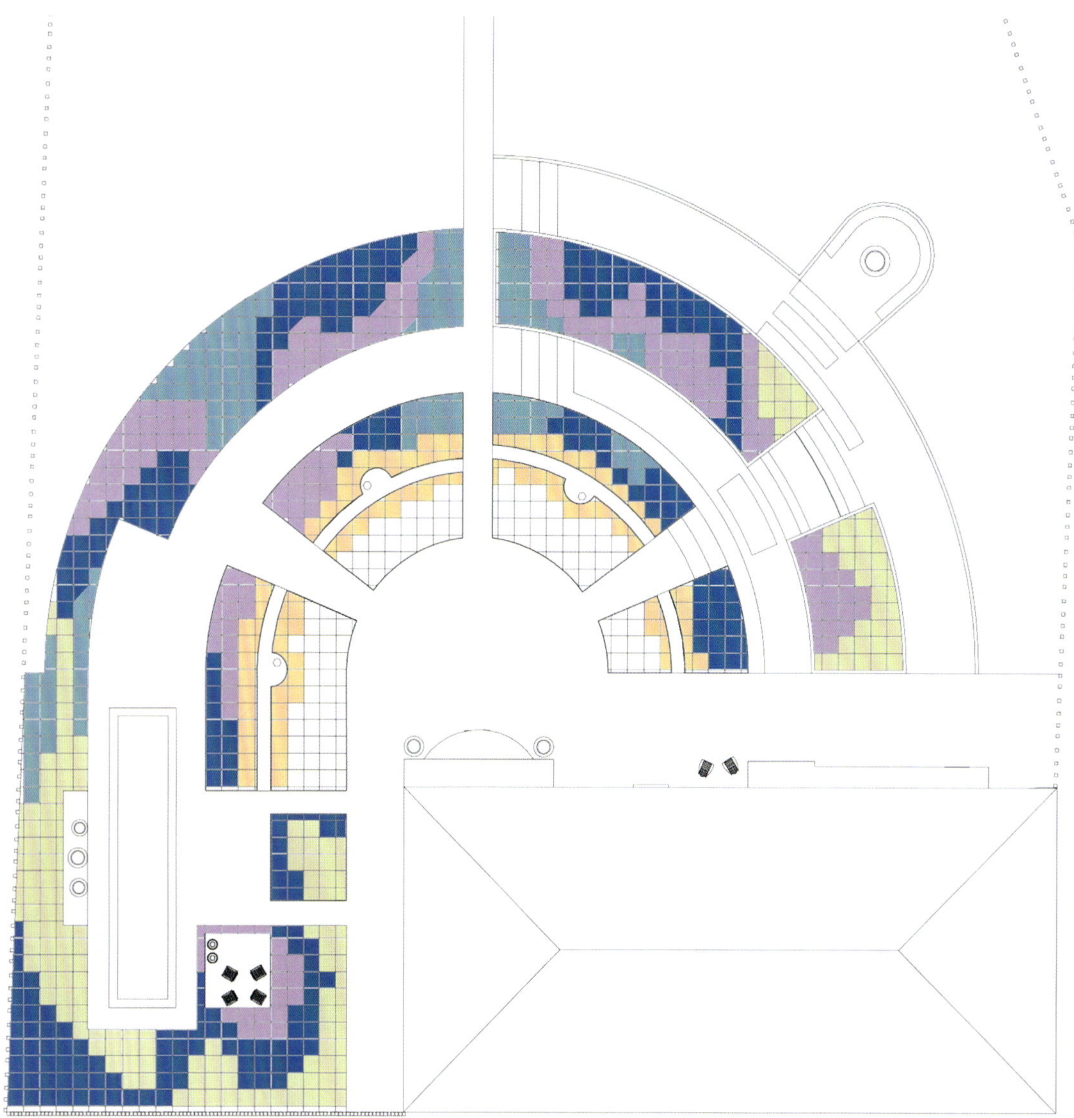

PLANTING - DEVELOPMENT

ANDREW SMITH-WILLIAMS, continued

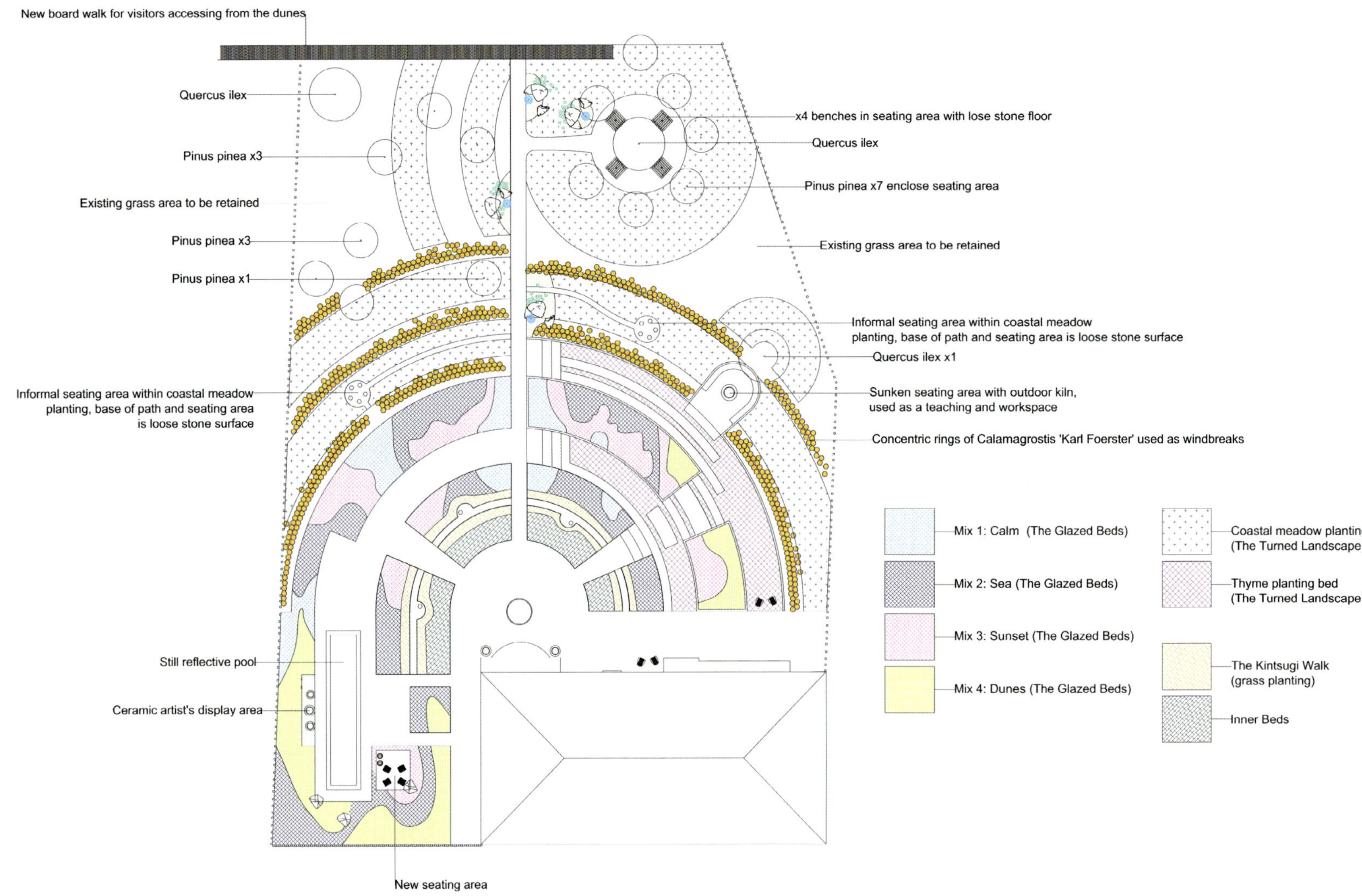

PLANTING DETAIL

Whilst this remains a project only on paper, it is included as a case study to illustrate how dynamic presentation methods can immediately connects the viewer with the design. The images shown are just a part of the whole design presentation, but are chosen to show a number of ways in which the designer has created a compelling narrative for a very unique site and building, and draws us into his vision for a new garden and planting.

Evergreen grass matrix: Helictotrichon sempervirens, Poa labillardierei

Cynara cardunculus, semi-evergreen structure

Perovskia atriplicifolia 'Blue Jean Baby', drifts of texture

Eryngium x zabelii, dark blue used a backdrop

Eryngium maritimum, coastal native

Phlomis tuberosa, used to lighten the palette

Artemisia 'Powis Castle', delicate foliage to offset more robust species

Origanum laevigatum 'Herrenhausen'

Iris 'Black Swan', strong punctuation

AFTERWORD: YOUR CAREER IN PLANTING DESIGN

◂ A plan for a planting in France, by the author. The narrative of 'through a woodland gently' led to a very simple seed mix being used, broadcast amongst existing trees and upon the surface to establish plants within a highly sensitive site.

Whilst landscape design has seen a strong shift towards a preference for greater areas of planting, trends alone are not enough to convince clients of the need for those intensive areas of plantings to be well designed; we must continue to advocate for our profession. A changing climate is also having an impact on how people view planting, however, casting our work into the public consciousness. There is a new enthusiasm amongst designers for sustainable approaches if they are given free rein to experiment with new ideas rather than regurgitate old ideas of what any given type of planting 'should' look like. How sustainable they truly are will be tested by time as much as methods and choices, but efforts towards sustainability should be celebrated. We are experiencing dramatic changes in climate and biodiversity loss, and it's here where the professional planting designer can make a real contribution.

Please use what you have learned here as a starting point for your own planting designs. Look at others' designs, too, with an analytic eye. More than anything else, experiencing completed planting projects will build your understanding and skills of the planting design profession. If you find yourself fascinated by a detail that leads you down an unusual or different path, be prepared to follow your curiosity and see what you can discover. Become an advocate for better planting design wherever you see a need, whether along public streets, in your local park, or in your own private projects.

When your own designs have matured, revisit your work to gauge success and add to your experience of how plants actually behave, and especially to engage with your client to get their opinion of the work. Review how you have connected people and plants. Consider if you've pushed your own boundaries, whether you've innovated in your work? How biodiverse and ecologically sound are your choices? How adaptive or resilient is your planting? Evaluating where our design started against how our planting has developed is the best education.

It is a great privilege to work with plants on exciting projects in different places, and I am lucky to do it every day. I work alongside remarkable people dedicated to making our landscapes better. Sometimes it feels too much fun to be a career, but I hope that you too will get a lifetime of enjoyment from designing with plants, as I do.

FURTHER READING

Planting Design Books

Throughout this book, references have been made to useful resources for your work. This is by no means an exhaustive list, but these are all well-regarded. Climate change has had an impact on the current relevance of books that are primarily about plant choices—always buy the most up-to-date revised editions.

Diblik, Roy. *The Know Maintenance Perennial Garden*. Timber Press, 2014.

Dunnett, Nigel. *Naturalistic Planting Design*. Filbert Press, 2019.

Filippi, Olivier. *Bringing the Mediterranean into Your Garden: How to Capture the Natural Beauty of the Mediterranean Garrigue*. Filbert Press, 2019.

Hodgson, Ian. *New Wild Garden: Natural-style planting and practicalities*. Frances Lincoln, 2021.

Lucas, Neil. *Grasses for Gardens and Landscapes: Design, Selection, Cultivation*. Timber Press, 2023.

Rainer, Thomas, and Claudia West. *Planting in a Post-Wild World: Designing Plant Communities for Resilient Landscapes*. Timber Press, 2015.

Reif, Jonas, Christian Kress, and Jurgen Becker. *Cultivating Chaos: How to Enrich Landscapes with Self-Seeding Plants*. Timber Press, 2015.

Stewart, Angus, and AB Bishop. *The Waterwise Australian Native Garden*. Murdoch Books, 2019.

Thompson, Jo. *The Gardener's Palette: Creating Colour Harmony in the Garden*. Timber Press, 2022.

Wilson, Andrew. *Contemporary Colour in the Garden*. Timber Press, 2011.

Weaner, Larry, and Thomas Christopher. *Garden Revolution: How Our Landscapes Can Be a Source of Environmental Change*. Timber Press, 2016.

Plant Encyclopedias

Definitive plant books exist for many, but not all, regions. These will help you identify plants that will work in your area, and contain useful information on hardiness zones and plant identification. The best known are:

The Royal Horticultural Society Gardeners' Encyclopedia of Plants & Flowers. Dorling Kindersley, for United Kingdom.

The American Horticultural Society Encyclopedia of Plants & Flowers. Dorling Kindersley, for the United States.

The Essential Plant Guide for Australian and New Zealand Gardens. Global Book Publishing.

Horticulture Books

Brickell, Christopher, ed. *Royal Horticultural Society Encyclopedia of Gardening*. Dorling Kindersley, 2022.

Capon, Brian. *Botany for Gardeners*. Timber Press, 2022.

Willgoose, Garry. *Principles of Soilscape and Landscape Evolution*. Cambridge University Press, 2018.

Sustainable Design Books

Cook, Thomas W., and Ann Marie VanDerZanden. *Sustainable Landscape Management*. Wiley, 2011.

Dunnett, Nigel, and Andy Clayden. *Rain Gardens: Managing water sustainably in the garden and designed landscape*. Timber Press, 2007.

Norris, Kelly D. *New Naturalism: Designing and Planting a Resilient, Ecologically Vibrant Home Garden*. Cool Springs Press, 2021.

Vogt, Benjamin. *Prairie Up: An Introduction to Natural Garden Design*. 3 Fields Books, 2023.

Additonal Design Books

Albers, Joseph. *Interaction of Color: 50th Anniversary Edition*. Yale University Press, 2013.

Floud, Roderick. *An Economic History of the English Garden*. Allen Lane, 2019.

Norling, Ernest R. *Perspective Made Easy*. Dover Publications, many editions available.

Sullivan, Chip. *Drawing the Landscape: The Art of Hand Drawing and Digital Representation*. 4th ed., Wiley, 2013.

Zetterman, Annika. *New Nordic Gardens: Scandinavian Landscape Design*. Thames and Hudson, 2017.

OTHER RESOURCES

Botanic gardens are very useful sources of information on plant science, names, and diversity. You will find a particularly rich vein of resources at the Royal Botanic Gardens, Kew; Harvard University Herbaria & Libraries; and the Australian National Herbarium. They collaborate on the International Plant Names Index, IPNI.org.

Community organizations can be very powerful, and cultivating an enthusiasm for plants through social media and in 'real life' can be very rewarding. Almost everywhere I travel in the world, I find groups of engaged professionals and enthusiasts who want to talk about plants. On many occasions I have announced that I've arrived in a country only to be contacted by followers who want to show me around their gardens and landscapes. Garden shows and festivals are a hub for these people, and it's where I have met lifelong friends and colleagues.

Horticulture courses are available in so many locations, from general introductions to specialised subjects. I started this book by recommending that a great start to any land-based career is to study horticulture. Just like you would source any other service or product, go out and get recommendations for the courses you can study in-class and online. You will have a ball.

Plant nurseries are useful resources and often have online availability lists for commercial customers. These will only show you what they have in stock, however, so cultivate a relationship with them and see what they might grow for you.

Online Resources

The following are online resources that come well-recommended, especially in support of sustainable planting design ideas.

Plant hardiness zones can be found with a simple search, but if you are in North America cec.org (for the U.S., Canada, and Mexico) is useful, as is planthardiness.ars.usda.gov. For other regions, try gardenia.net. Köppen-Geiger Climate Classification can be found by searching for your region online.

British Ecological Society: britishecologicalsociety.org

The British Entomological and Natural History Society: benhs.org.uk

The Ecological Society of America: esa.org

The Ecology Society of Australia: ecolsoc.org.au

The Ecological Society of Japan: esj.ne.jp

The Global Biodiversity Standard: biodiversitystandard.org

Plants of the World Online: powo.science.kew.org

Royal Entomological Society: royensoc.co.uk

Trees & Design Action Group: tdag.org.uk

ACKNOWLEDGEMENTS

I am fortunate to be surrounded by many amazing people who have supported me in realising the many planting designs that have led to this moment. I would especially thank Jo Thompson and Nina Baxter, who provided the impetus to write in the first place, and my editor, Stacee Gravelle Lawrence, who immediately understood the vision for this book and gave me the freedom to write what I have experienced and learned over a career in planting design.

My colleagues at London College of Garden Design (LCGD) are unflinching in their focus on providing the best for our students. It is a joy to work alongside Nina in the UK and Brent Reid in Australia; they challenge what I understand about the rich diversity of plants and sustainable solutions; my fellow founding partner Andrew Wilson has always supported my passion for innovating in what we deliver for our students; Marco Ambrosi and Kate Wilford are the best support team you could wish for.

The Planting Design Diploma that we deliver wouldn't be the same without the contributions of Graham Bodle, Nigel Dunnett, Neil Lucas, Amanda Patton, Carolyn Willitts and Sarah Wilson—to a backdrop of planting at Kew Gardens by Richard Wilford. They are amongst other inspirational designers and plant experts who give their time to help train the next generation of designers. Follow these people on social media, as they are as equally generous there.

The enthusiasm of Andrea Fowler at the Royal Horticultural Society, and Tim Hughes and Richard Barley at the Royal Botanic Gardens, Kew, means that I get to work with their horticultural students, for which I am eternally grateful. Thank you also to Gwendolyn van Paasschen and Mike Palmer, who gave me the space and peace to write some of this book at the renowned Denmans Garden, and to Dr Mima Taylor for all the critiques of approaches and sustainability.

My design partner Dan Bowyer has let me off working on a good many other projects to pursue my passion for plants, and his good nature and support over twenty years is much appreciated. He's running the shop now, but I will forever suggest new ideas as long as he keeps asking.

I am indebted to the great plantspeople I've met throughout my career, especially my nurseryman Peter Tilbury of Jacksons of Chobham. Those plants have been planted by a surprisingly small group of dedicated landscapers over many years, especially Stephen Quallington, Rupert Samuelson, Ryan Eldridge, Tom Bartholomew, and Steve Jimenez. Thank you to the many gardeners who have looked after them both in the UK and overseas. You make us designers look good.

My students arrive with open minds and great expectations, they take me at my word, experiment, innovate, and have great plant conversations. They are the test bed for the ideas in this book, and whether they are at our own colleges or studying elsewhere, they never fail to inspire me with their enthusiasm and ideas. Thank you to those who have contributed their work, including Tom Bannister, Carolina Briones, and Andrew Smith-Williams, and for the support of Sally-Ann Rees, Alice Cairns, Sarah McLauchlan and Luke Marshall, amongst many others.

Whilst writing this book we very sadly lost our colleague Sam Taylor-Hunt, an innovative professional and an inspiration for anyone wanting to follow a career in planting design. Sam will be sorely missed.

Two other LCGD graduates have made significant contributions. Duncan Cargill has supplied all the illustrations for the book, and Helen Olney has contributed her graphic design knowledge. Both have become good friends—how great is that?!

The planting designers who have contributed all their wonderful projects to help illustrate the book's ideas have been exceedingly generous in their contributions and delivered inspiration to me in spades. Some have worked with me in our design office at the start of their careers and then gone on to plough their own furrows around the world, of which I am immensely proud. I cannot thank them enough.

This all started with my mum and dad getting me interested in gardening from an early age, in an East Anglian clay-bound garden and down the allotment. More recently, it's been exciting to help Mum re-wild her garden and to talk about plants with her neighbours. Another neighbour, Catherine Bailey, ignited a flame in me for horticulture and landscape design in the 1980s, and then Chris Cox made those first years of training possible. These are important people in the journey, as is the companionship of Rostock, David & Graham, John, Sally & Gary, Fältskog, Malmo, Jeremy and Sam.

Finally, but most importantly, in all my horticultural efforts there has been one person who has always been there and been a major part of them. This book is dedicated to Shaun Cole, the person I garden and laugh with. After all, the best gardener in the world is the one who helps you have the most fun.

IMAGE CREDITS

Caitlin Atkinson: 46
Courtesy Nina Baxter: 102
Richard Bloom: 25
Marion Brenner: 2, 54, 55 bottom left, 55 top right, 55 bottom right, 56, 57, 58, 59, 94, 95, 97, 143 top, 143 bottom
Carolina Briones: 227, 232, 236, 237
Dave Burk Photography: 60
Courtesy Duncan Cargill: 31, 80, 81, 83, 84, 85, 87, 88, 89, 90, 104, 105, 106, 107, 110, 113, 118, 119, 123, 187, 218 top, 218 bottom, 219, 231 top, 231 bottom
Courtesy Sophie Clare: 130 top, 130 bottom
Courtesy Susan Cohen: 180, 181 top, 181 bottom
Courtesy CW Studio: 240, 241 all, 242, 243 top, 243 bottom
Dreamstime.com | © Joe Sohm: 19
Andrew Fisher Tomlin: 11, 13, 34, 43, 91, 186, 213, 237 all, 248
GAP Photos/Richard Bloom: 184
GAP Photos / Mark Bolton: 122
GAP Photos / Elke Borkowski: 14
GAP Photos / Rebecca Bernstein: 69
GAP Photos/Mark Bolton: 149, 151
GAP Photos / Matteo Carassale: 22
GAP Photos / John Glover: 98
GAP Photos / Marcus Harpur: 65
GAP Photos / Dianna Jazwinski: 109
GAP Photos / Andrea Jones: 78
GAP Photos / Fiona McLeod: 144
GAP Photos / Clive Nichols: 103, 168, 209 top
GAP Photos / Neil Overy: 191
GAP Photos /J S Sira: 12
GAP Photos / Nicola Stocken: 71
GAP Photos / Stephen Studd: 206
Courtesy Green Over Grey: 196, 197
Amanda Grimes: 202 all
Courtesy Todd Haiman: 210
Courtesy Hashiuchi Landscape Design: 74, 75 top, 75 bottom, 76, 77
Holly Lepere: 221 all
Marcelo Lopes: 93 top, 93 bottom
Marianne Majerus: 8, 20, 72, 73 bottom left, 73 top right, 73 bottom right, 116 bottom, 173 right, 178, 179 top, 179 bottom
Phil Mann: 134, 135 left, 135 right
Courtesy Gavin McWilliam and Andrew Wilson: 92, 93 top left
Courtesy Alexa Ryan Mills: 121
Courtesy RIOS: 220
Shutterstock / 4thebirds: 42 top
Shutterstock / allouphoto: 70 bottom
Shutterstock / Colleen Ashley: 172 right
Shutterstock / AustralianCamera: 38
Shutterstock / Zuzanna Bedlinska: 209 bottom
Shutterstock / Violeta Beigiene: 233 top left
Shutterstock / berni0004: 42 bottom
Shutterstock/ittisak boonphardpai: 201 left
Shutterstock / crbellette: 18
Shutterstock/Dave Cowe: 68
Shutterstock / crystaldream: 214
Shutterstock / Michael Cowled: 207
Shutterstock / R. de Bruijn_Photography: 16–17
Shutterstock / Drovnin: 35 right
Shutterstock / Ron Ellis: 128
Shutterstock / Roberto Epifanio: 30 top left
Shutterstock / Fahroni: 40 top
Shutterstock / Golden Shark 2: 233 top right
Shutterstock / gothiclolita: 203 bottom
Shutterstock / Margrit Hirsch: 236 bottom
Shutterstock / Viktoriia Hnatiuk: 35 left
Shutterstock / irakite: 40 bottom
Shutterstock / Clare Louise Jackson: 215
Shutterstock / John_T: 172 left
Shutterstock / Jurga Jot: 36 right
Shutterstock / Sergey V Kalyakin: 33 bottom, 132, 158 left
Shutterstock / Oleksandr Khmelevskyi: 146
Shutterstock / Yoshihide KIMURA: 62
Shutterstock / Piotr Krzeslak: 39 top
Shutterstock / LesiChkalll27: 182
Shutterstock / Leonardo da: 211
Shutterstock / Limbitech: 29 top left
Shutterstock / M Rose: 39 bottom
Shutterstock / MAkirar: 53
Shutterstock / MCorfield: 30 bottom left
Shutterstock / Minoru K: 64 right
Shutterstock / Munimara: 36 left
Shutterstock / Juan Carlos Munoz: 176
Shutterstock / Tatyana Mut: 114
Shutterstock / n.k.junky: 28, 29 bottom right
Shutterstock / Rene Notenbomer: 198, 200
Shutterstock / Photodigitaal.nl: 204 left
Shutterstock / Prettyawesome: 116 top
Shutterstock / Princess_Anmitsu: 177
Shutterstock / quiggyt4: 174
Shutterstock / Robert Harding Video: 204 right
Shutterstock / Mariana Serdynska: 201 right
Shutterstock / Shebeko: 50
Shutterstock / SimonTheSorcerer: 173 left
Shutterstock / EMJAY SMITH: 208
Shutterstock / SNEHIT PHOTO: 212
Shutterstock / T.Kai: 129
Shutterstock / Teo Tarras: 29 top right
Shutterstock / tolobalaguer.com: 33 top
Shutterstock / Hannah Tor: 233 bottom right
Shutterstock / Torjrtrx: 236 top
Shutterstock / trabantos: 125
Shutterstock / Joanna Tkaczuk: 115
Shutterstock / ungvar: 64 left
Shutterstock / Virrage Images: 239
Shutterstock / Yolanta: 171
Shutterstock / Alena Veasey: 205
Shutterstock / VOJTa Herout: 63
Shutterstock / Wlad74: 37
Courtesy Andrew Smith-Williams: 244, 245, 246, 247
Nicola Stocken: 136, 137, 138, 139
Derek Swalwell + Mitch Lyons, Courtesy Bethany Williamson: 216, 217
Claire Takacs: 140, 141 top, 141 bottom
Courtesy Jo Thompson: 222
Unsplash / Andrew Ridley: 70 top
Courtesy Jo Wakelin: 26, 101
Rachel Warne: 48, 112 bottom
WikimediaCommons/Supanut Arunoprayote: 203 top
Richard Wilford: 108, 148 left, 148 right, 150 top, 150 bottom, 152 left, 152 right, 153, 154, 155, 156, 157, 158 right, 159 top, 159 bottom, 160 top, 160 bottom, 161, 162, 163, 164, 165, 166 top, 166 bottom, 167 left, 167 right, 175 left, 175 right, 193 top, 193 bottom, 194, 195 top, 195 bottom
Courtesy Annika Zetterman: 44, 45 top, 45 bottom

INDEX

Note: Page numbers in *italics* indicate photographs and illustrations.

ABOUT THE AUTHOR

Andrew Fisher Tomlin has over forty years of planting design experience. He is widely acknowledged as leading the development of a distinct professional career path in planting design through his own work at Fisher Tomlin & Bowyer and at the internationally renowned London College of Garden Design, with branches in London and Melbourne. He has mentored some of the most exciting new designers coming out of the U.K. and Australia over the past twenty years.

He is currently Director of Environmental Design at the college, leading studies in planting design, ecology and sustainability. In 2012, he launched the Planting Design Diploma programme; to this day, it remains the only specialist course on this subject and attracts an international student enrolment. The programme has the support and involvement of some of the design world's leading plant experts and focuses on developing creative, innovative design skills that serve both people and their place within nature.

Andrew is highly regarded within the design and plant nursery world for encouraging innovation and new thought from his students, questioning the status quo and championing the principle of including creative planting design in new-build landscapes. He also teaches planting design to diploma students at the Royal Botanic Gardens, Kew, and the Royal Horticultural Society, Wisley Garden, and has delivered papers and training for institutions such as the Smithsonian in Washington DC and at the Victoria & Albert Museum in London. He has also served as Chair of Selection and Judging for the RHS Chelsea Flower Show and at other international garden shows around the world.

Andrew is a chartered horticulturist and has been recognised as a fellow of the Chartered Institute of Horticulture and the Society of Garden and Landscape Designers in the U.K., and has received awards for his design work in the U.K., U.S., Australia and New Zealand. His current work focuses on being the planting lead as part of collaborative design teams with landscape design and architecture offices on a diverse range of private and public projects worldwide.

First published in the United States of America in 2025 by
Rizzoli International Publications, Inc.
49 West 27th Street
New York, NY 10001
www.rizzoliusa.com

Publisher: Charles Miers
Editor: Stacee Gravelle Lawrence
Design: John Clifford and Tim Littleton
Production Manager: Gloria Arminio
Managing Editor: Lynn Scrabis

ISBN: 978-0-8478-4677-1
Library of Congress Control Number: 2025935220
Printed in China
2025 2026 2027 2028 / 10 9 8 7 6 5 4 3 2 1

The authorized representative in the EU for product safety and compliance is
Mondadori Libri S.p.A., via Gian Battista Vico 42,
Milan, Italy, 20123,
www.mondadori.it

Visit us online:
Instagram: @RizzoliBooks
Facebook.com/RizzoliNewYork
X: @Rizzoli_Books
Youtube.com/user/RizzoliNY

Cover graphics courtesy Andrew Smith-Williams